My Friend, the Holy Spirit
Intimacy with God

Gift Zawadi Love

My Friend, the Holy Spirit
Intimacy with God
All Rights Reserved.
Copyright © 2019 Gift Zawadi Love
v2.0

The opinions expressed in this manuscript are solely the opinions of the author and do not represent the opinions or thoughts of the publisher. The author has represented and warranted full ownership and/or legal right to publish all the materials in this book.

This book may not be reproduced, transmitted, or stored in whole or in part by any means, including graphic, electronic, or mechanical without the express written consent of the publisher except in the case of brief quotations embodied in critical articles and reviews.

ISBN: 978-0-692-04271-7

Cover Photo © 2019 www.gettyimages.com. All rights reserved - used with permission.

All scripture is from the World English Bible Version (WEB) unless otherwise noted. Scripture quotations marked (KJV) are from King James Version of the Bible. Scripture quotations marked (NKJV) are from the New King James Version of the Bible. Scripture taken from the New King James Version®. Copyright © 1982 by Thomas Nelson. Used by permission. All rights reserved. Scripture quotations marked (NLT) are taken from the Holy Bible, New Living Translation, copyright © 1996, 2004, 2007 by Tyndale House Foundation. Used by permission of Tyndale House Publishers, Inc., Carol Stream, Illinois 60188. All rights reserved. Scripture quotations marked (AMP) are taken from the Amplified Bible, Copyright © 1954, 1958, 1962, 1964, 1965, 1987 by The Lockman Foundation. Used by permission. Scripture quotations marked (NIV) are taken from the Holy Bible, New International Version®, NIV®. Copyright © 1973, 1978, 1984, 2011 by Biblica, Inc.™ Used by permission of Zondervan. All rights reserved worldwide. Scripture quotations marked (WE) are taken from THE JESUS BOOK - The Bible in Worldwide English. Copyright SOON Educational Publications, Derby DE65 6BN, UK. Used by permission. Scripture taken from The Expanded Bible. Copyright ©2011 by Thomas Nelson. Used by permission. All rights reserved. Scripture taken from *The Message*. Copyright © 1993, 1994, 1995, 1996, 2000, 2001, 2002. Used by permission of NavPress Publishing Group.

PRINTED IN THE UNITED STATES OF AMERICA

Gift Zawadi Love is also known as Gift Zawadi, and is the author of the life changing book...

Your God-Given Task.
What did God put in you during creation?

The book is found as Paperback, Kindle, or Audio book format.

For Ministry booking please contact me via email at:

giftloveministries@gmail.com

Endorsements

I am elated and full of gratitude for the impact this book has had on me personally. It has challenged me time and again as I read through the pages. Beloved, I can guarantee without fear of contradiction that this book is a life changing experience to those who are yearning for more. I am truly grateful to God for using my wife to unpack and impact lives with such great wisdom. I bear firsthand experience to many of the accounts she narrates, and even though at the time we were ignorant and naive, I now feel blessed and inspired by the revealed truth of powerful living through the leadership the Holy Spirit. I am very hopeful that many lives will be impacted and changed as mine has been, and together, as the body of Christ, we can be empowered to bring positive change into this world through the great leadership of God the Holy Spirit. It must no longer be business as usual! As children of God we must rise to the occasion and become all that God created us to be. May God help us to realize that we desperately need the Holy Spirit, ask for Him, receive Him, and allow the Holy Spirit to lead us by faith into fulfilling our destinies. Zawadi, you make our family proud and we pray that God will continue to use you to transform many more lives in the future. I love you dearly and you'll always have our support and Love, God bless.

—Isaac Love Kiriga

During the six weeks we spent in the hospital, I learned what it meant to have faith. I met Gift Zawadi about three weeks into the ICU (Intensive Care Unit) stay. The day she first entered my husband's hospital room, the impression I got of her was, "that the woman was of God!" She asked if she could pray for my husband and I gladly agreed. She began to pray, placing her hand on my upper back and **immediately** I felt overwhelmed with peace and all I could do was cry. She stayed a little while and spoke to my daughter and I about God. She encouraged me to believe and trust in God. She told me how mighty God was; that if He could raise Lazarus from the dead after three days, bring the weeping mother's son back from the dead, and resurrect the dry bones in desert, then my husband's issue was nothing to Him. She encouraged me to pray and believe. I thought, "my God! Where did this woman come from? She's been here all along, but never interacted with me until now?" I thought she was just a monitor tech, I didn't even know she was a nurse until after my husband was discharged from the hospital. But Oh what timing God has! God sent this woman, Gift Zawadi, to be my pillar of hope in the middle of the fierce storm. To bless me, encourage me, and to help me continue believing when everyone else around me had given up hope including the doctors and nurses. When everyone else said my husband was dead, she said he was alive! I chose to believe what God said through His servant Gift, and my husband lived! This amazed everyone. As 2 Chronicles 20:20 says that when we believe in the Lord our God, we will be able to stand firm and if we believe in His prophets, we will succeed. God sent me help, and I believe that God is sending you help today as well, through His daughter in this heaven sent book. I am forever grateful for Gift.

—Alica Jefferson

This book has definitely peaked my interest to explore the dimensions of the Holy Spirit. This read has been eye opening and triggered some deep thought as I found myself in the category of Christians that still needs growth. It's inspiring to know that it's not too late to work on my spiritual growth since God is always welcoming for those who want to thrive in His Kingdom. I pray that this book will reach many all over the world like me, who need this amazing person of the Holy Spirit whom Gift has found and unveils so profoundly and personally as her friend.

—Donna Manio BSN, RN

It with humble honor that I write this. I have observed Gift as a professional, a wife, a mother, a dedicated daughter, a student, and a cheerleader. She has always displayed great work ethic in all I have seen firsthand. I appreciate the remarkable acts of giving, the qualities of devotion and her innate ability to be a source of strength. She perceivably avails to the Holy Spirit allowing Him to rest, rule, and abide. May I convey what a perfectly divine privilege it is to be a part of what I feel will become vital and impactful to the body of Christ. Her methods of articulation provide a sense of light which the darkness cannot comprehend. As the Spirit of the Lord is being poured out on all flesh, we experience the period of the afterwards (Joel

2:28). Gift shares the word of God daily, and when I open the daily correspondence, I often feel the anointing as the words of encouragement and the scripture have positive bearing in my life and daily challenges. The word is always inspirationally relevant, uplifting, encouraging, edifying, contextually powerful, and a present help in times of need. The process of her craft will promote a lifestyle driven towards achieving a constant presence of the Holy Spirit. Gift, thank you for your diligence, your splendid gracefulness, and steadfast willingness to serve God. Most importantly the visionary you embody, and the fortitude you display as a career woman, an author, a minister of the gospel, and overall the brilliance of your gifts clearly reveals God the Holy Spirit at work in and through you.

—Kristine Wilson

Acknowledgments

My deepest appreciation to…

My Father God, my beloved bridegroom, Jesus Christ, and my FRIEND, God the Holy Spirit without whom I am NOTHING! To my husband, partner, and best friend, Love, I count my blessings daily and thank God for using you to change, and mold me into what He created me to be. It's so much fun being your wife and friend. Our precious princes; Trevor, Tevin (Big T.), and Amani, I love you more than you can ever imagine, I am extravagantly blessed to be in your life. It a BLAST and a great TREAT being your mom! My dad and mom, John and Rev. Priscilla K.J., My precious grandma Anne, my brother Godwin, sisters Favor, Pendo, Blessing, and all extended family. Thanks for being my family and FRIENDS. I love you unconditionally.
To all who stood with me in prayer and encouragement, May the beautiful seeds you've planted grow into a great harvest for God's Kingdom, may your reward be great.
Thanks to all who have helped make this book possible. May God bless you abundantly.

Dedication

I dedicate this book to…..

God the Father, God the Son, and God the Holy Spirit. Because of Your Agape Love for all humanity this book is written. You loved us extravagantly that You came up with the perfect plan (package) for our salvation. Yet most of us still do not understand this great plan. We often pick and choose the package not knowing that it is an all or none package. God the Father, God the Son, and God the Holy Spirit play an active and inseparable role in our salvation. The Father gave us the Son, the Son gave us His life, and God the Holy Spirit mentored the Son through this amazing plan. With this plan, we have the power to become sons of God by the same helper and mentor (the Holy Spirit) which Christ had. The Holy Spirit teaches us Kingdom living. Father in Jesus' name, Open our hearts to understand this perfect plan and will. Show us how to live in the fullness of this powerful plan. Thank You for Your love which has called upon the writing of this book. For giving me Your Son and Your Holy Spirit. Thank You Jesus for loving me so much that you are always fellowshipping with me. Thank You Holy Spirit for being my mentor and friend. Holy Trinity, Your inspiration and Grace has birthed this book. May we hunger and thirst after You. Help us to seek and understand what Your will is. May we be doers of Your word and not just hearers. Place a great urgency in our hearts to do Your will. May our lives be Your glory. Help us to number our days, That we may, like David said in Psalm 90:12, 'gain a heart of wisdom' to do YOUR PERFECT WILL in Jesus' holy, mighty, magnificent, powerful, and precious name I ask, believe, and receive with thanks giving! Amen!

Table of Contents

Chapter 1	God Speaks	1
Chapter 2	Who Is My Friend, The Holy Spirit?	20
Chapter 3	Knowing God Through My Friend The Holy Spirit	145
Chapter 4	The Fruit and Gifts of My Friend The Holy Spirit	157
Chapter 5	The Work of My Friend The Holy Spirit	168
Chapter 6	My Friend The Will Executor	186
Chapter 7	My Friend The Bride Seeker, Preparer, and Perfector	200
Chapter 8	Sins Against My Friend The Holy Spirit	221
Chapter 9	My Friend The Holy Spirit and I	234
Chapter 10	Baptism of My Friend The Holy Spirit and Fire	352

Introduction

Hello, world! Hello, church of Jesus Christ! Ladies and gentlemen, boys and girls, may I have your attention, please . . . I want to introduce to you someone VERY SPECIAL. He is the reason why I'm in your presence and on this platform today. I credit my life to Him. I thank God the Father and God the Son for graciously giving Him to me. What a priceless gift! Thank you!

I am nothing without Him. I'm totally lost without His guidance and leadership. I am fully dependent upon and yielded to Him. He is A TREASURE to me because I am engaged for marriage to a very high-ranking Man, who, together with His Father and my special friend, created and own everything you see. My bridegroom's name is the highest ranking name and title in heaven and earth. This is the name I am getting ready to take on, "Mrs. Christ." In order to be a compatible mate, my friend is in my life, as high ranking as He is, to help prepare me for our wedding supper which our Father is preparing. He was sent to me by my bridegroom and our Dad.

I am so excited because I am guaranteed to be perfect and

ready for my bridegroom's return as long as I have my friend in my life. My friend was my bridegroom's personal assistant, advisor, mentor, and trainer. He is now my mentor, advisor, councilor, helper, personal trainer, spiritual lawyer, intelligent agent, and so much more which He explains through me in this book. Most importantly, my friend is God!

Now, without further ado, with an unveiled heart, mind, spirit, and soul in Jesus' name, let us meet and get to know MY SPECIAL FRIEND . . . Ladies and gentlemen, boys and girls, I am EXTRAVAGANTLY BLESSED, HIGHLY FAVORED, EXTREMELY HUMBLED, AND HONORED to introduce to you the THIRD PERSON OF THE TRINITY. Please, help me welcome MY BEST FRIEND AND MENTOR, GOD THE HOLY SPIRIT!!

I don't know about you, but when I find great treasure, I try it out first and then share it with everyone I know. Jesus said many things while He walked on earth, but one of the greatest promises He gave was this:

"I have said these things to you, while still living with you. BUT the Counselor, the Holy Spirit, whom the Father will send in my name, HE WILL TEACH YOU ALL THINGS, AND WILL REMIND YOU OF ALL that I said to you." (John 14:25–26; emphasis added)

TEACH ALL + REMIND ALL = GUARANTEED SUCCESS IN ALL

If I stopped writing this book now, my work would be done. The formula for GUARANTEED, UNDISPUTED success in this life and in the life to come is found in the verse above. When a professor teaches a student and then reminds them of the lessons taught as they are taking a test, the student is guaranteed to succeed. This perfect help which Christ used to fulfill His assignment on earth successfully is the same help God wants us to have.

Who can teach and remind you of ALL things apart from God? Are you experiencing this kind of detailed, personal leadership from God? Being taught all things and reminded of all things? Do you feel cheated that you have been living in stress and defeat, while you could be worry and stress free, living daily in wisdom, peace, and victory?

If you were like me, you would be angry with yourself for not seeking God's wisdom daily. You would choose to study the Word of God for yourself with God the Holy Spirit as your personal instructor, guide, and revelator instead of relying on the preacher to feed you only when you attend church. Receiving the baptism of God the Holy Spirit should be the desire of all God's children after accepting Christ as their Lord and Savior.

God is the greatest giver of all! He not only gave us His Son. He also offered us His Spirit. What a God! We now can be successful just like Christ was. The Holy Spirit reveals to us the thoughts and ways of God the Father just like He did with Christ. As a result, Christ spoke and acted like God the Father, as instructed by God the Holy Spirit. The Holy Spirit is the overflow of God's power through a believer to others, for the benefit of the Kingdom of God.

This overflow is called baptism. That was why Christ received the baptism of the Holy Spirit and fire before beginning His earthly ministry. Likewise, all followers of Christ must be baptized by the Holy Spirit in order to overflow and impart to the world as they fulfill their God-given task. Are you living a life fully led by the Holy Spirit? Is Christ through the Holy Spirit overflowing through you, impacting the church and the world as a whole?

To live a successful life as a child of God, you must receive Christ in you through conviction from the Holy Spirit. When Christ comes inside you, He breathes the Holy Spirit into you. This is the first dimension of the Holy Spirit, the infilling of the Holy Spirit, where He works inside you and transforms you.

The next dimension of the Holy Spirit is the baptism of the Holy Spirit, where the Father pours out on you the overflow of His Spirit if you ask Him. This anointing flows from your life, reaching out to others through your transformation.

The third dimension of the Holy Spirit is the baptism of the Holy Spirit's fire for impartation, ministry, and for the successful fulfillment of your God-given task. Here, the Holy Spirit is the fire within you. He operates in the fullness of who God is in power through you.

God is a consuming fire. When you have His fire within you, you will operate as god on earth. When you have the three dimensions of the Holy Spirit, you have the fullness of God living in you. Many people have only one dimension of the Holy Spirit; some just two; very few live in the third dimension of the Holy Spirit. That is why other people run to those in the third dimension for miracles, signs, and wonders, just like in the time of Christ because they know they will receive their miracle.

Christ operated in the third dimension without measure. The secret of this third dimension is fully yielding to God the Holy Spirit, and, in turn, the Holy Spirit works through us in His fullness to perform miracles, signs, and wonders. This is the dimension which Christ told His disciples to wait for before beginning their ministry—their God-given task—They became popular for miracles, signs, and wonders after Pentecost when they entered the third dimension. Only the Father gives this level. This can be yours too!

As I finished publishing my first book, *Your God-Given Task: What did God put in you during creation?* The Holy Spirit told me that God the Father has chosen me to introduce God the Holy Spirit to the world. The Father told me to prepare the church for the Second Coming of Jesus Christ just as John the Baptist did, by introducing the most ignored and misconceived Godhead to the church. In doing so, people will receive the Holy Spirit, and He will transform them into ready brides for Christ. Once I had a dream and Christ was telling me in urgency that He is coming the next day, meaning very soon, just like it was tomorrow. That was how urgent it was.

When I began writing this book, I had it titled, *God the Holy Spirit*. But one day, as I stood in my front yard meditating upon God's love and goodness, fellowshipping with the Holy Spirit, He said, "I don't want the title of the book to be *God the Holy Spirit*."

"No?" I responded.

"No," He said. "I want the title of the book to be *My Friend the Holy Spirit* because I'm your friend!"

I was taken by surprise! I wept in humility and accepted this great title of being called a friend of God. God the Holy Spirit did not doubt that I had made Him my friend. I however, did not know that He called me His friend. How humbling it is to be called a friend of God.

As I write this book, I will refer to God the Holy Spirit as my friend, because this is what He wants us to know Him as. What an honor that He also calls me His friend. When you make Him your friend, He will call you His friend too because this is the kind of intimacy He longs to have with us. As I introduce my friend to you, I hope that you will hunger for and desire this kind of intimacy and friendship, launching you deeper in Christ through Him.

CHAPTER 1

GOD SPEAKS

"Babe, I had a dream last night. I dreamt that I was pregnant, and I was working with a lady who was months further in pregnancy than I was, and I wished I was her," I said to my husband one morning on our way to work.

"It's just a dream . . ." he responded.

Not giving it much thought, we changed the topic and went about our day. A few months later, I resigned from where I worked and found another job. At the same time, we found out that we were expecting a child. At my new workplace, I met a woman who was three months ahead of me in pregnancy. I admired how much she enjoyed her pregnancy. She ate anything she desired while I was sick all day and could not hold anything down. I wished I was three months pregnant like her, so I could be done with the sick phase of pregnancy. IMMEDIATELY, I remembered the dream. It happened just as I saw it in the dream I had months before. Wow! God truly speaks in mysterious ways.

Someone once said that we must be careful about what we wish for because we just might get it. Five months into my pregnancy, the night before my ultrasound, which was to reveal whether we were expecting a boy or girl, I had another dream. I dreamt that I was going to have a very HEALTHY BABY BOY BUT WITH TUBES RUNNING ALL OVER. As we prepared to go for the ultrasound, I told my husband about the dream, but this time, he said nothing because the first dream had come true.

I understood the HEALTHY BABY BOY part of the dream, but the TUBES RUNNING ALL OVER part was a great mystery to me. I, therefore, ignored the mysterious part of the dream and chose to stay with what I knew. This was the wrong decision, as you will see later. We went in for the ultrasound, and as sure as the dream revealed, the ultrasound confirmed that we were expecting a healthy baby boy! Oh, what joy! However, I had not been wise and prayerful enough then because if I had been, I would have asked God to reveal what the mystery in the dream was. This would have probably avoided a lot of pain later on, or we would have been better prepared for what was about to come.

Six months into my pregnancy, I was about to know what the "TUBES RUNNING ALL OVER" meant. That Thanksgiving Day, November twenty third evening in the year two thousand, a relative we had not seen in a long time happened to visit our home but missed us the first time. She came back again as she said she felt a powerful urge to see us. She also happened to be pregnant. She saw how much pain and agony I was in that evening, and she insisted that I must go to the Emergency Room because having an excruciating stomachache during pregnancy was not normal according to her doctor.

At twenty-eight weeks of pregnancy, my husband hesitantly rushed me to the Emergency Room. They took my blood pressure and immediately rushed me to the Labor and Delivery unit. I had very high blood pressure (hypertension), which did not respond to any medications the doctors gave me. The doctors diagnosed me with HELLP syndrome, and they said that I had to have an emergency C-section to cure it.

HELLP syndrome is a life-threatening disorder of the liver. "It is severe preeclampsia characterized by hemolysis (destruction of red blood cells), elevated liver enzymes (which indicate liver damage), and low platelet count" (www.emedicinehealth.com/hellp_syndrome_and_preeclampsia-health/article_em.htm).

The doctors, about five of them, were consulting with one another that night in my room. One of them came to my bedside, called my name, and said, "Coming to the hospital when you did was the best decision you have ever made in your life! Because, if you stayed home tonight, you would have been dead by morning."

I thought to myself, *Wow! God truly loves me!* Receiving Jesus Christ in my life was the best decision I had ever made in my life because He sent help at just the right time. However, had I died that night, I would have been with my Jesus in heaven!

Without further delay, I was rushed to the operating room (OR) for delivery to avoid severe complications and/or death to both my son and me. My husband gowned up for the OR as he ran down the hallway to be with me in the operating room. Once in the OR, the doctors said that because my blood pressure was very high, if they put me to sleep for surgery, I would not wake up. I would die.

The physicians said that the only other option was to give

me an epidural to paralyze me from the waist down, but because my liver enzymes and clotting factors were all messed up due to the HELLP syndrome, it was very likely that I would remain paralyzed for the rest of my life. They asked me to choose my fate. I told them that I had lived my twenty-one years at the time and that the baby in me deserved a chance to live. I said to them, "Whatever you do, make sure my baby lives and give him to his father."

Pointing at my husband who stood in disbelief of how life had taken such a quick turn for the worst, we were now choosing between life and death. Who would live and who would die if it came to that—his wife or his child. Earlier that evening, when I told my husband that I was going to the emergency room as advised by our God-sent relative, he did not see the need for it because, according to him, it was too soon to deliver a baby. Besides, I had been sick throughout my pregnancy, so my stomach ache seemed like a normal part of my pregnancy . . . until he almost lost both his wife and son.

Our first baby was born the day after Thanksgiving prematurely. He was one pound and fifteen ounces at birth and was immediately sent to the NICU (Neonatal Intensive Care Unit). When I got to see him, he was a tiny thing that fit on the palm of my hand; I could see through him . . . his tiny veins and so many tubes ran all over his tiny body. Tubes ran into his throat, nose, mouth, little arms, and feet. Wow! The dream had come true again. The mystery part of the dream finally revealed itself.

In the end, our son came home weighing four pounds after spending two months of his life in the NICU. Trevor was a healthy baby boy just as the dream had revealed. That was the part of the dream I held on to regardless of what the doctors said . . . "healthy." Our son is a track and field runner and a basketball player who is very fit and healthy. I bless God for the promise He kept of my baby being healthy. Because of how much oxygen he required in NICU, the doctors thought his eyesight would be adversely affected. However, nothing was amiss with him. The doctors were amazed at his outcome. He is our miracle child. He caught up very fast developmentally. He made the varsity running team as a freshman. What a mighty God we serve!

God spoke about his running when he was still in the hospital through a pastor who would visit him at the hospital, and he would prophesy over our son. He said that our son would grow very fast, and before long, he would be running, and I would chase him but not catch him. The pastor spoke what was in our son: the gift of running. Our son ran one time in elementary school in California, not knowing he had this gift of running, and without having trained anywhere, he was the fastest kid in his elementary school and maintained his position as the fastest kid in the whole district throughout his middle school years. From this, we knew that he possessed the gift of running. He runs real fast to this day! And, yes, I still can't catch him.

What was happening to me? I thought. How come my dreams were becoming a reality? How is it that I was dreaming about the future? Who was behind it all? Who was talking to me? Who was revealing these things to me, and how could I get that information to work for my benefit? What is the point of knowing the future if I cannot do something about it? Was I using this intelligence entrusted to me wisely, or was I undermining it? Who can help me understand?

The answers to these questions are evident in God's Word. Job said:

FOR GOD SPEAKS AGAIN AND AGAIN, THOUGH PEOPLE DO NOT RECOGNIZE IT. HE SPEAKS IN DREAMS, IN VISIONS OF THE NIGHT, WHEN DEEP SLEEP FALLS ON PEOPLE AS THEY LIE IN THEIR BEDS. He whispers in their ears and terrifies them with warnings. He makes them turn from doing wrong; he keeps them from pride. He protects them from the grave, from crossing over the river of death. (Job 33:14–18, NLT; emphasis added)

"It will happen afterward, that I WILL POUR OUT MY SPIRIT ON ALL FLESH; and your sons and your daughters will PROPHESY. Your old men will DREAM DREAMS. Your young men will SEE VISIONS. And also on the servants and on the handmaids in those days, I will pour out my Spirit." (Joel 2:28–29; emphasis added)

The Holy Spirit has already been and continues to be poured out on all flesh. Whoever you are, you can receive the Holy Spirit. He is the giver of dreams, visions, and prophecy. He is available to all children of God. Your title on earth doesn't matter. Once you are in Christ Jesus, ask for the Holy Spirit and you will receive Him. He is the precious gift from God.

Notice what happens when the Holy Spirit of God is poured out to all people, men and women alike. They both will:

- PROPHECY
- DREAM DREAMS
- SEE VISIONS

These are some of the manifestations of the Holy Spirit of God. Prophecy, dreams, and visions are ways God the Father uses to communicate with His children, the church of Jesus Christ. Glory to Jesus! It is happening now. We are living in the fulfillment of Joel's prophecy. God is using both men and women in the body of Christ with no limitations to preach, teach prophecy, work miracles, dream dreams, and see visions for the benefit of the church. God speaks all the time. He asks us to pray without ceasing, and He answers our every prayer. God has given us all we need for life and godliness through His Holy Spirit.

Do you know the Holy Spirit? Do you have access to the highest spiritual intelligence in heaven and earth? Do you have direct access to heaven's WILL which Christ left for us? Do you have God the Holy Spirit living inside of you? Do you have Him overflowing to the world through you? Has the Father baptized you with the Holy Spirit and fire?

If you answered 'no' to any of the questions, then get ready to break free from every limitation of the flesh and the world's systems. This book will bring you into complete freedom if you act upon God's Word. You will know who the Holy Spirit is and why He was a MUST-HAVE for Jesus Christ the Son of God and His disciples, and why He is now a MUST-HAVE for you. You will understand why no matter how hard you have tried in the past, you don't seem to get to a place of perfect rest and liberty. You may have Christ as your Savior for many years or for a short time, but you will never get satisfied or enter into the rest of God without the guidance of God the Holy Spirit. Jesus is made manifest to us and in us through God the Holy Spirit.

If you answered "yes" to all these questions, then you are in for a treat because you will enhance your knowledge of God the Holy Spirit. You will be able to actively and purposefully access the will of God for your life, His present needs, and desires for you at any time and place. You will learn how to receive and tap into what is going on in the spiritual realm so that you can wage war where it matters. You will experience what heaven is experiencing in the now and enforce it on earth. You will learn how to be successful in your position as a king and priest, holy and belonging to God as we see in the OLD, NEW, NOW, AND REVELATION of what is to come. Remember, we are supposed to live in heaven and operate on earth because we are seated with Christ in heavenly places. (See Ephesians 2:4-6 and Colossians 3:1.)

"If then you were raised together with Christ, seek the things that are above, where Christ is, seated on the right hand of God." (Colossians 3:1)

" But God, being rich in mercy, for his great love with which he loved us, even when we were dead through our trespasses, made us alive together with Christ (by grace you have been saved),and raised us up with him, and made us to sit with him in the heavenly places in Christ Jesus." (Ephesians 2:4-6)

And YOU SHALL BE to Me a kingdom of priests and a holy nation.' These are the words which you shall speak to the children of Israel." (Exodus 19:6 (NKJV)

"But YOU ARE a chosen generation, a royal priesthood, a holy nation, His special people, that you may proclaim the praises of Him who called you out of darkness into His marvelous light." (1 Peter 2:9, NKJV)

"And HAS MADE us kings and priests to His God and Father, to Him be glory and dominion forever and ever. Amen." (Revelation 1:6, NKJV)

Notice what the three time frames say:

i. The Old Testament promised us future glory: *"And you shall be"* is a promise of future-making.
ii. The New Testament reveals who we are: *"But you are"* is the confirmation of the present process of making.
iii. The Future Testament, (Revelation) reveals who we will become after the Holy Spirit is done perfecting us: *"And has made us"* is the completion and perfection of our making which makes us entirely like Christ!

We are not just a rib from Christ like Eve was from Adam. We are the complete body and bride of Christ. When Adam was promised a helper, he was put into a deep sleep, and when he awoke, he found a complete helper who came from himself. Likewise, Christ was promised a bride, He was put into a deep sleep (death), and His side was pierced to reveal His bride. Notice that His side was pierced after he slept in death because they wanted to make sure that He was dead and this was their proof, and out of His side came forth His bride, the church. The bride could not come before death.

The bride of Christ was not flesh from the rib. His bride was spiritual, made from water and blood, which is what came from His pierced side. We, therefore, become the brides of Christ from the cleansing power of His blood and the Word (living water) by the power of the Holy Spirit of God. We cannot understand the Word of God and be purified without revelation of the Word by my friend the Holy Spirit. We must die to self to be brides of Christ.

Nothing just happened to Jesus. The Father planned his piercing. The soldiers and the kingdom of darkness had no idea that they were fulfilling prophecy. The second helper of Christ, His bride, was waiting to be released from Him, the body of Christ, where the life of the church is in His blood. We are to help Christ carry the cross as His helpers, to draw many unto Him.

We help Christ to operate on earth in His fullness through us. We have dominion and authority over all kingdoms and powers of darkness in Jesus' name. Christ took back the dominion which the first Adam lost to the devil in the Garden of Eden. He rose from the dead and is coming back to receive His perfected bride whom my friend the Holy Spirit is perfecting. The second Adam, that is Christ, defeated the enemy forever by my friend's help.

> When Jesus therefore had received the vinegar, he said, "It is finished." He bowed his head, and gave up his spirit. Therefore the Jews, because it was the Preparation Day, so that the bodies wouldn't remain on the cross on the Sabbath (for that Sabbath was a special one), asked of Pilate that their legs might be broken, and that they might be taken away. Therefore the soldiers came, and broke the legs of the first, and of the other who was crucified with him; but when they came to Jesus, and saw that he was already dead, they didn't break his legs. However one of the soldiers pierced his side with a spear, and immediately blood and water came out. He who has seen has testified, and his testimony is true. He knows that he tells the truth, that you may believe. For these things happened, that the Scripture might be fulfilled, "A bone of him will not be broken." (John 19:30–36)

The Old Testament was a shadow of things to come. Jesus came to perfect the shadow and bring great light. The end point is the Promised Land, which is entering into the REST OF GOD. No one can get into this place of perfect rest without one thing: a change of mind and spirit. The children of Israel all went through the Red Sea, they all saw miracles, signs, and wonders through Moses, but they, including their leader Moses, never entered the Promised Land. Only two men, Caleb and Joshua, whom God testified well about entered the land of promise. They entered into rest.

Joshua was chosen to take over for Moses. He saw what God did and was in close relationship and encounter with God, and Moses, his leader. Not so for Caleb. Caleb was among those who FOLLOWED THE LEADERSHIP of God through Moses from Egypt. However, God saw and hand picked him from the multitude of followers who were in the wilderness. Imagine the ratio of one in a million. It is so sad that God found only one in more than a million who grasped the fact that God will not entrust His Kingdom to slaves, but to those with another spirit—a spirit of sonship . . . God's own Spirit. Sons and daughters—not slaves—rule kingdoms.

> For if you live after the flesh, you must die; but if BY THE SPIRIT YOU PUT TO DEATH THE DEEDS OF THE BODY, YOU WILL LIVE. For AS MANY AS ARE LED BY THE SPIRIT OF GOD, THESE ARE CHILDREN OF GOD. For you didn't receive the spirit of bondage again to fear, but you received THE SPIRIT OF ADOPTION BY WHOM WE CRY, "ABBA! Father!" The Spirit himself testifies with our spirit that we are children of God; and if children, then heirs; heirs of God, and joint heirs with Christ; if

indeed we suffer with him, that we may also be glorified with him. (Romans 8:13–17; emphasis added)

When you allow my friend to indwell you, change you, and lead you into God's perfect ways, you will not be just a number to God. God will see and handpick you from a multitude. Don't think that you are too small, insignificant, or inferior for God to use. God is not looking for the high and mighty, for big titles and high intelligence in academics, skill, and/or proficiency; rather, He is looking for yielded vessels to use for His glory. He will use those who will yield to His leadership and guidance through His Holy Spirit.

Joshua was entrusted to help Moses lead the Israelites because God said that the Holy Spirit was in him.

Yahweh said to Moses, "Take Joshua the son of Nun, a man in whom is the Spirit, and lay your hand on him." (Numbers 27:18)

Caleb had not been chosen as a leader, but he learned God's ways through the wilderness experience which they all, the children of Israel, encountered. The others did not allow that experience to mold them and change their spirits, but Caleb did, and the change in him resulted in him having a different spirit. He believed in God fully and was led by God's own Spirit. God, therefore, spoke of Caleb and said that only he, out of the other followers who left Egypt with him, will enter the Promised Land because he had "ANOTHER SPIRIT WITH HIM." (See Numbers 14:22–24)

The Spirit of God is not a spirit of bondage or slavery. He is not one of an inferiority complex which views sinners as giants and God's children as grasshoppers. The Spirit of God is not a Spirit that limits us. Caleb had been transformed by the renewing of his mind, and he learned to have faith in God. He believed in God as his source of truth. What God said was his truth. It did not matter what his eyes saw or his physical senses felt or smelt. Caleb's truth was whatever God said it was.

As a result, God handpicked Caleb from the crowd of millions, because of the Spirit of God within him. It is not hard to pick out light in the darkness. God sees this light of His Spirit in those who yield to Him. God will never give His WILL or share His Kingdom with slaves. He only rules with sons and daughters. That is why Jesus came so that those who believe in Him may have the power and right to become children of God. (See John 1:12.)

God has His part to play in our freedom, and we have ours just like the children of Israel. God freed the Israelites from the Egyptian slavery by the supernatural signs and wonders in the destruction of their enemies, including opening the Red Sea for them to escape through and using their escape path to trap and destroy their enemies forever. This was an instant change of title, position, and location. This means that the Israelites were no longer slaves, and they were free to leave Egypt.

The Israelites, on the other hand, had to free themselves from their slave ways and mentality. They had to unlearn how to think like slaves and become sons and daughters, inheritors of God's promise through obedience and the guidance of my friend the Holy Spirit. It was up to them to allow God to give them a new Spirit and yield to God's Spirit to teach them how to think and act as sons and daughters, rulers, kings, and priests.

No wise man will give his inheritance or kingdom to a slave thinker, because the slave will only bring slavery and defeat to the kingdom. Only those who are free and are confident of who they are, and of who God is, can be entrusted to rule and reign with Christ in His Kingdom. Caleb was that follower; Joshua was that leader. It doesn't matter if you are in a leadership position or follower position; you can have a different spirit. You can yield to and be led by my friend the Holy Spirit.

"because all those men who have seen my glory, and my signs, which I worked in Egypt and in the wilderness, yet have tempted me these ten times, and have not listened to my voice; surely they shall not see the land which I swore to their fathers, neither shall any of those who despised me see it. But my servant Caleb, because he had another spirit with him, and has followed me fully, him I will bring into the land into which he went. His offspring shall possess it." (Numbers 14:22–24)

The promise was fulfilled for Caleb in Joshua 14:6–15.

"Joshua blessed him; and he gave Hebron to Caleb the son of Jephunneh for an inheritance. Therefore, Hebron became the inheritance of Caleb the son of Jephunneh the Kenizzite to this day BECAUSE HE FOLLOWED YAHWEH, THE GOD OF ISRAEL, WHOLEHEARTEDLY. Now the name of Hebron before was Kiriath Arba, after the greatest man among the Anakim. Then the land had rest from war." (Joshua 14:13–15; emphasis added)

My friend helped Caleb to follow God fully, and Caleb entered into the REST of God. He took over a city named after the greatest man among the giants. Wow! An eighty-five-year-old man took over the territory of the greatest giants! Do you have this Spirit residing in you? Do you want to be so different that God handpicks you in the midst of millions or even billions and gives you the territory of giants? Great name, fame, and wealth for His glory? My friend will do that for you!

Last Christmas, 2018, the Sunday before Christmas, I was

in church just about to preach, when God the Holy Spirit showed me a vision of what was happening in the spirit. I saw heaven's gates with people who had entered standing at the gate. I saw the humongous heaven's dining table with God the Father sitting at the table looking at the gate where His children stood. He was waiting for His children who were His guests to come in and dine with Him. He had everything prepared for them, but the people entered heaven, and they did not go any farther. They just stood at the entrance and did not move any closer. I saw the sadness in the Father's eyes as He waited in hunger, longing for His children so He may fellowship with them.

The Father said to me that these are the Christians who got born again but never progressed in their relationship with Christ because they have ignored the Holy Spirit. The Holy Spirit is the Kingdom tour guide; yet, people have refused to listen to or follow Him. There are those who do not even ask for Him, and there are those who ask for Him but refuse to yield to Him. The Holy Spirit was at the gate, longing to lead God's children to the Father's feast, but He was totally ignored.

The people were busy speaking to each other, paying attention to each other and never once asked where to go or even desired to move any farther. The Father told me to tell them about the Holy Spirit and introduce to them their Kingdom guide. He said that no one could gain access to the Kingdom without being given access by the Holy Spirit. Just like on earth, when one is invited to the president's house, or a king's palace, they do not know where to go. They cannot be allowed to wander around because the doors and entry have to have badge access or some other kind of secure access due to many treasures in the palace or mansion.

In heaven, access to our inheritance is granted only by the Holy Spirit. No one can gain access to any room or door without the Holy Spirit's access activation. Heaven is very much protected. Earth copies what heaven does. The secret service intelligence in heaven is the Holy Spirit. Without Him, all we can do after accepting the invitation for salvation is to take the blood of Jesus to heaven's gate for entry. After that, Christians are stuck. No more progress, growth, or movement can be made without God the Holy Spirit.

The Father hungers for and is eagerly waiting for our fellowship. He is longing to feed and grow us in Him. The Father wants to show us all He has for us. He wants us to receive access to everything that Christ paid for . . . our healing, deliverance, restoration, wealth in Christ, revelation, miracles, signs and wonders, and all the promises of God we have in Christ Jesus, including the wisdom of God.

When man fell in the Garden of Eden, it was because he started operating outside the wisdom of God. Satan succeeded in making man trade God's wisdom for the wisdom of this world. That was why God kicked them out of His glorious Kingdom, His divine provision, and protection. As long as we operate in the wisdom of this world, or demonic wisdom, we forfeit the right to rule and reign with Christ.

> Who is wise and understanding among you? Let him show by his good conduct that his deeds are done in gentleness of wisdom. But if you have bitter jealousy and selfish ambition in your heart, don't boast and don't lie against the truth. This wisdom is not that which comes down from above, but is earthly, sensual, and demonic. For where jealousy and selfish ambition are,

there is confusion and every evil deed. But the wisdom that is from above is first pure, then peaceful, gentle, reasonable, full of mercy and good fruits, without partiality, and without hypocrisy. (James 3:13–17)

We cannot rule in God's Kingdom without the wisdom of God given by the Holy Spirit of God. Isaiah 40:13 makes it clear that no one can teach or advise the Holy Spirit. Isaiah also mentions the first thing that the Holy Spirit has and gives us when He rests upon us is the wisdom of God. The Holy Spirit is the one who gives us the authority to get back into the Garden of Eden, the place of divine provision and rest. The Holy Spirit gives us wisdom, understanding, counsel, might, knowledge, and the fear of the Lord (Isaiah 11:5).

My friend the Holy Spirit is a MUST-HAVE to enter into the rest of God, the Garden of Eden, the Promised Land, back to divine provision, protection, overflow, and constant fellowship with the Father, Son, and the Holy Spirit. The keys to the Kingdom, divine access, and revelation are only found in the Holy Spirit. He is the one who convicts the soul of man to turn to God, and only He can lead us into the presence of God.

My friend is the only designated Kingdom trainer and guide. God teaches His children. He does not entrust them to strangers or other people because He wants to make sure that His children feed on the healthy organic Kingdom food. No steroids or unhealthy food with additives and the harmful cancerous doctrine of men and religion. Only the Holy Spirit has our best interest at heart. If you do not have the Holy Spirit, you will be deceived with every doctrine. That is why we have many cults, false teachings, and religions which create bondage, encourage hatred, discrimination, and partiality.

The Holy Spirit gives us the spirit of discernment, which reveals any counterfeits and dangerous doctrine so that we, God's children, may remain healthy, growing in Christ and in the knowledge of God. Just as people live miserably and eventually die from disease because of their diet, it is so in the spirit. Some people get doctrine poisoning, sick from false doctrine, and many have had stunted growth. Some, sadly, have died eternally from these diseases in the spirit realm. Many are, and have been, wounded because they refuse to rely on the Holy Spirit.

Beloved, are you tired of suffering and struggling, but failing in working out your salvation? Are you spiritually starving and malnourished, or spiritually obese from spiritual junk food of false doctrine, religion, and theology without the power of God? Spiritually obese people are full of religious doctrine but void of an intimate relationship with Christ. This intimacy is what Christ died and paid for . . . the restoration of the relationship between God and man.

Intimacy with God results in the immense growth of spiritual muscle and height. Are you confused about which religion or doctrine is right? Do you really want to know what God thinks about it and what He desires? Are you tired of hearing from human beings with the thousands of religious doctrines and man-made laws that cause bondage? Are you done with human tradition and are now ready to be taught by God? Child of God, you must get to this point of hunger and thirst for more like I did, and say:

> ENOUGH IS ENOUGH! *God, if you don't teach me yourself, I will be lost. You promised me in John 14:18 that you would not leave me as an orphan, but you will come to*

me. You promised to send me a helper, your Holy Spirit. Where is He? I need Him now in Jesus' name! Holy Spirit, you were there during creation. You saw what was put in me. Reveal it to me and help me to accomplish it successfully like you helped Christ in Jesus' name I pray, believe, and receive, with thanksgiving, amen!

CHAPTER 2

WHO IS MY FRIEND, THE HOLY SPIRIT?

MY FRIEND, THE Holy Spirit is God. He is not an "it." He is a He. Jesus made this clear when He spoke of my friend and said:

> I have many more things to say to you, but you cannot bear [to hear] them now. But when He, the Spirit of Truth, comes, He will guide you into all the truth [full and complete truth]. For He will not speak on His own initiative, but He will speak whatever He hears [from the Father—the message regarding the Son], and He will disclose to you what is to come [in the future]. He will glorify and honor Me, because He (the Holy Spirit) will take from what is Mine and will disclose it to you. (John 16:12–14, AMP)

My friend is the Spirit of truth. Who is Truth? Jesus Christ is the truth. My friend is, therefore, the Spirit of God who reveals Jesus Christ. He is the witness of Christ, the Son of God.

> Who is he who overcomes the world, but he who believes that Jesus is the Son of God? This is he who came by water and blood, Jesus Christ; not with the water only, but with the water and the blood. It is the Spirit who testifies, because the Spirit is the truth. For there are three who testify: the Spirit, the water, and the blood; and the three agree as one. If we receive the witness of men, the witness of God is greater; for this is God's testimony which he has testified concerning his Son. (1 John 5:5–9)

Jesus said to him, "I am the way, the truth, and the life. No one comes to the Father, except through me." (John 14:6)

My friend is part of the Godhead. God is three in one, just like we are three in one. We are created in God's image, and like He is; God the Father, God the Son, and my friend, the Holy Spirit; we have a spirit, soul, and body. God is Spirit, in three different parts, yet working together in harmony just like our spirit, soul, and body work together in harmony. Your body cannot work without the soul or the spirit.

"For God is Spirit, so those who worship him must worship in spirit and in truth." (John 4:24, NLT)

To know my friend, we must understand the Holy Trinity. We know that the Father is the head of the Son and my friend the Holy Spirit. The Great I AM, the Father, speaks the Word, who is His Son, and my friend manifests the Word (Son).

Who then is the Son? JESUS CHRIST, the Word.

"In the beginning, the Word already existed. The Word was with God, and the Word was God. He existed in the beginning with God. God created everything through him, and nothing was created except through Him. The Word gave life to everything that was created, and his life brought light to everyone. The light shines in the darkness, and the darkness can never extinguish it." (John 1:1–5, NLT)

> He came into the very world he created, but the world didn't recognize him. He came to his own people, and even they rejected him. But to all who believed him and accepted him, he gave the right to become children of God. They are reborn—not with a physical birth resulting from human passion or plan, but a birth that comes from God. So the Word became human and made his home among us. He was full of unfailing love and faithfulness. And we have seen his glory, the glory of the Father's one and only Son. John testified about him when he shouted to the crowds, "This is the one I was talking about when I said, 'Someone is coming after me who is far greater than I am, for he existed long before me.'" From his abundance we have all received one gracious blessing after another. For the law was given through Moses, but God's unfailing love and faithfulness came through Jesus Christ. No one has ever seen God. But the unique One, who is himself God, is near to the Father's heart. He has revealed God to us. (John 1:10–18, NLT)

This scripture reveals to us who Jesus was before creation, and who He was on earth after a body was created for Him.

We cannot know or receive my friend, the Holy Spirit without receiving the sacrifice which God the Father made through His Son Jesus Christ. We cannot know God the Son, Jesus Christ, without the revelation of Him from the Father through my friend the Holy Spirit. We can never know God the Father without the revelation of Him through God the Son and God the Holy Spirit.

You see, my friend is the middleman and can never be eliminated from the equation. If we are to know God and have the fullness of Him living in and through us, we must be taught by and remain yielded to the leadership and guidance of my friend. You cannot ignore my spirit and have a relationship with my body, or ignore my soul and have a relationship with my spirit, or ignore my body and have a relationship with my soul. It is impossible! You either get all of me or none of me. You will never be a successful Christian if you ignore any one of the Godhead. You will be the joke of the enemy, which many Christians are; comedy to the devil and his demons.

"Turning to the disciples, he said, 'All things have been delivered to me by my Father. No one knows who the Son is, except the Father, and who the Father is, except the Son, and he to whomever the Son desires to reveal him.'" (Luke 10:22)

In Genesis, we read about God creating the earth. We see God the Father and my friend the Holy Spirit here. I always asked, "Where was God the Son?"

God the Son was very present. In the beginning, God the Son is the WORD that was with God the Father. In Genesis, He had no physical body; a body had not been created for Him yet (see Hebrews 10:5). John, the disciple of Jesus Christ, through the revelation of my friend, reveals Jesus clearly to us in the scriptures we just read. He speaks of God the Son, who existed in the beginning as God the WORD, whom God the Father spoke, and my friend the Holy Spirit manifested.

Power of life and death is in the tongue. Words are spirit. A spirit is not visible, but its actions are. We cannot see the words we speak, but we see the manifestation of our words. The world was created with the power of the spoken Word. The Word God spoke out in the beginning was Christ, and the power that manifested Christ, the Word, was the Holy Spirit. We have been given the same creative power.

The Word of God, being Spirit, is part of the full armor of God discussed in Ephesians 6. It is the only offensive weapon we have against the enemy. All others are defensive armors. Therefore, without the Word, there is no way any believer can be victorious over the enemy.

"Death and life are in the power of the tongue, and those who love it and indulge it will eat its fruit and bear the consequences of their words." (Proverbs 18:21, AMP)

In the beginning God (Elohim) created [by forming from nothing] the heavens and the earth. The earth was formless and void or a waste and emptiness, and darkness was upon the face of the deep [primeval ocean that covered the unformed earth]. The Spirit of God was moving (hovering, brooding) over the face of the waters. And God said, "Let there be light"; and there was light. (Genesis 1:1–3, AMP)

Then God said, "Let Us (Father, Son, Holy Spirit) make man in Our image, according to Our likeness [not physical, but a spiritual personality and moral likeness]; and let them have complete authority over the fish of the sea, the birds of the air, the cattle, and over the entire earth, and over everything that creeps and crawls on the earth." So God created man in His own image, in the image and likeness of God He created him;

male and female He created them. (Genesis 1:26–27, AMP)

Moses in Genesis and John the disciple of Jesus in the book of John speak of the same thing. John explains who Christ was in Genesis. God the Father needed both God the Son and God the Holy Spirit to create.

"You hide your face: they are troubled; you take away their breath: they die and return to the dust. You send out your Spirit and they are created. You renew the face of the ground." (Psalm 104:29–30)

"The Spirit of God has made me, and the breath of the Almighty gives me life." (Job 33:4)

God never created anything apart from the WORD—Jesus. God is a God of order. Have you wondered about this? If God can think and act, why did He have to SPEAK out the WORD before it manifested? Why say what He wants to do, and then do it? Can you picture yourself speaking out loud what you want to see, and it happens? We possess the same power because we have been created in the image and likeness of God.

I find it very fascinating and eye-opening that God the Father saw the darkness on earth and instead of Him speaking out what He saw or acknowledging the reality of the situation, He spoke out what He wanted to see, or the situation to become. He never called out to the angels or even out loud to Himself, and neither did He say to the Holy Spirit, "Hey, Holy Spirit! It is too dark out there!"

God did not do this because He does not endorse evil. He is not a God who acknowledges darkness, giving it power to rule. He is a holy, all-powerful God! Remember what He did with Gideon? When God saw Gideon hiding from his enemies, He did not speak out what He saw Gideon doing, nor did He acknowledge the fear that was in Gideon at the time. Instead,

God spoke what He had placed in Gideon during creation and what He wanted Gideon to do and become: A mighty man of war!

"Yahweh's angel came, and sat under the oak which was in Ophrah, that belonged to Joash the Abiezrite. His son Gideon was beating out wheat in the wine press, to hide it from the Midianites. Yahweh's angel appeared to him, and said to him, "Yahweh is with you, you mighty man of valor!"" (Judges 6:11–12)

God renamed Abraham and Sarah, his wife. He called them a father and mother of many nations while they were still BARREN. He never once acknowledged their barrenness or even called them by it.

> When Abram was ninety-nine years old, Yahweh appeared to Abram, and said to him, "I am God Almighty. Walk before me, and be blameless. I will make my covenant between me and you, and will multiply you exceedingly." Abram fell on his face. God talked with him, saying, "As for me, behold, my covenant is with you. You will be the father of a multitude of nations. Your name will no more be called Abram, but your name will be Abraham; for I have made you the father of a multitude of nations. I will make you exceedingly fruitful, and I will make nations of you. Kings will come out of you." (Genesis 17:1–6)

"God said to Abraham, "As for Sarai your wife, you shall not call her name Sarai, but her name will be Sarah. I will bless her, and moreover I will give you a son by her. Yes, I will bless her, and she will be a mother of nations. Kings of peoples will come from her." Then Abraham fell on his face, and laughed, and said in his heart, "Will a child be born to him who is one hundred years old? Will Sarah, who is ninety years old, give birth?" (Genesis 17:15–17)

Jesus is the WORD of God; therefore, when God spoke, He spoke Christ Jesus, who was and is the WORD; and the Holy Spirit manifested Christ, the WORD, in creation. That is why John said that Christ Jesus, the WORD, came down to His creation, because nothing was made apart from Him; yet, His own creation did not recognize or receive Him.

Hebrews 3:1 says that Jesus Christ is the High Priest of our confession. What we confess according to His Word, Christ speaks it to the Father, the Father acknowledges and endorses the Word by speaking it out for the Holy Spirit to manifest it. Whenever we confess negative from what Christ says, He will not speak the negative word to His Father because He is not a creator of evil. He cannot deny Himself at all.

Instead, the negative words we speak are taken by the enemy, and he runs with the words to God the Father in the courtroom of heaven. The devil then quotes the Word of God that says that power of life and death is in the tongue, and they that love talking too much will reap the harvest of their words, just as Proverbs 18:21 states. He then advocates for the negative words spoken to come to pass in your life according to the laws in the spirit realm and the principle in God's Word. Because God honors His Word over His name, the negative word must come to pass.

Psalm 138:2b, King James Version (KJV) says, ". . . for thou hast magnified thy word above all thy name."

God explained this to me one day as I was meditating on all the evil I saw and heard on earth. He said that the heavens belonged to Him but the earth He has given to men. Therefore, He will not do what we do not ask Him to do on earth. He can, but He won't do it because He will not violate His word and invade earth without our invitation.

"The heavens are the heavens of Yahweh; but the earth has he given to the children of men." (Psalm 115:16)

"God said, "Let us make man in our image, after our likeness: and let them have dominion over the fish of the sea, and over the birds of the sky, and over the livestock, and over all the earth, and over every creeping thing that creeps on the earth." (Genesis 1:26)

God will not take back the authority He gave to man. He never included Himself in having dominion over all the earth. When things go wrong in a company or an organization, the first person to question is whoever is in authority. When evil prevails on earth, it is our fault, not God's. Have you taken charge through prayer and fasting? Have you changed your ways and your thinking? Have you given yourself, your time, and resources to help the needy or get involved in improving the community? Or are you just confessing what you see and enforcing evil with your words instead of taking authority over the evil on earth? Whom are you blaming for not staying on your knees as a watchman and enforcing the Kingdom of God on earth?

We possess what we confess. The power of life and death is in what we speak. When we pray according to God's Word, confessing what He has already declared, we invite Him to operate on earth on our behalf. We permit Him to bring heaven down to earth. Just as Jesus taught us to pray, "Your Kingdom come, and Your will be done on earth as it is in Heaven." God's Word never fails. Just like when one breaks the law and the consequences of breaking the law are activated, so do the consequences of your words get activated.

As we speak, our words begin to create, manifesting our confession on earth. We then turn around and blame God for our problems, and those in the world around us while we created the problem because we have the same creative power which God has. However, instead of fixing the problem, we use our tongues to create greater problems. The devil has no power to create at all. Remember, he is just a servant, an angel who has no portion in the inheritance of God's Kingdom. He was never created in the image and likeness of God. He, therefore, cannot curse or bless just as much as an angel of God cannot curse you or bless you.

The angel has no creative power apart from what God has given him from being at God's service. Angels do what they are commanded by God to do. Even Satan himself only does what God allows him to do. That is why it is critical that we live according to God's Word so that the enemy does not use it against us. There is nowhere in God's Word where we see the devil cursing anyone. In fact, even the angel of God who came to fight Satan over Moses' body could not curse Satan. He referred him back to God, saying, "The Lord rebuke you!"

"But even Michael, one of the mightiest of the angels, did not dare accuse the devil of blasphemy, but simply said, "The Lord rebuke you!" (This took place when Michael was arguing with the devil about Moses' body.). (Jude 9:9, NLT)

This is because the power of life and death is in the tongue of God and those created in His image—humans. God knew that if He saw the darkness on the earth and acknowledged it, darkness would prevail. Therefore, we must speak as God speaks. Look at the situation, ask what God thinks about it, and then speak God's will over the situation for manifestation.

One lady, a believer I worked with, felt sad as she told me how one time she had been wounded by a certain man, and out of anger, she wished death upon him. She spoke out loud, saying, "I wish he would die and go to hell!"

Needless to say, the following day, she found out that the man had died that night of a heart attack. She felt very guilty afterward, but the damage had already been done. This is what the tongue does. She acted like a witch and cursed the man, instead of acting as a priest and blessing and interceding for the man who hurt her, that he may be forgiven and come to the knowledge of Christ, just like Christ commanded us to do. See how much power we have in our tongue? With our tongue, we empower the kingdom of darkness or the Kingdom of light. Who are *you* empowering? God or Satan? We need to pray like David did and ask God to "Take control of what I say, O Lord, and guard my lips. Don't let me drift toward evil or take part in acts of wickedness. Don't let me share in the delicacies of those who do wrong." (Psalm 141:3–4, NLT)

"Whoever speaks, let it be with God's words. Whoever serves, do so with the strength that God supplies, so that in everything God will be glorified through Jesus Christ. To him belong the glory and the power forever and ever. Amen." (1 Peter 4:11, NET)

We must have the mind of Christ to think and talk like God. How do we attain this? Only by the help and power of God the Holy Spirit.

"These things we also speak, not in words which man's wisdom teaches but which the Holy Spirit teaches, comparing spiritual things with spiritual. But the natural man does not receive the things of the Spirit of God, for they are foolishness to him; nor can he know them, because they are spiritually discerned. But he who is spiritual judges all things, yet he himself is rightly judged by no one. For "who has known the mind of the Lord that he may instruct Him?" But we have the mind of Christ." (1 Corinthians 2:13–16, NKJV)

We cannot be successful in thinking or speaking right without my friend. He is the most excellent help we have from God. He teaches us the things of God, the secret things of God.

"He who didn't spare his own Son, but delivered him up for us all, how would he not also with him freely give us all things?" (Romans 8:32)

The only way the devil can have creative power is if we allow him to use our mouths by confessing what he shows us or brings to mind. He can only give us ideas because he speaks into our minds. We are creators on earth. We create good or bad. We create light or darkness. God has given us a choice. Before you speak, think of what your words will create.

Before you speak, stop and compare your words with God's Word and will. Ask yourself: "Would God say what I want to say?" If not, don't say it. Rebuke the thought and replace it with God's Word. Say what Christ would say in that situation. We are supposed to enforce God's will on earth, not the devil's. Heaven is the Supreme Court, and we are the branches of the Supreme Court, and we enforce what the Supreme Court of heaven has ruled. We don't make our own rules. Instead, we enforce rules that God has already put in place.

As a child, when my parents took me to the physician for a visit, the first thing the doctor said to me was "Stick out your tongue for me." He or she would then look at my tongue and down my throat for signs of sickness. Just like the physicians then, when we go to our Father God in prayer, He first tells us to stick out our tongues so He can see the words we have been speaking. This is because what we say, we create. What have *you* been speaking? Life or death? Have your words been creating or destroying?

One day, I was praying to God about a specific situation, and as I knelt in my living room, in the middle of my prayer, God the Father stopped me and said, "Stop! What did I say about that situation?"

I stopped and repeated to Him what He had said. Then He said, "Then stop praying about it and declare it! Just say what I said."

I did exactly that, and it came to pass! God wants us to believe in what He says and place a demand on it. Take Him at His WORD. In other words, we must return His WORD to Him for manifestation. Just like the scripture says:

"For as the heavens are higher than the earth, so are my ways higher than your ways, and my thoughts than your thoughts. For as the rain comes down and the snow from the sky, and doesn't return there, but waters the earth, and makes it grow and bud, and gives seed to the sower and bread to the eater; so is my word that goes out of my mouth: It will not return to me void, but it will accomplish that which I please, and it will prosper in the thing I sent it to do." (Isaiah 55:9–11)

We return God's Word by declaring it out loud, and as it goes back to God to report that it has completed its mission, it accomplishes and prospers in what it was sent to do. When we pray, we should ask God to reveal His will to us so we can pray His will on earth. That is what prayer is supposed to be. God communicates His will to us through the Holy Spirit. We all need my friend's help in prayer to represent heaven faithfully. Remember what Jesus said? The Holy Spirit reveals the will of the Father to us. He tells us of things to come. (John 16:13)

My friend the Holy Spirit was there in the beginning, hovering over the chaos of the earth. He never brought anything to order on His own accord or will. He saw what was happening on earth. He saw the darkness, chaos, and disorder; yet, He never did anything about it. Why? Isn't He God? Isn't He in charge of all that is happening? Isn't He powerful and mighty and can do all things? Isn't He a God of order, and nothing is impossible with Him? Then why even record Him hovering in the chaos? Does God live in chaos?

My friend the Holy Spirit was on earth surveying the chaotic situation and coming up with a plan to fix the chaos. The Holy Spirit was the architectural wisdom of God in creation. He was deployed first because He is the Kingdom designer. He is the one who makes things beautiful, more like the female part of God. If you send a man and woman to organize a chaotic office, most times the man will organize, but the woman will both organize and design the office. A home without a good woman is not as lively as one with one. Why is this so? Because men and women see things differently. That is why the combination of man and woman brings completion in a home. Fruitfulness and multiplication come from this union alone. The Holy Spirit was God the Father's helper in creation, just as Eve was supposed to be for Adam.

The Holy Spirit is symbolic of the dove that Noah sent to see if the earth was dry enough for them to get out of the ark. The dove guided Noah's next move in history. This move meant life or death. God did not speak to Noah and tell him it was all dry. The Holy Spirit did this for Noah as symbolized by the dove. After bringing them to safety and dry ground, the dove left and never returned to the ark. The dove knew that life was limited in the ark and wanted them to follow it into the fullness of what God was saving for them.

They were saved from death so that they could enjoy the earth which God so thoughtfully created for them. The dove knew that Noah would remain in the ark if he returned to the ark, so he had to lead them out of their temporary shelter in this way. The Holy Spirit appeared as a dove at Jesus' baptism and stayed with Christ, guiding Him until He fulfilled His created purpose. The indwelling Holy Spirit is a gift from God for which we must be very grateful. He leads us to spiritual safety by changing us and making us like Christ that we may have everlasting life and enjoy the fullness of God's Kingdom, which is why God saved us from death.

Noah's ark is symbolic of being in hidden Christ (John 3:16, that those who believe in Christ shall not perish but have eternal life). The dove in the ark was symbolic of the Holy Spirit, being led by the Holy Spirit into abundant life, life everlasting (see the story in Genesis 8:6–12). Those who entered the ark represent those who believe in God's sacrifice, Jesus Christ, who is the ark of our refuge and salvation from the impending destruction of eternal death.

The dove was inside the ark with Noah; then it was sent out to survey the land, just as the Holy Spirit was doing in the beginning at creation, but it returned to Noah in the ark, and he accepted it back because it was not yet safe for them to get out of the ark. Then after seven days, the dove was sent again. After a survey, it was time for the dove to lead them into the next stage of life because it was safe. The dove never returned to the ark so that Noah and his family, including all the animals, could get out of the ark and follow the dove into greater territory.

The dove did not return to stay in the ark once it was safe for them to go out, just as the Holy Spirit will not stay in Christians who do not want to progress and be ambassadors for God's Kingdom. Those who follow the dove's guidance are those who enjoy life more abundantly and are free to enjoy the freedom and fullness of God's Kingdom. Had Noah, his family, and the animals chosen to remain in the ark, ignoring the guidance of the dove (the Holy Spirit), they would be limited and never enjoy the earth or the fullness of it (God's Kingdom and its fullness).

They would eventually outgrow the ark, deplete their supplies and resources, and probably result to attacking and destroying each other for their survival. They would end up spreading infection due to poor sanitation, leading to illnesses, diseases, and or death.

In this case, the Ark that had saved them from the flood would end up being the trap that destroys them. This situation would be unfortunate and devastating, where one would consider those destroyed by the floods better off since their destruction came as a penalty for their disobedience and sin towards God. However, Noah and all who were with him would have perished for lack of understanding that the situation had changed, and it was time for them to move to the next phase. The dove therefore served the purpose of guiding them into their new world where they would thrive without limits. Sadly, this is the case today where people refuse to grow in Christ through the leadership and guidance of the Holy Spirit, making the scripture spoken by Hosea true that "people of God perish for lack of knowledge." (Hosea 4:6)

Doesn't that sound like the church today? Old and tired in the ark? Someone spoke this reality, that "the church is the only army where soldiers attack each other." They get on each other's nerves; they destroy each other's marriages, businesses, and reputation; they get tired of each other and infect each other with gossip, slander, adultery, fornication, abortions, and hatred—which is murder, backstabbing, and jealousy, judging each other and ridiculing those who are trying to grow. They discriminate and show partiality. They have a false sense of security, thinking that because they are Christians, they are guaranteed heaven, eternal life. They, therefore, take the grace of God as a license to sin and end up dying eternally.

The ark was only good for a short-time rescue; it was not built for long-term survival. The dove led them to their survival phase with greater access to the earth and life more abundantly. In the church, Jesus' blood is the requirement for getting into the "Ark," but the blood alone cannot sustain us and make us holy, for the Word says that without holiness, no one shall see God (Hebrews 12:14). God the Father, God the Son, and God the Holy Spirit all play an active role in the redemption plan. The plan comes as a package that cannot be separated. It's an all or none package.

However, Satan has sent out a counterfeit spirit which has deceived many people and made them separate the redemption package to form different false religions. This gives them a false sense of security and hope of redemption only to be destroyed in the end. We cannot create our own redemption plan because we are not qualified to redeem ourselves. Anyone who does not believe in the Father, the Son, and the Holy Spirit is headed for destruction. There is no way around it. Beloved, do not accept religion ignorantly. Ask my friend the Holy Spirit, and He will help you to discern this counterfeit spirit. Jesus never promised us religion; He promised us a Helper to teach us relationship and intimacy with God and Kingdom living.

How do we know if we are enrolled in the right redemption package? There are three who bear witness for redemption: the water, the blood, and the Spirit. The blood of Jesus on its own will sustain you for a short while, but it is not enough for the Christian lifestyle. How many Christians do you know who do not live like Christ? They are actually worse than non-believers. Does this make sense now? If you just accept Christ and ignore the Holy Spirit, you will be destroyed. Remember, it is all or none. Don't die in the ark; follow the Holy Spirit. The disciples got the water; the Word of God cleansed them; then the blood of Jesus on the cross; and the baptism of the Holy Spirit and fire at Pentecost. Christ's disciples had to wait for and receive the Holy Spirit. When they did, they were led out of their "ark" into their assigned places for training and deployment, to conquer the enemy's kingdom and take back the territory for God's Kingdom. This is how it must be with us.

Jesus was very careful to warn His disciples not to ignore the third witness. He made it clear to them that although they knew the Word and were cleansed by His blood, they still lacked the final redemption witness. The disciples had to wait for the Holy Spirit, who, when they obeyed Christ, longed for the Holy Spirit, and received Him, became successful witnesses for Christ. That is why the gospel is still alive today because their witness was that effective. They had the full redemption package to offer to the world. What about *you*? Are you an effective witness of Christ? Do you have the full redemption package?

A successful Christian must have in them the full redemption package at all times in order to be a faithful witness. We cannot survive with only one witness; God the Father, God the

Son and God the Holy Spirit are inseparable.

Before believing:

1. You hear **God's Word** (water); you realize you are a sinner.
2. You receive Christ, and **the blood** of Jesus cleanses you.
3. You ask for and receive the baptism of **the Holy Spirit**.

After believing:

1. You must continue a lifestyle of studying **God's Word** daily for continuous cleansing and deliverance.
2. You must continue a lifestyle of applying **the blood** of Jesus daily for continuous righteousness.
3. You must continue a lifestyle of yielding to **the Holy Spirit** for continuous guidance into God's will and obedience, receiving spiritual intelligence, wisdom, knowledge, and understanding.

All the three witnesses are a MUST-HAVE continually for redemption and to be successful witnesses of Christ. This is who a real Christian is, one who operates in the full package.

"**Who is he who overcomes the world**, but he who believes that Jesus is the Son of God? This is He who came by **water and blood**—Jesus Christ; not only by **water**, but by water and **blood**. And it is the **Spirit** who bears witness, because the Spirit is truth. For there are three that bear witness in heaven: *the Father, the Word, and the Holy Spirit*; and **these three are one**. And there are three that bear witness on earth: *the Spirit, the water, and the blood*; and **these three agree as**

one." (1 John 5:5–8, NKJV; emphasis added)

In the same way, the children of Israel's action of sacrificing the Passover lamb and applying the blood of the lamb on the doorposts only saved them from the spirit of death. Crossing the Red Sea saved them from their enemies, but refusing to follow the leadership of the Holy Spirit led to their death in the wilderness. They had the blood of the lamb, the water of the Red Sea, and God's Word (the Ten Commandments), but they rejected the third witness, the Holy Spirit.

Needless to say, they died in the wilderness after all the trouble they went through. It would have been better if they died in Egypt as slaves than to die in freedom like fools because they lacked the knowledge of the THIRD WITNESS. However, we see two men, Caleb and Joshua, who embraced the third witness. They followed the leadership of the Holy Spirit and were transformed, receiving a new Spirit and the mind of God, which gave them access to the Promised Land. Do *you* have a new Spirit and the mind of Christ? This is a must-have to enter into the Promised Land.

Beloved, let us not be deceived. Being born again is not just a one-step process. Receiving Christ is enrolling into spiritual warfare in God's Kingdom against the kingdom of darkness. It is vowing to protect and serve the Kingdom of God. This alone doesn't make you a trained military commander ready to be deployed. You need a military trainer who will teach, train, and equip you for Kingdom warfare, give you your assignment and deploy you.

It is similar to enrolling into the earthly military. When you enroll, you are assigned a trainer to teach, train, and equip you to be ready for battle and ultimate victory over the enemy. Without training, you will be destroyed by the enemy. Your country cannot help you because you refused to be equipped to protect and serve. They have the right to dismiss you because you are a liability to them and their military as you might sell them out to the enemy.

Because you do not know the rules of engagement, you will break under pressure, giving the enemy the upper hand. You are, therefore, no good to the country or yourself. It is better for you to remain a civilian than to enroll as a militant, go to war untrained, and die as a fool because of lack of knowledge. You will only have yourself to blame for your death.

The third witness of Christ, my Friend the Holy Spirit, is last but not least. He is here for the final run because the first witness, water, in the Old Testament law that came through God the Father, has already come. The second witness, the blood, in the New Testament that was shed by the Son, is a done deal. Now, the grand finale . . . The third witness, the Holy Spirit outpouring, in the Now Testament, has already been poured out by the Father on all flesh to complete the work of the Holy Trinity.

The three witnesses are one and inseparable: God the Father (The **water,** the Old Covenant, the Ten Commandments), God the Son (the **blood** of the New Covenant), and God the Holy Spirit (the anointing and power of God by His **Spirit**). There is no other argument about this. The three witnesses complete the redemption work. Without one, you cannot be redeemed. Remember, you are going to live in their home; therefore, you might as well get to know all three God heads, appreciate and accept their work of redemption for your sake. It is all or none. Just like you cannot love and accept me but despise and reject my husband and children and be welcome in my home. For you to be accepted in my home you have to love and accept all of us. It is all or none.

One time, years ago, my mother saw how much anger and rage was in me over a particular issue she was trying to help reconcile. At the time, I had begun a close walk with the Holy Spirit, and she knew that my friend was living in me. After the situation was settled, she said in surprise, "Wow! I didn't know that the Holy Spirit can live in such a hostile environment!"

I was surprised too! I did not know that I had such anger in me either. I now understand why my friend the Holy Spirit was still in my chaotic being and why He was still in David's sinful nature when he committed adultery with Bathsheba, and why He is still in your chaotic self today.

The Holy Spirit is the spiritual organizer and designer of our spiritual chaos. He came to the chaos of earth after the devil's fall, which caused darkness over the earth. There, He brought order and design. In the same way, the devil causes chaos in our spirits before we receive Christ, and after we are born again in Christ, the Holy Spirit comes in us to organize and design our spirits and souls from the chaos caused by the kingdom of darkness.

The Holy Spirit first brings light; that is, He illuminates Christ to a nonbeliever. Just as we look for the light switch as soon as we enter a dark room, the Holy Spirit turns the light on first before He does anything in us. He is a Spirit of the light, not of darkness. When a nonbeliever is convicted of sin and receives Christ into their hearts, His light shines so brightly, putting out the darkness in their hearts (spirits).

At creation, the Holy Spirit never designed anything before He brought the light which chased away the darkness. Before designing anything, light has to be created first; then order must be established, and then design and beautification follow. Which stage are you in? Chaotic phase, still in darkness, with no Christ in your life? Or are you a believer who is not cooperating with the Holy Spirit; you are backslidden and living in sin? Or are you in the organization stage, where you are allowing the Holy Spirit to organize, rearrange, prune, uproot, throw away, tear down, destroy, and overthrow evil from your life? In other words, are you being delivered from all evil within you? Or are you in the design stage where you are born again, delivered, completely sold out to God? Are you living under the complete guidance and leadership of my friend the Holy Spirit? Are you allowing my friend to beautify you and make you a prepared bride for Christ?

The Holy Spirit is there to stir your spirit and soul up to reveal the evil in you, that you may, with His help, deal with it. This is the process of deliverance. Deliverance is a continuous process. You cannot deal with what you do not know, just like you can't fix what you don't know is broken. Some sins are hidden from us unless God the Holy Spirit reveals them.

This is because the devil is evil and sly! He wants to hide your sin from you so that you continue to live under a curse, and then he convinces you that God is a liar and does not keep His Word, and that is why you are unsuccessful or sick or broke, which causes you to sin even more by resenting God. These are the sins which David, with the help of the Holy Spirit, prayed for God to reveal to him. No wonder David cried and asked God not to take His Holy Spirit from Him, because he knew that the only way he would know the Father's heart is through my friend the Holy Spirit.

"How can I know all the sins lurking in my heart? Cleanse me from these hidden faults." (Psalm 19:12, NLT)

An example of this for me was the traditional naming of

children in my culture. I grew up in the Kikuyu tribe, and some things my tribe traditionally does that seem innocent are a sin. Like naming children after family members to carry on the name is ancestral worship. This naming pattern gives the enemy a bridge access to the child through the name. God was and still is very particular with names. He never called anyone after another. Instead, God often changed people's names when He wanted to bless them.

Like He did with Abraham, the father of many nations, or Sarah, mother of many nations, and Gideon, a mighty man of war. What about Jacob—trickster—to Israel—a ruler with God, to mention just a few? God named people according to their assignment. Just like we name objects after their purpose. If I ask for a knife, you know that I want to cut something. If I ask for a nail clipper, you know that I want to clip nails. Our names, therefore, should point us to our God-given tasks. For example, Jesus means "savior" (Matthew 1:21), and He lived up to His name. He came to save us from our sin. What about Nabal? (1 Samuel 25) His name means "fool," and he also lived up to his name and died a fool. What does *your* name mean? Are you living up to it?

At work, people are distinguished by their name tags that spell out their title, which is connected to their job description. In the same way, we were created and given a title (name) that is connected to our job description in God's Kingdom. Do you know your created title? Are you living according to your assignment? Does your life match your created name and job title? How would you know this? Are you still searching because your parents named you traditionally and did not care to ask the creator what He calls you, or what He created you to do?

Just because we do not know that something we are doing

is sin, that doesn't mean that this hidden sin will not open doors to the demonic realm to operate freely in our lives. Remember the hidden sins? That is why we need my friend the Holy Spirit to reveal them to us because ignorance is no defense. Just because you did not know the speed limit on a street doesn't mean that you will not get a ticket if the police catch you. The law works at all times; it never takes a break nor does it makes exceptions. The law is there to administer punishment to lawbreakers. I share more on this in my book, *Your God-Given Task*.

When you invite some professional cleaner to clean your house, they will move furniture around and clean up, exposing all the hidden dirt so that the house can be spotless. In my young life, I went through so much heartache and pain that I harbored many soul wounds and anger in me which I did not realize. I had not dealt with my heart. I had suppressed a lot, and because I had asked for the Holy Spirit to indwell me, rearrange His new home, and empty me of everything that is not of God, He sure got on to it one by one.

When I was a young girl in Africa, we fetched water from the well. We often waited for the dirt to settle down in the container to filter the water and then boil it. Looking at the water from the top, it looked clean, but when it was stirred up, all the dirt was revealed, which made the water unsafe for human consumption until proper filtration occurred. The Holy Spirit works similarly. He stirs up our hearts to reveal the evil in us so that we can be aware of the sins hiding inside us which keep us from inheriting all that God has for us.

The Holy Spirit hovering over the chaos and not doing anything about it is because there is order in heaven. God operates in harmony. He is three in one, and each Godhead has his role.

God is not an author of confusion. He runs a vast and prosperous Kingdom—the most powerful and wealthiest Kingdom in heaven and earth. He is the ruler and creator, the Alpha and the Omega, the Beginning and the End, the First and the Last. He is all in all. He exists and operates in order.

God the Father speaks the Word, who is God the Son, and the Word (Christ) is made manifest by God the Holy Spirit. Without God the Father speaking His Son (the Word), God the Holy Spirit has nothing to work with. Remember, the Holy Spirit never does anything on His own accord. He only does what the Father speaks (John 16:13). He manifests God the Son, who is explained clearly by John, the disciple of Christ.

In John 1:1, John records that in the beginning was the WORD (JESUS), and the WORD was with God, and the WORD was indeed God. In the beginning, nothing was made apart from Him (the WORD). Through the Son (Word), all things were made. Just like you exist in harmony as three in one that is; spirit, soul, and body, and your spirit cannot do the work of your body or the work of your soul, God is a God of order with each Godhead performing their work in harmony. That is why God the Son was the one who had to die, and not God the Father or God the Holy Spirit.

Why God the Son? Because God the Father wanted to produce more sons and daughters. In order to do this, He had to sow a seed of a child to get many children. If you want corn, you sow corn seeds and not mango seeds. You sow what you want to reap. It is a principle on earth. God's Word says in Luke 6:38, to give and it will come back to you, good measure, pressed down, shaken together and running over.

No one could do Jesus' work; only He could. The Holy Spirit responds only to God's Word and manifests it. He does not speak His own words; He speaks what the Father speaks. What belongs to the Father belongs to the Son. Jesus said this so clearly in John 16:12–14. The Holy Spirit, therefore, works to manifest the power of God through His WORD (Jesus Christ).

"These signs will accompany those who have believed: in My name they will cast out demons, they will speak in new tongues; they will pick up serpents, and if they drink anything deadly, it will not hurt them; they will lay hands on the sick, and they will get well." So then, when the Lord Jesus had spoken to them, He was taken up into heaven and sat down at the right hand of God." (Mark 16:17–19, AMP)

"And they went out and preached everywhere, while the Lord was working with them and CONFIRMING THE WORD BY THE SIGNS THAT FOLLOWED." (Mark 16:20, AMP; emphasis added)

The Holy Spirit responds and confirms God's Word with signs and wonders! He confirms or manifests the Word who is Jesus!

"[and besides this evidence] God also testifying with them [confirming the message of salvation], both by signs and wonders and by various miracles [carried out by Jesus and the apostles] and by [granting to believers the] gifts of the Holy Spirit according to His own will." (Hebrews 2:4, AMP)

The Holy Spirit of God was hovering in the chaos, not in the perfect earth. He, however, perfected it at God's Word. The lesson here is that God the Holy Spirit comes to purify and cleanse us according to the Father's desire and standards. Without Him, order would not have been accomplished in the chaos. He raised Jesus from the dead and changed the chaos of death into victory over death.

The Holy Spirit knows God's perfect will, so He exists to reveal and perfect it in us who believe and receive Him. Therefore, if you are born again in Christ and have chaos in your life, it doesn't mean that the Holy Spirit is not around. All you need to do is speak to the chaotic situation and declare God's will over your life as revealed to you by my friend, and watch the Holy Spirit put things in order according to the Word of God.

The Holy Spirit's act of bringing order into chaos only after God the Father released the Son (the Word) was symbolic of the order which was going to come to earth through Christ in a dark, chaotic world of sin. The light of Christ's salvation was going to shine into the darkness as the Father released the Son to earth, and God the Holy Spirit manifested Him in conception, trained Him as He grew up, equipped Him for His assignment, strengthened Him even unto death, and raised Him up again at resurrection to give Him victory over death. My friend illuminates Christ into the hearts of men and women who seek to know God.

The structure of the Holy Trinity

1. God the **Father thinks** it (The Mind/**Wisdom** of God)
2. God the **Son speaks** it (The **Word**/Wisdom of God)
3. God the **Holy Spirit manifests** it (The Wisdom/**Acts or Power of God**)

God the Father is the mastermind. He thinks of the plan, as we see in Genesis, then God the Son puts it into Words, and then God the Holy Spirit puts the Words into action. Therefore, my friend, the Holy Spirit manifests God the Father's will through

God the Son. This is just like we operate. The spirit gives life, the soul feeds from the spirit, and the body manifests what the soul and spirit have agreed upon. They work in agreement.

The body is the action part of the spirit and soul. It is their manifestation. Your spirit may be bubbling with praise, your soul takes it and interprets it, puts it into feelings and words, and the body acts it out . . . lifts up your hands, dances, kneels, cries, shouts praises, etc., all in manifestation of what your spirit willed and your soul interpreted. The body acts it all out for others to see.

If someone is paralyzed and mute, there is no way of knowing how they feel because the body does not manifest it, unless they can speak and put it into words. Otherwise, they are powerlessly trapped in their own body. In the same way, a Christian without God the Holy Spirit is a spiritually paraplegic Christian. No one can see any manifestation of God through them. They are powerless Christians, no good for the Kingdom of God as they introduce disability which the enemy uses against God's Kingdom. Paul condemned these powerless Christians when he said, "But I will come—and soon—if the Lord lets me, and then I'll find out whether these arrogant people just give pretentious speeches or whether they really have God's power. For the Kingdom of God is not just a lot of talk; it is living by God's power." (1 Corinthians 4:19–20, NLT)

We can never win anyone to Christ without my friend's help. We can never be faithful or successful witnesses for Christ without Him because the Holy Spirit is Christ's witness. Now, I know why Jesus never performed a single miracle before He was baptized with the Holy Spirit.

Jesus, who was the Word, was sent by God the Father, but He needed someone to manifest Him. The Holy Spirit had to be present, or the ministry of Christ would be a paralyzed ministry. The first sign that John the Baptist was told to look for as a witness of the messiah was the dwelling presence of the Holy Spirit. My friend is the perfect witness of Christ. Jesus knew this, and He did not dare start His ministry without the baptism of God the Holy Spirit. That is why Christ told His disciples not to go preaching until they received the baptism of the Holy Spirit because the Holy Spirit would manifest Jesus, the Word, with signs and wonders following. That is why we have the book of Acts. He is the Acts of God.

The Holy Spirit will not move before the Word is spoken, the Word will not be spoken before God the Father wills it, and the Word cannot be manifested or brought to pass without God the Holy Spirit. The Word will not come forth without the Father, and that was why God sent His Word, Jesus, to be conceived or made manifest by God the Holy Spirit. Jesus Christ never went back to God the Father void. He accomplished all that He was sent to do through God the Holy Spirit. Nothing God has willed and Christ has spoken will fail to be manifested by the Holy Spirit. That is why Jesus kept saying over and over again that the words He spoke and actions He performed were not His own, but the Father's. Christ never took credit for the Father's mastermind, planning, and thinking. Instead, He always acknowledged the Father, giving Him all the glory.

God the Holy Spirit is on earth now in this last testament to bring chaos into order through Jesus Christ, whom God sent. The Holy Spirit is the power of God! That is why no one can ever know God or Jesus Christ without Him because He is the one who illuminates them. You do not see Him, but you see His works; what God the Father has released to us through

His Son (the Word).

The Holy Spirit is now on earth because this is the last testament, and this generation is the most chaotic generation since the beginning of creation. He is here to bring back order through the Father's sacrifice of Christ. He is here to perfect and complete the work which God began in us through the sacrifice of His Son, to present to Jesus a prepared bride, and to the Father, mature sons and daughters.

"being confident of this very thing, that he who began a good work in you will complete it until the day of Jesus Christ." (Philippians 1:6)

The Holy Spirit is preparing us for Jesus' return. That is why He is here on earth to perfect us in Christ. When the Word became flesh and was given the name Jesus, the Holy Spirit did what He did in the beginning but now in the Spirit. God saw that the human race was dark and void. The Father spoke Christ into the human race to bring light into the darkness within us to restore man unto Himself.

The Holy Spirit conceived Christ in Mary's womb and brought light into darkness and order into chaos; life into a dying world. There is no Holy Spirit without Christ. God gives the Holy Spirit only to those who receive Christ as their Lord and Savior. The Holy Spirit is the personal trainer for kingdom living. We do not know how to live in God's Kingdom because we came from the kingdom of darkness. Laws and principles are different in every kingdom.

For instance, if you go to a country you have never been to before, you will need a map and someone to advise and guide you on the laws of the land. You will need to know what is required of you to live successfully and to prosper in that land. To be a citizen of the country, you will need to know what is expected of you and about your rights as a citizen. You may need to read a book or take a class which informs you of the country's expectations of its citizens.

But if you go to the country ignorantly with no one to guide you, you will find yourself in trouble most of the time. You will get frustrated living there in your own wisdom because you cannot live in the new country using the same laws you had in your former country. If you do, you will struggle, fail, and get in trouble with the law. You will be deported or voluntarily go back to your former country instead of staying in the country where you could have been very successful. You may even lose your life there, perishing for lack of knowledge because you have rejected knowledge. You refused to learn their laws.

Likewise, if you try living in God's Kingdom with the wisdom of the world, you will be frustrated and will fail miserably. You will live under a curse instead of blessings. You will not know how to live in God's Kingdom and succeed like Christ did. You will perish for lack of knowledge because you have rejected the guidance of the Kingdom guide, my friend the Holy Spirit. This is the mistake many Christians make. We become citizens of God's Kingdom by the blood of Jesus, receiving Him as our Lord and Savior. We even get the manual for the Kingdom, the Bible, but we do not ask to receive our tour guide and Kingdom mentor—God the Holy Spirit. When a student ignores their instructor, they will fail. We then go about God's Kingdom in our worldly wisdom and wonder why we are not prosperous or blessed.

No one can succeed in another country by using their former country's laws, rules, and regulations. I was born in Kenya, East Africa, and learned to drive on the left side of the road.

I came to the United States of America (U.S.A.), and even though I had a Kenyan driver's license, I was not allowed to drive in the States without training and learning about their driving laws. I had to take, and pass, a written test as well as a behind-the-wheel driving test. If a country on earth that will one day come to an end requires this kind of training and competency to succeed in it, how much more does the eternal Kingdom require training and competency to succeed?

What if I were ignorant and failed to get familiar with the laws of driving in the U.S.A.? Several things would have happened. I would drive on the wrong side of the road, I would not know what to do at an intersection while making a left turn because I was used to roundabouts in Kenya, and I would get in on the wrong side of the freeway. I would at the least get a ticket, but most likely, would get into a deadly accident and be killed or kill others, and if I survived, I would never enjoy the privilege of driving again. I would perish for lack of knowledge because there is no defense in ignorance.

Unfortunately, many Christians live this way in God's Kingdom. They think that getting a visa into the Kingdom and acquiring citizenship is enough. This is so wrong, and that is why most Christians struggle and suffer because they lack the knowledge required to live successfully as Kingdom citizens. There are citizens of the U.S.A. locked behind bars for breaking the laws. Being a citizen does not guarantee your freedom, but being a law-abiding citizen does. How do you live in victory and freedom in God's Kingdom without yielding to your instructor? Are you a free citizen, a citizen on probation, one under house arrest, or a citizen behind bars? The devil takes advantage of ignorant Christians.

God said in Hosea 4:6 that . . . "My people are destroyed for lack of knowledge. Because you have rejected knowledge, I will also reject you, that you may be no priest to me. Because you have forgotten your God's law, I will also forget your children."

What a scary thing for God to forget our children and us! I would never survive with this curse. Are you walking under this curse because you have rejected knowledge by wrongfully judging who God the Holy Spirit is? Have you despised knowledge that you don't read God's Word with your instructor's help in guiding you and taking you through competence like He did Christ in the wilderness? To graduate and begin ministry, Jesus had to pass the test of Kingdom stewardship. The Holy Spirit had trained Him through the years, and now it was time for Christ's baptism and ordination.

Christ was already filled with the Holy Spirit at conception. It was now time for the Holy Spirit to come to earth for the first time since creation to stay on a Man—Jesus Christ—through baptism. Christ could not accomplish His Kingdom assignment in a human body and flesh successfully without the supernatural assistance and constant overflow of God in His life. He needed the Holy Spirit to stay and remain on Him for His great commission from the Father. The Holy Spirit was already in Christ, and now He was going to stay and remain on Him continually, overflowing through Him to the world. This is the baptism of the Holy Spirit and fire . . . the overflow of God through us to human life. The constant presence of God.

The same Holy Spirit led Jesus to the wilderness to test the Word of God which He had taught Christ while He was in Him. Just like on earth, your driving instructor takes you to the department of motor vehicles to be tested. Why? It is necessary for your next level of licensing and responsibility. Yes! Now, you know that not all test and trials are of the devil. In fact, the devil never tempts you without authorization from God, **IF** you are a child of God. If you are not God's child, the devil has unlimited, direct access to you like a friend does.

The difference between testing and temptation is that the Holy Spirit will lead you to test for growth, that He may grant you even greater territory and jurisdiction in God's Kingdom, but the devil will tempt you to sin so you may lose your promotion, influence, jurisdiction, and territory that he may enslave you. The devil wanted to tempt Jesus into sin, but the Holy Spirit wanted to test Jesus on the Word which He had learned—same experience but different motives.

You do want to be tested because without a test, there is no growth or promotion. You must pray against temptations, not against tests. Pray that you will endure and come out victorious in Jesus' name. Jesus taught the Lord's Prayer and said we should pray not to be led into temptation; instead, we should ask God to deliver us from all evil (Matthew 6:13). Jesus said this because temptation is evil. He never prayed against testing. Jesus proved this when He predicted Peter's denial of Him three times. Jesus never prayed for Peter not to be tested, but He prayed for Peter's faith not to fail Him. In tests, the prayer Jesus prays for us, and which we should pray for ourselves and others, is that our faith will not be lost. Then when we are restored from the wilderness experience, we should work for the Kingdom's sake by strengthening others who may be going through a similar situation.

Christians end up envying sinners because of their success, forgetting that a sinner's success is short-lived and their wealth will be soon transferred to the righteous. However, you will never get the wealth transfer without the Holy Spirit because without Him, you can never be righteous. Our righteousness is as filthy rags to God, but the righteousness of Christ is only found in Him through His blood and His Holy Spirit. Jesus explained this perfectly clear to Nicodemus the night which Nicodemus came secretly to see Jesus. Jesus told him that he must be born again by water (baptism unto repentance) and Spirit (filled with the Holy Spirit for righteousness living). Water which cleanses, and Spirit which anoints and teaches us kingdom living. Jesus was cleansed and anointed during His baptism.

"As for you, the anointing which you received from him remains in you, and you don't need for anyone to teach you. But as his anointing teaches you concerning all things, and is true, and is no lie, and even as it taught you, you will remain in him." (1 John 2:27)

> Now there was a man of the Pharisees named Nicodemus, a ruler of the Jews. The same came to him by night, and said to him, "Rabbi, we know that you are a teacher come from God, for no one can do these signs that you do, unless God is with him." Jesus answered him, "Most certainly, I tell you, unless one is born anew, he can't see God's Kingdom." Nicodemus said to him, "How can a man be born when he is old? Can he enter a second time into his mother's womb, and be born?" Jesus answered, "Most certainly I tell you, unless one is born of water and spirit, he can't enter into God's Kingdom! That which is born of the flesh is flesh. That which is born of the Spirit is spirit. Don't marvel that I said to you, 'You must be born anew.' The wind blows where it wants to, and you hear its sound, but don't know where it comes from and

where it is going. So is everyone who is born of the Spirit." (John 3:1–8)

By seeing the Kingdom of God, Jesus meant seeing signs and wonders of God. It means seeing God at work within us, and us partnering with Him. It meant God's Kingdom coming, and His will being done on earth as it is in heaven through us. We must be born of WATER (the cleansing power of the Word of God) and SPIRIT (the anointing of the Holy Spirit) to accomplish God's will successfully. I cannot emphasize enough that God the Holy Spirit will not come apart from our Lord Jesus Christ. John the Baptist made this clear when he said . . .

"Therefore produce fruit worthy of repentance! Don't think to yourselves, 'We have Abraham for our father,' for I tell you that God is able to raise up children to Abraham from these stones. Even now the ax lies at the root of the trees. Therefore, every tree that doesn't produce good fruit is cut down and cast into the fire. I indeed baptize you in water for repentance, but he who comes after me is mightier than I, whose shoes I am not worthy to carry. He will baptize you in the Holy Spirit." (Matthew 3:8–11)

"Jesus, when he was baptized, went up directly from the water: and behold, the heavens were opened to him. He saw the Spirit of God descending as a dove and coming on him. Behold, a voice out of the heavens said, 'this is my beloved Son, with whom I am well pleased.'" (Matthew 3:16–17)

John the Baptist baptized men unto repentance. Repentance not of the mouth only, but he said they must change their actions too. We must turn from our evil ways and bear fruit that shows repentance. But there is one who baptizes with the Holy Spirit and fire, Jesus Christ. The Holy Spirit does not come apart from Jesus. Jesus was baptized by John the Baptist and then with the Holy Spirit by His Father God. Only God can fill you with Himself—not man.

The baptism of the Holy Spirit is God immersing you in Himself that all we eventually see and hear is Him living through you. He transforms you into the likeness of Christ. If Christ needed to be baptized by the Holy Spirit, and after that, His ministry began with great power, and he was successful in completing it with signs and wonders, how much more do we need my friend? The Holy Spirit is God given to man only through Christ, the Son of God. Simply put . . . no Christ, no Holy Spirit.

John the Baptist said that God the Father who sent him to prepare the way for Jesus told him how he would recognize the Messiah. Jesus looked ordinary; no one could tell Him apart from men his age. The Holy Spirit of God being in Him and coming to stay on Him was extraordinary. If Jesus Christ, God's only begotten Son, could not be told apart by only looking at Him but by His righteous living, holy lifestyle, and signs and wonders done by God the Father through God the Holy Spirit, how much more must we have the Holy Spirit to distinguish us from the world as ones who belong to God? As children of God and brides of Christ? Without the Holy Spirit, you and the world look alike. The Holy Spirit cleanses us, transforms us, and distinguishes us from the world. He reveals Christ to us, making us like Jesus. He is the presence of God in us. That was the same supernatural presence which Moses interceded for in Exodus 33:14-16. The personal, tangible presence of God.

"The LORD replied, "I will personally go with you, Moses, and I will give you rest—everything will be fine for you." Then Moses said, "If you don't personally go with us, don't make us leave this place. How will anyone know that you look favorably on me—on me and on your people—if you don't go with us? For your presence among us sets your people and me apart from all other people on the earth." (Exodus 33:14-16 NLT)

"John testified, saying, "I have seen the Spirit descending like a dove out of heaven, and it remained on him. I didn't recognize him, but he who sent me to baptize in water, he said to me, 'On whomever you will see the Spirit descending, and remaining on him, the same is he who baptizes in the Holy Spirit.'" (John 1:32–33)

The Holy Spirit remained on Jesus Christ after the Father baptized Him with the Holy Spirit, just like one gets water on them after water baptism. In the Old Testament the Holy Spirit never remained on anyone. He came temporarily on the specific individuals, empowered them to do the supernatural, and then left. An example of this was when Samson fought against his enemies.

"Then went Samson down with his father and his mother to Timnah, and came to the vineyards of Timnah; and behold, a young lion roared against him. **Yahweh's Spirit came mightily on him**, and he tore him as he would have torn a young goat; and he had nothing in his hand, but he didn't tell his father or his mother what he had done." (Judges 14:5–6 emphasis added)

The Holy Spirit never stayed because of man's sinful nature.

"Yahweh said, 'My Spirit will not strive with man forever, because he also is flesh; so his days will be one hundred twenty years.'" (Genesis 6:3)

Jesus said that the Holy Spirit would confirm the Word of God with signs and wonders following those who believe. The plan of redemption was not possible without God the

Holy Spirit. He made the conception of Jesus possible through Mary. He took Jesus through His ministry on earth doing the work of God the Father. He took Him through the wilderness and suffering and then raised Him from the dead. The Holy Spirit made the God-given task of Jesus possible and successful because Jesus relied on Him to guide Him, for He knew the heart of God and the will of the Father.

When Mary received the news that she was going to have a baby, she was shocked and wondered how she would conceive without knowing a man. The Holy Spirit stepped in because it was not by the might or power of a human being to carry out God's will on earth, but by the power of my friend the Holy Spirit. Even now, we must have God the Holy Spirit's help to fulfill God's will on earth.

"Mary said to the angel, "How can this be, seeing I am a virgin?" The angel answered her, 'The Holy Spirit will come on you, and the power of the Most High will overshadow you. Therefore also the holy one who is born from you will be called the Son of God.'" (Luke 1:34–35)

The Spirit that raised Christ from the dead lives in us!

"But you are not in the flesh but in the Spirit, if it is so that the Spirit of God dwells in you. But if any man doesn't have the Spirit of Christ, he is not his. If Christ is in you, the body is dead because of sin, but the spirit is alive because of righteousness. But if the Spirit of him who raised up Jesus from the dead dwells in you, he who raised up Christ Jesus from the dead will also give life to your mortal bodies through his Spirit who dwells in you." (Rom. 8:9–11)

We cannot live a victorious Christian life without God the

Holy Spirit. The Bible confirms that all have sinned and fallen short of the glory of God in Romans 3:23. But looking at it all after redemption and living in Christ, the glory of God has been bestowed back to us through Christ for those who are hidden in Christ in God. The latter glory is greater than the former glory.

Like the children of Israel who had built God a temple that had great glory, when they began sinning, the enemy came and took them captive, destroyed the temple, and took all the precious things belonging to God from the temple. In Haggai 2:1–9, God encouraged them to continue working on rebuilding the temple and promised them that His Spirit would never leave them, and that the glory of the latter temple would be much greater than the former. This would be made possible only by His Spirit.

God the Father said in Zechariah 4:6b, "'Not by might nor by power, but by My Spirit,' says the Lord of hosts."

Jesus would not have been manifested on earth without God the Holy Spirit. We cannot see or know Jesus apart from the Holy Spirit revealing Him to us. If you take the Holy Spirit out of the picture, then you just took Jesus out of the picture, and there is no hope for your salvation. Jesus is made manifest and real to us only by my friend the Holy Spirit.

Jesus was mightier than anyone who ever came to earth because He was conceived of the Holy Spirit, filled with the Holy Spirit, and baptized by the Holy Spirit when the Holy Spirit came down on Him from heaven and STAYED. This was a first, where heaven came to earth and three Godheads operated on earth at the same time. The Father came to baptize Christ with the Holy Spirit. He is the only one who can baptize us with this same Holy Spirit and fire! The same power that Christ had to help Him fulfill His work successfully and raised Him from the dead is the same power and Spirit He will give us so that we may fulfill our Kingdom assignments successfully too.

When we believe in Christ and receive Him in our lives as the Holy Spirit convicts us, we become born again of the Spirit. This is the conception and birthing in the Spirit, then the Holy Spirit fills us and takes the place of the evil spirits that dwelt in us before salvation, as we allow Him to teach us Kingdom living. After being born of the Holy Spirit at our spiritual birth, we then get baptized in water as a symbol of dying to sin and raising up unto the righteousness of Christ. Then we need to be baptized by the Holy Spirit and fire. This is for those who ask and want to get to the next level in the spirit. This is a gift given by God the Father to those who ask for Him in Jesus' name. This gift then gives us the same power and authority which Jesus Christ had while on earth. It helps us to be powerful and successful in fulfilling our purpose on earth. It is never by our might or our power but by the Spirit of the Living God.

"If you love me, keep my commandments. I will pray to the Father, and he will give you another Counselor, that he may be with you forever—the Spirit of truth, whom the world can't receive; for it doesn't see him, neither knows him. You know him, for he lives with you, and will be in you." (John 14:15–17)

Christ promised us that we would do greater things than He did because He will live in us and do the work through us who believe. Because the Holy Spirit can be in all places at the same time, we who are born again, baptized, and filled with the Holy Spirit can operate in the same power Christ did all over the world at the same time because of the Holy Spirit. Jesus said . . . "Most certainly I tell you, he who believes in me, the works that I do, he will do also; and he will do greater works than these, because I am going to my Father. Whatever you will ask in my name, that will I do, that the Father may be glorified in the Son. If you will ask anything in my name, I will do it." (John 14:12–14)

The Holy Spirit's fullness exists and manifests in sevenfold. The reason why God instructed Moses to build a lamp with seven branches branching out from it is because these seven Spirits all come from the same source, the Holy Spirit of God. This lamp was located in the Holy Place in the temple where the table of showbread and the incense were. The light in this Holy Place was from the lamp. This is because the Holy Place is a place of faith and total surrender to and reliance on the leadership of the Holy Spirit, who illuminates the Word of God, Christ, who is the bread of life.

"I saw in the middle of the throne and of the four living creatures, and in the middle of the elders, a Lamb standing, as though it had been slain, having seven horns, and seven eyes, which are the seven Spirits of God, sent out into all the earth." (Revelation 5:6)

"Out of the throne proceed lightnings, sounds, and thunders. There were seven lamps of fire burning before his throne, which are the seven Spirits of God." (Revelation 4:5)

"John, to the seven churches which are in Asia: Grace to you and peace from Him who is and who was and who is to come, and from the seven Spirits who are before His throne, and from Jesus Christ, the faithful witness, the firstborn from the dead, and the ruler over the kings of the earth. To Him who loved us and washed us from our sins in His own blood, and has made us kings and priests to His God and Father, to Him be glory and dominion forever and ever. Amen." (Revelation

1:4–6, NKJV)

The Father, the Holy Spirit, and the Son are mentioned in the scripture above, giving grace and peace to the seven churches in Asia. Here, the Holy Spirit is called the "seven Spirits" who is always before God, so He knows everything about God and what God's desire is. He is then entrusted to give us that information and mentor us into God's presence and dwelling place, into the Kingdom. When God filled Christ with the Holy Spirit, He gave Him the Holy Spirit without limit or measure. That tells you that you can have the Holy Spirit **with** measure, which is the infilling, not the baptism. The baptism is without measure. The Holy Spirit of God has the sevenfold Spirit of God in Him. That is why Jesus was given the Holy Spirit WITHOUT MEASURE. We too must pray for the Holy Spirit without measure.

"For he whom God has sent speaks the words of God; for God gives the Spirit without measure." (John 3:34)

The Holy Spirit is responsible for the seven churches of Christ. When Christ spoke to the churches in Revelation, He referred them back to the Holy Spirit for help by saying, "He who has ears let him hear what the Spirit is saying to the Church." That meant, they must listen and follow the leadership of the Holy Spirit. These seven churches represent the types of Christians we have today. We are the church which Christ is coming for. We must listen to the Holy Spirit if we are to fix our shortcomings and overcome. I will refer to these churches as Christians. In Revelation 2 and 3, we see the different types of Christians and what Christ says about us, including what we need to do to be made right with God by the help of my friend the Holy Spirit. He gives us the problem and answer and refers us to a private tutor. If we fail, we only have ourselves to blame.

Christ loves us so much that He does not hesitate to say that if we do not listen to and follow the leading of the Holy Spirit, we will be destroyed. We will not be His brides; we will be cut off. He is talking to Christians, not nonbelievers. He is like a parent who disciplines their children, not children of a stranger. Beloved, salvation is not guaranteed without the Holy Spirit's assistance. He is one who changes us and makes us ready and acceptable brides for Christ.

Read Revelations Chapter 2-3. The church or Christians here are revealed in seven categories, which one do you fall into? Beloved, let us open our ears and hear what the Holy Spirit is saying to us.

1. The Loveless Christian
2. The Persecuted Christian
3. The compromising Christian
4. The corrupt Christian
5. The Dead Christian
6. The Faithful Christian
7. The Lukewarm Christian

The fullness of the Holy Spirit exists in sevenfold.

"A shoot will come out of the stock of Jesse, and a branch out of his roots will bear fruit. Yahweh's Spirit will rest on him: the spirit of wisdom and understanding, the spirit of counsel and might, the spirit of knowledge and of the fear of Yahweh. His delight will be in the fear of Yahweh. He will not judge by the sight of his eyes, neither decide by the hearing of his ears." (Isa. 11:1–3)

THE SEVEN SPIRITS OF GOD FOUND IN THE HOLY SPIRIT ARE:

1. The Spirit of God
2. The Spirit of wisdom
3. The Spirit of understanding
4. The Spirit of counsel
5. The Spirit of might
6. The Spirit of knowledge
7. The Spirit of the fear of the Lord

Without the fullness of the Holy Spirit, who carries the fullness of God the Father, which God the Son had during His stay on earth as man, a believer in Christ will not succeed in their God-given task. When Christ came to earth for His assignment, He was empowered by all these Spirits from God through the Holy Spirit. One thing that truly stands out is that Christ delighted in the Spirit of the fear of the Lord. My life turned around, and God started using me profoundly when I prayed for and received this Spirit. I did not know that the fear of God was a spirit.

Fear is a spirit. There are two kinds of spirits of fear. There is one from God called "the fear of God," which helps us to live righteously and there is another spirit of fear which comes from the devil called "spirit of fear." The reason why it does not specify what kind of fear it is, is because it is responsible for all other kinds of fear. This spirit makes us live in sin. God has not given us this spirit of fear but a spirit of power, love, and a sound mind. (2 Timothy 1:7) Power, love, and a sound mind are spirits too, but they are from God that counterattack the spirit of fear from the devil. When we succumb to the spirit of fear, we get robbed of our power, love, and sound mind. People who live in fear cannot be productive. They are afraid to start things or try something new. They fear what others may think or say or what they may lose, and so on. These people displease God because they have no faith.

Fear is a lack of trust in God. It is a spirit that insults God, calling Him names like: unfaithful, powerless, liar, and abuser. Fear is an insult to God's ability and intelligence. Fear will make a believer get less than what God has in store for them and have less Kingdom authority because a fearful person can sell out the Kingdom. The devil gives people the spirit of fear to paralyze them so that they cannot fulfill their purpose on earth. He does it to protect himself from them because he knows if they truly knew who they were in Christ, and the power they possess in Him, his kingdom would be defeated. Fear is his greatest weapon against anyone.

Many mental health issues which people suffer from come as a result of this spirit of fear. Fear brings anxiety, hopelessness, helplessness, depression, anger, rage, paranoia, insecurities, jealousy, malice, suicide, and murder. Fear is a wicked spirit! An example of this is the story about the fearful servant that exposes fear as a wicked spirit which robs us of our dominion and power.

'I was afraid I would lose your money, so I hid it in the earth. Look, here is your money back.' "But the master replied, 'You wicked and lazy servant! If you knew I harvested crops I didn't plant and gathered crops I didn't cultivate, why didn't you deposit my money in the bank? At least I could have gotten some interest on it.' "Then he ordered, 'Take the money from this servant, and give it to the one with the ten bags of silver." (Matthew 25:25–28, NLT)

The authority in the kingdom is what gives you power over principalities and powers of darkness. Without this authority, the enemy has the upper hand. Have you accepted this spirit of fear to your detriment? Or do you live a life of victory, righteousness, and holiness with the fear of God? Because of fear of man, we tell lies so that we don't get in trouble with fellow humans instead of telling the truth and being right with God. We fear what people will say if they saw our sinful habits, so we hide these evil acts and play righteous in people's presence, while we remain filthy in our eyes, in God's eyes, and the devil's eyes.

The enemy will always have power over us in the spiritual realm as long as we live in fear of others because we sin and fall short of God's glory and power. Fear of people leads to sin; fear of God leads to righteousness. May God give us the spirit of the fear of God that we may delight in Him so that we, like Christ, may live righteous, pure, and holy lives in God's eyes.

"The fear of the Lord is the beginning of wisdom, and the knowledge of the Holy One is understanding." (Prov. 9:10, NKJV)

"Fear of the Lord is the foundation of true wisdom. All who obey his commandments will grow in wisdom." (Ps. 111:10, NLT)

"And this is what he says to all humanity: 'The fear of the Lord is true wisdom; to forsake evil is real understanding.'" (Job 28:28, NLT)

When we live and delight in the fear of God, we get wisdom, which leads to knowledge and understanding, giving us might and counsel for daily work that we were created to do.

When we delight in the spirit of the fear of God like Jesus Christ did, we will attract all these other spirits of God into our lives, and we will be fully equipped to fulfill our God-given assignments. Jesus was successful because He had the seven Spirits of God in Him.

"'And to the angel of the assembly in Sardis write: "He who has the seven Spirits of God, and the seven stars says these things: "I know your works, that you have a reputation of being alive, but you are dead."' (Rev. 3:1)

"From the throne came flashes of lightning and the rumble of thunder. And in front of the throne were seven torches with burning flames. This is the sevenfold Spirit of God." (Rev. 4:5, NLT)

"But the Helper, the Holy Spirit, whom the Father will send in My name, He will teach you all things, and bring to your remembrance all things that I said to you." (John 14:26, NKJV)

And the Lord spoke to Moses, saying: "Speak to Aaron, and say to him, 'When you arrange the lamps, the seven lamps shall give light in front of the lampstand.'" And Aaron did so; he arranged the lamps to face toward the front of the lampstand, as the Lord commanded Moses. Now this workmanship of the lampstand was hammered gold; from its shaft to its flowers it was hammered work. According to the pattern which the Lord had shown Moses, so he made the lampstand. (Numbers 8:1–4, NKJV)

These seven lamps are to give light in front of the lampstand. The lampstand supports or holds the lamps and the oil supply where the lamps feed from to shine their light. Without the lampstand, the lamps cannot stand, nor can they have the oil to produce light and keep on burning. The lampstand is the

Holy Spirit, and the seven lamps are the seven churches, who can only shine the light of Christ and know Christ by feeding on the revelation from the Holy Spirit of God. They cannot stand alone; otherwise, they will fall. Beloved, we cannot support ourselves. We will fall. We must rely on the Holy Spirit to help us stand.

The Holy Place was dark and without windows so the natural sunlight could not shine in. The light in this Holy Place is found in the seven lamps also representing the seven Spirits of God who illuminate Christ, the Word of God, to the seven churches of Christ. Remember the Psalm of David that states, "Your Word is a lamp unto my feet and a light unto my path"? (Psalm 119:105)

The temple was purposely made in that way with those specifications because it was important to know that the way to the Father is only through Jesus Christ His only begotten Son, who is made manifest by God the Holy Spirit. Only by the Holy Spirit can anyone be convicted of sin, righteousness, and judgment. No one can be born again unless the Holy Spirit does the work of conviction in them. No one can stop sinning by their strength. It is only by the Holy Spirit that we put to death the deeds of the flesh. We must be led and get support and the oil of anointing from my friend the Holy Spirit.

Only by the guidance of God the Holy Spirit can we know the will of the Father through His Son who is the Word of the Father. Many of us struggle to live righteously because we think we can do it on our own. We walk in darkness because we ignore the light that should light our way, and the support we need from the Holy Spirit. Like little children need to hold their parent's hand for support as they learn to walk, we need to hold the Holy Spirit's hand and learn to walk in the Kingdom.

We cannot be born and start running. There is a process, and this process only the Holy Spirit knows and is assigned to take us through it.

Let us not be like stubborn children who do not want to hold their parent's hand. They keep stumbling, falling, and running into danger. Some Christians act like these children, and it's no wonder we stumble and often fall, getting injured by the enemy and the traps he sets on our way. Only those led by the Holy Spirit and spend time in the Word of God can overcome because they live in the light. They see things through God's eyes, not through the eyes of the enemy.

Does the Holy Spirit light your life, or are you still walking in darkness? Are you a stubborn child or a yielded child? Remember the Holy Spirit is the one who works in us both to will and to do what God desires (Philippians 2:13). We cannot see the spiritual realm where our battles are, through our natural eyes (the eyes of the flesh). Without my friend the Holy Spirit, we are disadvantaged because we are fighting an unseen enemy, but the enemy can see us. In this case, we are defeated before we even begin fighting. Therefore, let us allow the Holy Spirit to lead us so we can win this battle.

There is a reason why we have the Old Testament. It was a shadow of what was to come. If we are to understand who God is and how to worship Him in the fullness of His glory, in Spirit and in truth, we cannot ignore the Old Testament. The temple and the set rules and rituals tell us so much about God and which route we must follow to get to Him.

These different stages and places of worship, the Outer Court, the Inner Court, or the Holy Place, and the highest level which is the Holy of Holies, symbolize the different dimensions of Christianity or relationships with Christ. Remember,

Christianity is not a religion; rather, it is a personal relationship with God the Father through Jesus Christ His Son, by the help of God the Holy Spirit.

The dimensions of the outer court were much bigger than those of the Holy Place. This was because the outer court had many people who could enter and offer sacrifices on the altar, which was located there. The light which illuminated this place was the sun. Many Christians are comfortable in this dimension where they live by sight, not by faith. Meaning, they believe what they see, feel, or sense with their physical body to be their source of truth instead of what God says, which faith is. When something happens in their life, they confess what they see and believe in what they see, feel, or experience with their physical senses.

God the Father is not found in the outer court, but the Son is found here because this is where He cleanses all who come to Him by faith in need of a savior. Not all who get born again live by faith in the Word of God. Most people like to stay here in the outer court. They do not desire to go deeper in Christ. However, they admire those who do and rely on them to bring food and fellowship from the Holy Place and the Holy of Holies, but they are not willing to sacrifice and go deeper themselves. These are the lazy, lukewarm Christians who never enter God's rest; yet, they are jealous of or admire those who have entered God's rest.

These Christians want the mantle that someone else has gone deeper to get, but they are not willing to work at getting the mantle from God themselves. Only God gives the mantle. If you do not know the cost of it, you cannot value it. Even Elijah told Elisha that if Elisha wanted the mantle upon his life, which he had asked to get a double portion of, Elisha would have to go through what Elijah would be going through until God takes Elijah home. If Elisha was able to endure till the last minute and see Elijah go home, then he would get the double portion anointing that was upon Elijah's life. There were some occasions when Elijah asked Elisha to remain behind, but Elisha refused and said he would not take his eyes off Elijah. Elisha endured it all, and when it was time for Elijah to go with the chariots of fire, Elisha was there to witness and receive Elijah's mantle. Elisha passes the test and did not bail out when difficulty arose.

Are you ready to pay the price for the mantle you admire? Has God called you into the same ministry? Remember, Elisha was called by God to take over Elijah's ministry. The mantle was given through God's instruction, not human reasoning. Don't just follow and admire someone's anointing; you must be called into the same ministry by God for you to receive the same anointing. If you are out of your assignment, God will not give you the mantle. You will be wasting your time. Stop admiring what God is doing through others and neglect your calling. Seek God's calling over your life through my friend the Holy Spirit, and you will succeed. (See 2 Kings Chapter 2.)

The outer court does not have the word "holy" in it because one cannot be holy in this place. What is holiness? According to Christ, holiness is an attitude and character of God that is found in His Spirit. This character is referred to as fruit. Just like we know a tree by its fruit, we know who a person is by their character in public and in private. The fruit of holiness is the fruit of the Holy Spirit of God which is so rich in nine godly characters as Galatians 5:22–23 states: love, joy, peace, patience, kindness, goodness, faithfulness, humility, and self-control.

You have heard the law that says, 'Love your neighbor' and hate your enemy. But I say, love your enemies! Pray for those who persecute you! In that way, you will be acting as true children of your Father in heaven. For he gives his sunlight to both the evil and the good, and he sends rain on the just and the unjust alike. If you love only those who love you, what reward is there for that? Even corrupt tax collectors do that much. If you are kind only to your friends, how are you different from anyone else? Even pagans do that. But you are to be perfect, even as your Father in heaven is perfect. (Matthew 5:43–48, NLT)

In order to obey Christ's command above, we must, by the Holy Spirit, possess all the nine fruits of the Spirit or character of God. With this knowledge, can you call yourself holy? Do you now see why the Holy Spirit is a must-have?

"So prepare your minds for action and exercise self-control. Put all your hope in the gracious salvation that will come to you when Jesus Christ is revealed to the world. So you must live as God's obedient children. Don't slip back into your old ways of living to satisfy your own desires. You didn't know any better then. But now you must be holy in everything you do, just as God who chose you is holy. For the Scriptures say, "You must be holy because I am holy." (1 Peter 1:13–16, NLT)

Holiness comes from spending time with God. Just like you would spend time with someone and learn their behavior or go to school and learn new knowledge and skill. The outer court is a place of enrollment in the school of holiness. If one enrolls in school but never meets the teacher or never goes to class, they will never gain the knowledge they went to school for. No matter how much has been paid for them to go to school, they will never be the doctor they signed up to be because they will never graduate. The tuition will just be a waste of resources. You can be a student enrolled in school and tell everyone about it, but you will never graduate or be successful in your studies without attending class and following directions from the instructors.

Some people enroll in school, but they are only part-time learners. They take one class at a time and sometimes withdraw from the class when it gets hard. Unfortunately, they have to keep enrolling into the same class because, just like any other school, they cannot skip a class and expect to graduate. These students never benefit from the knowledge because they do not make time to meet with their instructor to go through the difficult subjects to understand the concept.

Other students are lovers of school, instruction, and their instructors. They make good use of the available resources to help them succeed. They even form study groups to reinforce what they have learned and are not afraid to seek clarification or knowledge from their instructors. These full-time students go the extra mile and take extra credits to gain knowledge with a zeal of going out to practice that knowledge. As they do this, they get experience and promotion in their field of practice and enter into rest, as well as enjoy the fruits of their labor.

The preparation, testing, and relying on the instructor is not easy, but it pays off. Christ never promised us an easy time or easy life as we seek after Him to do His will. The enemy does not want us to succeed in becoming all that God created us to be. Satan wants us to walk blindly with false hope and assumption that because we are enrolled in school, success is therefore guaranteed. We all know that this is not true. Being born again, receiving Christ's sacrifice for us, and believing that He paid it all and He is now our Lord and Savior is only an admission process into the Kingdom.

The tuition is already paid for by the blood of Jesus. You have a full scholarship from the Father's sacrifice of His Son. Now, living in the Kingdom successfully and fruitfully is totally dependent upon your hunger and thirst after righteousness and losing your will to God's will . . . yielding completely to His leadership and taking the classes He has set up for your growth in the Kingdom. He is amazing because not only does He pay the full tuition, He provides a personal instructor who teaches us at our level of understanding. He is all-lingual and all-knowing. He teaches and then reminds us what we have learned during the test. If we fail, it will be our choice to fail.

The instructor only teaches what the curriculum of the Kingdom instructs. He does not look for His own curriculum. The Father prepares the lessons, and the instructor teaches them. The Father never gives His children more than they can handle. When someone wrongs me, and I feel like speaking some of my 'human wisdom' to them, the instructor reminds me that I am in a more advanced class, and I need not respond to the person's immaturity and lack of God's wisdom.

How many times have you wanted to give your opinion to someone, but you know that the person will not receive it as you meant it? You know that they will twist it to mean something else, and greater tension will then be created from that situation. Has it happened to you? When you know you are right, but your opinion will not be useful to the other person? Thank God for His wisdom in Christ when He said, "Don't give that which is holy to the dogs, neither throw your pearls to the pigs, lest perhaps they trample them under their feet, and turn and tear you to pieces." (Matthew 7:6)

OUTER COURT CHRISTIANS

As we know, the outer court dimensions are very large. This is because the majority of Christians make this their dwelling place. They do not progress. This reminds me of when we traveled using public means in Africa before they implemented public safety rules. Many people would board the bus and stand right by the entrance, holding on to the nearest pole. The bus conductor would then ask them to move in farther to make room for more people. The bus would often lean on one side because of people's weight. It was very unsafe to stand right at the door as one could be thrown out the bus accidentally when the doors open while the bus is at a curve or negotiating a corner. The bus doors could not be shut because of overcrowding, and the people stood at the doorsteps. Similarly, many Christians fall back or get thrown out when they face the cares, troubles, curves, and corners of this life. Beloved, we need to move deeper in Christ where there is safety and a guarantee of finishing well.

In the outer court, the Holy Spirit convicts us of sin, righteousness, and judgment. This is the beginning of a relationship with God in Christ. Here is found the altar of sacrifice where Christ is the sacrificial lamb (blood) and the Word that cleanses us (the water). Christ told His disciples that the word which He had spoken to them and they received had cleansed them. When the children of Israel got delivered from the Egyptians and crossed the Red Sea, many of them died in the wilderness because they refused to be led by the Spirit of God. Even now, many Christians, including leaders, dwell here. Just like a compound is larger than a living room or a bedroom, and one is not intimate with those who are far from them, Christians here never experience intimacy with God. They leave God starving in longing for intimacy with them. The outer court houses many because the human heart is wicked and hard to submit to the leadership of God the Holy Spirit. That is why many people get stuck here.

Also, this place is considered the introduction phase. Here, we meet and greet Christ. Christ is revealed as the only way to the Father. The journey begins here. We are acquainted with Him, but we do not commit to a relationship yet. We settle for "knowing about Him" instead of having a desire to know Him personally. We get to hear about the God of Shadrach, Meshach, and Abednego, the God of Abraham, Isaac, and Jacob, the God of David, Samson, Job, and many others, but we do not know Christ as our God. We settle for the crowd's assumption, knowledge, or lack of knowledge of who God is. This is a very dangerous place to live in because we can never use Christ's name effectively, for we do not understand His authority at this level.

We pray ineffective, irrelevant prayers due to a lack of knowledge. We do not get what we ask for because we ask selfishly or ask God to do what He already has done. We suffer from ignorance and laziness. We do not want to study and go deeper into God's Word. There are some things we need in life, but we do not have to pray about them. Instead, we are supposed to claim them from the spiritual realm into the physical manifestation with the authority of the finished work of the cross in Jesus' name! The devil enjoys Christians who dwell here because he can easily manipulate them and convince them that God does not care about them, and that is why their prayers have not been answered.

An example of this is when we need protection from God.

The people in the outer court will ask and pray hard for protection as they are living a life of sin. The people in the inner place will read the scripture that promises safety, and they will claim it by living in God's secret place, therefore activating their safety. Those in the Holy of Holies do not have to worry because a dead man is not afraid or worried about their safety. Nothing can kill them or harm them as they are no longer alive to this world and its pleasures; they are alive only to God, and God deals with their safety personally.

This is the place that Peter outgrew and was then given the name "rock" when Jesus asked them who people said He was. The other disciples only had crowd knowledge of Christ and not God's revelation of who Jesus was. However, it was revealed to Peter by God the Father through the Holy Spirit. As soon as God blessed Peter, Peter became the devil's target. The devil used Peter's mouth to discredit Peter and expose him as wishy-washy so that Peter would doubt what God said he was: a rock. The devil got Peter to deny Christ three times to seal the fact that Peter was a failure. No matter what the devil tried, Jesus restored Peter three times to confirm that Peter was forgiven and was still a rock chosen by God, not because of his good works but because of God's faithfulness and for the sake of the church. (See Matthew 16:13–20.)

People who dwell here do not get to discover their God-given task. These people die without knowing who they are in Christ and what they were created to do. Their destiny can be aborted, and they are prone to premature deaths. They are still alive to self, making God's power inactive in them.

In the outer court, God fights the initial war to rescue us from the enemy's hold by sacrificing His only Son. The shed blood is my salvation. It saves me and destroys my enemies. For the Israelites, it was the crossing of the Red Sea that saved them, but the same Red Sea destroyed their enemies. Supernatural authority and wealth transfer is found here. The enemy gives their wealth up to us for God's Kingdom.

This is the rescue phase where the body, which is the temple of God, is rescued from the enemy's kingdom into God's Kingdom. This is where the basin with water to wash the feet was located. The basin was made with the inside of it lined up with mirrors of women because the Word of God requires us to look at ourselves before looking at someone else like most people do, to fix the messes in our lives. When we look in the mirror, we see our image, not someone else's. When we look at scripture, we should see ourselves and not someone else; then once we take care of our mess, we can help others by the help of the Holy Spirit.

This is where we clean our dirty walk and get right with God. There is not much revelation here in the outer court. When you meet someone, you do not give them all your secrets or reveal yourself fully to them, because you have no intimate relationship with them. Therefore, this is a "meet and greet phase." Acquaintances live here, not brides. The soul and spirit can still die if one lives here. Living in this phase even after outgrowing it is called spiritual retardation. No growth or maturity exists in this phase.

The light or truth in this place is the natural sunlight. This represents facts, witnessed events, and historical evidence. The sun, when it is too much, can scorch and cause sunburn. It can cause skin cancer, droughts, and death. It can also cause fire that destroys homes, properties, people, and animals. The sun goes down at the end of the day, and darkness takes over, making it unreliable at night. It gives the enemy the upper hand when it goes down.

This tells us that if we live by sight, we will fall when trials come because our trust is in the temporary, unreliable evidence of human limitation. That which we trust in and hold on to as the light will go down, and we will go down with it. The enemy will have the victory at the end. As the saying goes, "he who laughs last laughs best." The enemy will have the last laugh on those who live by sight. On the other hand, those who live by faith go deeper in Christ, who is the light of the world, and He never goes down. Darkness has no place in Him, and the enemy cannot touch those who are in Christ. Beloved, let's go deeper!

Because this place is the earthly equivalent of the compound, anyone who acknowledges Christ can enter here. Whosoever believes in Christ and in His sacrifice (John 3:16) begins here. Like the first grade or preschool, this is the enrollment phase. It is meant for people to pass through, not to dwell here. We accept Christ as Lord and Savior, and start the journey, crossing the Red Sea. Do not end the journey here as many people do. We enroll into the Kingdom military because our Kingdom is at war with the enemy's kingdom, as in Matthew 11:12, "From the days of John the Baptizer until now, the Kingdom of Heaven suffers violence, and the violent take it by force."

Another thing about the outer court is that in this phase, God is just a renter of our bodies, His temple. Here we tell God what He can and cannot do with us. We limit God and His will for us. We, therefore, have limited access to Kingdom wealth because we do not want to invest in the Kingdom. My friend the Holy Spirit does not lead us here; therefore, we cannot be trusted. God will not give us any inheritance in this phase because we will squander it. We have no knowledge about how to run the Kingdom, therefore God will not invest in us because we are a risky investment.

The outer court is also the realm of the ordinary. No signs and wonders are found here, just an ordinary life. People believe in death more than life in this realm. Death can rule if we remain here. When it comes to religion in this place, we rely on people's interpretation of scripture, resulting in many different religions and beliefs which cause bondages. This is because people think that they can please God with their works and faithful practice of religion instead of obedience to God through His Spirit.

We also find that people in this place live by the sweat of their labor. They are still working for their food, leaning on their own understanding and the understanding of man which is wrong because true revelation of scripture only comes from God the Holy Spirit; He inspired the writing of the Bible. Because people in this realm do not rely on God's Spirit, they become slaves of religion, allowing others who are misled to mislead them too.

Outer court was the place where the Israelites asked for a golden calf, their own religion, because they did not want to seek God for themselves. They wanted something they could see, something that was familiar with their history, their gifting, their light or truth when they were back in Egypt. Remember when they were the builders and laborers of Egyptians who were idol worshipers, and the Israelites were professional idol carvers? They went back to use their familiar ways from slavery in their free lives. In Egypt, they had gifts of construction. They constructed great monuments and structures, including idols for their masters. Their God-given gifts were perverted and needed restructuring.

Many of us are in the same place the Israelites were. Our gifts are still perverted because we do not allow God to lead us into what He intended us to do with the gifts He gave us before the devil perverted it. Many new believers make this mistake. They want to change from the worldly lifestyle but still maintain some aspects of it, bringing it into the Kingdom of God for "modernization." One thing I need to make very clear is that, unless we are fully yielded to God the Holy Spirit's leadership and guidance, our "works," whatever we say we are doing for God's Kingdom, will never count. It will be an abomination unto God, just like the golden calf was an abomination. The Israelites were seeking to please and worship God using the golden calf as a visual image of God. But God condemned it. Do not use God's gift with your own understanding and strength. Allow the Holy Spirit to mentor you through it so it will be pleasing to the Father.

Which golden calf you have created, thinking that you are worshipping God? Are your gifts still perverted? Are you leading yourself? Are you following the world's leadership and trending styles, what is accepted by the culture and style? Have you taken God the Holy Spirit for granted and assume you are helping to bring to speed the gospel of Jesus Christ in a modern way? Have you have spent a fortune only to find yourself worshipping and dancing around a golden calf (idols in life) instead of worshipping and dancing before the Holy God, Yahweh?

The Egyptians did not have to kill the Israelites; the Israelites killed themselves in the wilderness because they refused to "unlearn" their historical, familiar, comfortable, and slave ways. In the same way, the devil does not have to kill you or cause you to go to hell; you will kill yourself and doom yourself to hell. The Israelites refused to follow God, and God said that He would leave them and assign them a new guide, an angel, to the Promised Land to lead them. God warned them that the angel is not like a parent. He is not God.

The angel would be there to enforce heaven's laws, just like the police enforce a country's laws. An angel would enforce Kingdom law with no emotional attachment or remorse. They will not negotiate or bend any rules. They were created to follow orders and punish disobedience of orders as it is written in scripture. Moses knew that this would be a disaster; therefore, he refused to be led by an angel and pleaded with God to lead them instead. He knew that he was leading a very rebellious people, and the angel would destroy them and would not accept any plead for mercy. See Exodus 33:2–4, 14–16. Remember, the angel who struck King Herod to his death when the king received glory from man and instead of giving it to God he kept it for himself? See Acts 12:23.

These outer court Christians do not live by faith or seek the one true God. Instead, they follow human rituals without understanding. They celebrate Halloween, with trick or treat in their churches although it is a demonic celebration. They celebrate Easter with the Easter bunny and eggs even though bunnies do not lay eggs, and they cannot explain why they do it. They lie to children that Santa Claus is real, even though he comes to take away the real meaning of Christmas, and the bunny and eggs distort the truth of Easter, watering down the most powerful event in human history. The devil was dethroned on Easter. He lost authority and dominion. Therefore, to keep people from celebrating his defeat, he diverts them to celebrating things that do not make sense. He takes away the spotlight from Christ on Christmas and Easter and puts it on Santa, bunny, and eggs. Churches celebrate this too! You cannot mix what is holy with that which is unholy. How can a parent then turn around and hold children accountable for telling the truth while they lie to their children? A lie is a lie, no matter what the context.

These "innocent seeming" characters come to dilute the most powerful Christian celebrations and the world's rescue from darkness. Why is Ramadan, Indian, or Chinese religious celebrations not distorted? Why just Christian celebrations? Have you wondered why? Why not distort Halloween? This is a strategic scheme of darkness, the devil's plan which the church has fallen for. These believers have no backbone, so they are afraid of what people will say more than what God thinks. Many people believe that Halloween costumes are meant to scare evil by dressing like demonic creatures. This actually makes the evil spirits feel welcome and at home not threatened. The real threat to evil is the light of God, the blood of Jesus, and living by the Holy Spirit. Righteousness.

The blood in the outer court is called the shed blood, which has cleansing power. It has been shed and is now waiting for my acceptance. People do not make the sacrifice, nor work at all here. All they do is accept that they are sinners and that Jesus' blood was shed for them, and sign up for cleansing. This blood only gives them hope that they can be saved and protected if they accept this sacrifice.

Just as a child is born and does not have to push or feel any pain, the one in pain is the mother, Jesus is the mother figure in this scenario and we the children. When we accept Christ's sacrifice, we say that we are in Christ, and He is pushing us out as belonging to Him. He felt the pain at the cross, and all we did was accept His pain for our birth. A child accepts the mother who went through pain and bled so they may live. The discomfort of pregnancy is what Christ went through until His midwife, Judas Iscariot, pushed Him to His birthing place. Our midwives may not be our friends. Many are just there to assist us in birthing the spiritual babies in our lives. After that, don't hold on to the midwife because you will suffer loss.

The midwife knows how to help with childbirth. If we activate a midwife in our lives before time, we will lose the child because they will coach us to deliver the baby prematurely. If we hold on to them longer than necessary, we will be frustrated because they can not help us continue with our regular health as it is not their specialty. Let them go! God will send the next midwife when the time for delivery comes. I love my midwives, some of whom were so mean to me that they pushed me to deliver my promotion! Glory to Jesus!

Hearers of the Word dwell here in the outer courts. They do not apply the blood in their lives or the Word of God. Therefore, they are in danger of destruction. Being a doer of the Word and not just a hearer is what brings life. The purposeful application is what brings about cleansing. If you fell in a pool of mud, then jumped into a clean pool and got out immediately, how clean will you be? Your clothes may look a bit clean, but you will still have evidence that you fell in the mud. You will have mud still lingering in your hair, body, and inner clothes, including your feet and inside your shoes.

For instance, if someone had some water for you to bathe in, and the water was available and warm, the choice is yours to accept that the water is indeed yours because it has been offered to you. Salvation is accepting the sacrifice God made by the shed blood of Jesus Christ. It does not deal completely with the inner man yet. That is why many are called, but few are chosen. The few are chosen because they decided to go further than the first stage of cleansing. They chose wisely and sought to be delivered from their old perverted ways and thought processes. These are the people who get to the next level in Christ.

Giving cannot be separated from Christianity. God displayed this by giving us His only begotten Son, Jesus Christ, to people who did not deserve it. However, Christians who dwell in this place are stingy and emotional givers. These Christians are in the toddler stage of giving. They are concerned with what they desire and want. They are very selfish and highly limited by people's opinion of them. They do things to fit in and be accepted by others. What people think of them is extremely important. They are afraid to stand alone for the truth at all times.

They are self and people pleasers who struggle to give anything toward the kingdom or obey God's Word on giving. They struggle to tithe and give offerings, but they have no problem spending their resources elsewhere, like shopping or other pleasures. They struggle with obedience and have a hard time saying no to sin. They have a "mine!" mentality. All they have belongs to them because they have worked very hard for it. To them, 100 percent is theirs, and 0 percent belongs to God. Because of this mentality, they don't give toward the Kingdom, and being a thief in God's Kingdom gives the devil access to their resources.

Some of these people own all the rights to their shares and are not willing to let go and invest any in God's Kingdom unless they think they can buy God's miracles. They get deceived by "Kingdom Tele or TV marketers" . . . Those who think they can help God to raise funds through deception. Peter warned us of these false prophets in 2 Peter 2:3 (NLT). "In their greed they will make up clever lies to get hold of your money. But God condemned them long ago, and their destruction will not be delayed."

Outer court Christians are also viewed as first-floor Christians. These Christians have a very limited view. It doesn't cost much to live here. There is a low ceiling height on this floor representing an extreme limitation. The enemy is comfortable with us here because we are easily accessible. We lack the knowledge of the full armor of God. We just got enrolled in the Kingdom military. We are Kingdom rookies who can easily be defeated since we lack enough experience or ground to support us. We live by sight, what we see, which the enemy can easily manipulate. We barely have our feet wet. We easily fall just as it is easy to trip a child who just started walking than someone who has been walking for a while.

God protects us as we meet Him here, but if we refuse to follow Him deeper, He will continue to meet and greet new people. However, you will be left behind where the enemy can get you. For example, if you have guests coming to your house, you meet them and welcome them to follow you in. But if some of them refuse to go in with you and they choose to stay in your outer court, how would you treat them every time your gate rings for new guests? Will you be concerned with them after a few times of trying to welcome them into your house, but they refuse? Will you not ignore their existence and eventually send them away to clear your court? This is why I say the outer court is a dangerous place to dwell in. It is only good for meet and greet and then move on in. There are no seats here to rest, no food to eat, and no roof for shelter or protection. Those who live here will hunger, thirst, starve, get hurt by changing seasons, the enemy, and they will eventually die spiritually.

After salvation, we are required to enter into God's Kingdom by following our Helper, my friend the Holy Spirit. If we do not follow Him, we will die here because we are not equipped for war, nor do we possess the full armor of God yet in the outer courts. We still have the old mind-set in us, the slave mentality, because that is all we know. Transformation only comes in the next level where we get our minds renewed by studying and meditating upon God's Word and putting it into practice.

Romans 12:2 (NLT) says, "Don't copy the behavior and customs of this world, but let God transform you into a new person by changing the way you think. Then you will learn to know God's will for you, which is good and pleasing and perfect."

This full armor is only found in the next level after enrollment, during training in the inner place. See Ephesians 6:10–18.

Outer court Christians only praise God during the good times but complain and murmur during the bad times. They are like the Israelites after crossing the Red Sea and receiving deliverance from their enemies and slave lifestyle. They praised and worshipped God, but when they faced hardships, they murmured and complained. These Christians only see God's goodness when things go their way, but when things are tough, they go back to their old life and way of doing things. Jesus explained this very well in the following parable . . .

> The farmer went out to sow his seed. As he sowed, some fell along the road, and it was trampled underfoot, and the birds of the sky devoured it. Other seed fell on the rock, and as soon as it grew, it withered away, because

it had no moisture. Other fell amid the thorns, and the thorns grew with it, and choked it. Other fell into the good ground, and grew, and produced one hundred times as much fruit." As he said these things, he called out, "He who has ears to hear, let him hear!" Then his disciples asked him, "What does this parable mean?" Now the parable is this: The seed is the word of God. Those along the road are those who hear, then the devil comes, and takes away the word from their heart, that they may not believe and be saved. Those on the rock are they who, when they hear, receive the word with joy; but these have no root, who believe for a while, then fall away in time of temptation. That which fell among the thorns, these are those who have heard, and as they go on their way they are choked with cares, riches, and pleasures of life, and bring no fruit to maturity. That in the good ground, these are such as in an honest and good heart, having heard the word, hold it tightly, and produces fruit with patience. (Luke 8:5–9, 11–15)

Here Christ speaks of a farmer, in this case, a preacher or teacher, who sows seed, which is the Word of God, and the receivers of the seed or the ground, meaning the people who hear the Word of God, receive it in four different ways and results.

- Along-the-road people

These are not Christians yet; these are people who belong to the world. They hear God's Word, but Satan does not want them to receive it in their spirits, so he makes them blind, deceives them, and steals the Word of God sown in their lives. Satan convinces them that they are "good" people, and that salvation is not for them. Or he makes them believe the lie that they are too bad to be accepted by God. The Word they receive is therefore trampled underfoot (goes to waste) because they hear it, but they don't believe and are not saved.

- On-the-rock Christians

These are born-again Christians who hear the Word, receive it with joy, believe in it, and then backslide or fall back in temptation. They have no ground to hold them. They are very shallow and blown about by every wind of doctrine. They are very quick to hear, but they do not practice the Word when temptation comes. They are quick to complain, and because they lack wisdom, they blame God for their problems.

- Among-the-thorns Christians

These are Christians who are busy making a living instead of living the making. They are consumed with trying to make a name for themselves, and the Word they hear never grows because they do not take time to nurture and practice it. This is where you will find many well-to-do Christians, who think that as long as they show up at church, support it financially, and look good in the eyes of men, all is well. They are quick to compromise to fit in with the majority, even when it is a sin. Their prosperity deceives them as they think they are right with God and that is why they are successful. They lack the perfect peace of God.

- Good-ground Christians

These God-fearing believers work out their salvation with fear and trembling. They live in the presence of God, continually led by His Spirit (Holy Place and Holy of Holies Christians). They yield to God the Holy Spirit, and with patience, they cooperate with Him and change their ways as He leads them into holiness and righteous living. When temptations come, they are patient because they believe in what God says over their situation. They know that God loves them, and He has great plans for them.

On the rock and among the thorns Christians are outer court Christians. They are shallow Christians who get very excited in the church but do not practice what they've learned. They do not take the Word of God as a cleansing agent; therefore, they do not work on their character. These Christians do not report for duty in prayer; instead, they tell God what they want Him to do for them as if they were the king, and God was their servant. They tell God their already made-up plans and ask Him to follow along and make it happen. They deploy God instead of them reporting to duty for God to deploy them. Beloved, we are supposed to follow God, not insist God follow us.

The outer court is a level where only new believers should be because they are still trying to figure out and distinguish between who the leader is and who the follower is. If you are counting years as a Christian and you are still in the outer court, you are in danger of destruction. It is like dating someone whom you never progress with in a relationship beyond meeting each other; yet, you still hope to marry that person someday without putting the work required into the relationship.

This is false hope. You cannot be the bride of Christ at this stage. Don't deceive yourself. Here, the Holy Spirit is not given full authority to lead because these Christians still like to lead themselves, like toddlers do. Outer court Christians are like a child who never grows up. They age in years, but their maturity level, which is represented by their character, remains the same.

> Why do you call me, 'Lord, Lord,' and don't do the things which I say? Everyone who comes to me, and hears my words, and does them, I will show you who he is like. He is like a man building a house, who dug and went deep, and laid a foundation on the rock. When a flood arose, the stream broke against that house, and could not shake it, because it was founded on the rock. But he who hears, and doesn't do, is like a man who built a house on the earth without a foundation, against which the stream broke, and immediately it fell, and the ruin of that house was great. (Luke 6:46–49)

Christ never promised us a stormless life, He actually warned us of the many storms we would face in life, but He asked us to be of good cheer because He has already overcome the world. If Christ already overcame, then those who are in Him are more than overcomers. Paul was led by the Holy Spirit, and he was warned of many tribulations which awaited him as he followed Christ. Christ also told Ananias that Paul would suffer for the Kingdom's sake in Acts 9:16. Beloved, we live in the finished work of the cross, in the hope of glory, Jesus Christ.

"Now, behold, I go bound by the Spirit to Jerusalem, not

knowing what will happen to me there; except that the Holy Spirit testifies in every city, saying that bonds and afflictions wait for me." (Acts 20:22–23)

"I have told you these things, that in me you may have peace. In the world you have oppression; but cheer up! I have overcome the world." (John 16:33)

The Holy Spirit is less active in the outer court. Just as an educational or a career growth is dependent upon the person's willingness to work hard, study more, try new challenging things, and researching to produce the best results, spiritual growth is dependent upon the individual's willingness to spend time with the Holy Spirit and learn more about Christ and the Father. Hours spent learning and obeying the lessons by putting them into practice leads to spiritual growth. Book knowledge is not enough. Even the world system knows that. When one goes to the university, they have attachments where they practice under a preceptor, who is an expert in their field. They do this to put into practice what they have learned in theory, in preparation for their new career.

Once they graduate and are now practicing on their own, they must increase their knowledge in their field of study to earn an even higher degree, allowing them to move higher in rank, pay, and skill. This is true too in the spiritual realm. What is done on earth was borrowed from heaven. Do you want to move higher in rank in the spirit realm that demons will know you and tremble because of how much you have died to self and allowed the Holy Trinity to live through you? If you do, you must make the Holy Spirit your BEST FRIEND. You must always consult Him and never make a move without His guidance and leadership.

Scripture tells us that the reason we have our bodies is that we were created to house God in them. When I accepted the Holy Spirit, He came and reorganized my life, beginning with my closet. He took me through my clothes and told me what He wears and what He doesn't wear. You can never go wrong with your dress code if you allow the Holy Spirit to select it for you. After all, it is He wearing it, not you. During this time, I asked the Holy Spirit why He was not telling my husband to change his closet too. My husband had old clothes which I unsuccessfully had tried to have him donate. The Holy Spirit told me to stop being concerned with my husband because He was working in me at the time, not my husband. Does this sound familiar? When we hear God's Word, we think about how it could benefit others, not us. We have the big log in our eyes, but it is amazing how we somehow manage to see past our log into someone else's speck.

In my situation, I had indecent clothes, the above-knee skirts which the Holy Spirit said He doesn't wear, the tight jeans, and other seductive outfits which, until my friend showed me the sin I was committing through His eyes, I had not seen it in His wisdom. As much as my husband advised me not to wear them, I had the wisdom of the kingdom of darkness, and I merely thought he doesn't want me to look attractive. In reality, I was attracting seductive spirits which attracted other people to me, provoking the spirit of lust in them, and we all harbored these demons, allowing them to operate and sin through us. I was the root cause of this demonic open door because of my clothes. When God comes inside you, He shows you things through His eyes. He takes away the wisdom of this world, unveils you, and gives you His wisdom. Oh, how wise I thought I was, only to find out that I was really foolish!

God speaks in many ways. When my husband had

mentioned to me not to dress in above-the-knee outfits, and I refused, God used an animal to speak to me. When God is interested in you, He will make the donkey speak before He allows you to be destroyed. In my case, He used a bee. One day after work, our maintenance man commented on how good my legs were and said jokingly, "and your husband lets you leave your house in that outfit?" It was above my knee, not too short but not modest either. As I drove home, listening to music with my windows down, a bee flew in. I did not know it was there until it stung me right up my right thigh, and as you know, my outfit was even shorter when sitting down. I jumped up in pain and pulled over to remove the stinger. I went home and repented, telling my husband what had happened and vowed not to wear short outfits again. My husband was so excited that he blessed God for the bee!

My asking the Holy Spirit why He was not telling my husband to change his closet was very immature and shallow because I was the one in sin by how I dressed while my husband was not committing any sin by wearing the same old and decent clothes he liked. I am glad my friend the Holy Spirit is in me to make me as wise as He is. Many of us question God about other people's destinies while He is trying to give us instruction on our own. Doesn't this sound familiar? Sounds like when we are dealing with little children, giving one of them an assignment or instruction, and they ask, "What about him or her?" (Pointing at a sibling or other child near them). Don't you then wonder, what does one child's assignment concern the other child for? I often reply, "Don't worry about them, you go do what I asked you to do."

I tell my son Amani, who is twelve now, when he asks me, "What about Tev? Or Trevor?" I respond, "I am not speaking to them but to you, and the assignments I give them, you cannot perform, so stop worrying about their assignments and do what I ask you to do."

This reminds me of what Jesus told Peter when Peter asked about John's destiny in John 21:18–22 (NKJV; emphasis added)

> Most assuredly, I say to you, when you were younger, you girded yourself and walked where you wished; but when you are old, you will stretch out your hands, and another will gird you and carry you where you do not wish." This He spoke, signifying by what death he would glorify God. And when He had spoken this, He said to him, "Follow Me." Then Peter, turning around, saw the disciple whom Jesus loved following, who also had leaned on His breast at the supper, and said, "Lord, who is the one who betrays You?" Peter, seeing him, said to Jesus, *"But Lord, what about this man?"* Jesus said to him, "If I will that he remain till I come, what is that to you? **You follow Me.**

God's desire is for people to worship Him in Spirit and in truth, which is only possible through the Holy Spirit. Worship of Yahweh is fully yielding our bodies, souls, and spirits to His Holy Spirit in Christ, and living sacrificially for the benefit, glory, and fulfillment of God's desires. It is the uncompromised, dedicated, unconditional love and service to God with no conditions or benefits attached, even though we know that God is a rewarder of those who diligently seek Him. People in the outer court dimension lack this selflessness and level of yielding to God. They only lend God their bodies once in a while when things are bad, and when things are good, they forget God and are consumed with the pleasures of the world. I used to live here, where I only went on my knees when my marriage was in chaos. That was my surrender point, but when things became good, I would ignore God and be busy with other things until things went bad again, forcing me back on my knees.

This lifestyle makes God a renter, not a homeowner. A rented house is not a home because it does not belong to you. Expensive furniture and valuables are not invested in rental properties because it is a temporary residence. The home owner can refuse to renew the lease agreement, forcing you out of the home. Therefore, renters tolerate the house even when they do not like certain things in it while they save up for a home they can buy to own.

Homeowners, on the other hand, have vested value in the home and can tear it apart and rebuild. They can make it over, repaint it, and invest in upgrades and treasures in their property because they own it. They have invested value in it. The renter has no invested interest in the rental property because they will never own it. That is why God cannot put His investment in these Christians. They are risky investments because the enemy has direct access to them. They will sell out the Kingdom like Adam and Eve did because they are not hidden in Christ in God. They have not pledged allegiance to God's Kingdom. They have nothing to lose, but the Kingdom has everything to lose.

These Christians may be ministers, preachers, evangelists, teachers of the Word, bishops, archbishops, prophets, and many more Christians with no such ministerial titles. These ministers look at ministry and their success of it from the world's point of view. They measure success in their ministries by how many members or followers they have, how much offerings they collect, how much publicity they get, the type of cars they drive, buildings they own, and their sophisticated church programs.

Many ministries whose ministers dwell here force their congregation to live here as well. I know this because I have been to churches like these—until I said enough was enough, and I wanted to go deeper! Many fleshy leaders are entertainers, not God-seekers. They hire intercessors to seek God for their ministry, which is very unwise because the intercessors are not the ones who should hear God for them. Moses, the Israelites' leader, went up the mountain to hear God for himself and bring God's Word to God's people. He never sent intercessors to go up the mountain while he went partying, eating, and drinking. He was the one fasting for forty days and nights while his congregation partied. How many leaders do we have who do the same today?

Look at Christ. The disciples reported that He *often* withdrew Himself to pray. Jesus prayed all night and through the day. He left them to go and pray. His lifestyle was that of prayer and fasting that no demon was any match for Him. He was criticized because His disciples never fasted while John the Baptist's disciples fasted. He was the leader; yet, He sought God for Himself! He was the ministry bearer. The assignment was His, and He never entrusted the success of His assignment to others. When He asked the disciples to pray at His most trying time, they fell asleep, and He went to intercede for Himself. The disciples fell into temptation when they faced it, but Christ never sinned when He could have. He was victorious. He was silent instead of cursing his persecutors when He could have. He remained obedient to God to the end.

Why do you entrust others to seek God for you? You will be answerable for the failure of your assignment, which will lead many astray. This would have been the result of Christ's assignment had He entrusted His ministry to others. Some ministers Google messages or listen to other people's revelations, then go and preach it because they do not have time to seek God for themselves, to get into a deeper dimension in God. They are in it for the fame and money, for what they get out of it—not for God's passion which He died for: souls. They live double lives and easily fall into sin. Their families suffer abuse from them because their character is not like Christ; yet, they want to lead others into the same dysfunctionality. They refuse to be led by the Spirit of God; therefore, they are not being transformed. These people will die in the wilderness because they have refused to have a different spirit.

Those under their leadership who do not seek God for themselves never grow. Those who go deeper end up with a deeper revelation than their own pastors and are directed elsewhere by God for more solid food. This happened to me. When my eyes were opened, for the first time, I saw our pastor as an entertainer. He kept the congregation entertained, but sin lived there. There was no spiritual growth or healing. I realized it was time to leave the outer court church and get deeper into the Holy Place.

INNER COURT CHRISTIANS

In the Holy Place, Christ reveals Himself more to us through the Holy Spirit. It is a more serious stage in the relationship with Christ. He shows you a side of Him you can never see in the outer court. He dines with you here. In a relationship, this is now the "dating stage." He invites you to know Him more. He reveals His likes, His desires, what pleases Him, what hurts Him.

However, Christ does not give you the deep secrets to begin with, but this gets deeper as you go into deeper levels in Him. This is a multilevel dimension, just as courting takes longer than meeting and greeting, and the relationship grows into different stages before marriage. Christ knows that many Christians bail out once persecution comes, or when they get attracted to the cares of the world, including money and making it. The Holy Place, therefore, is for God-seekers. Those who want more than just enrollment. Those who are ready to take a deep dive into the study and understanding of God and His Word. Those who need to get a strong foundation in God. This is a high dimension, higher than the outer court, and very few Christians live here.

Holy Place Christians are closer to God. They have allowed God to sign a lease agreement to rent with an intent of ownership. There is hope for owning these bodies for Christ. Very few people give God this opportunity. These people have a longer term contract and can be depended upon more than the outer court Christians. They have God's Word leading them; however, they are still limited to God's written Word. If God wants to display His glory anew, they miss it because they look for it in the written Word. They have not developed enough faith to know God in every form He decides to come in.

These Christians are very faithful in studying God's Word. They have a revelation of it, but they still lack the fullness of the Father. They are now friends with the Son, as they have gone deeper into friendship. There is promise here of engagement if they want to go deeper into intimacy and marriage. They just accepted an invitation to commitment and courtship, giving God an opportunity to be a homeowner. He is renting to own; if the seller agrees to the final terms, then ownership will be the final stage.

These Christians may be preachers, evangelists, teachers of the Word, bishops, archbishops, prophets, and many more who rely on God's Word for their daily living and direction. They can be Christians with no such ministerial titles but seek God for themselves and get into the Holy Place because of their hunger for more. People here launch deeper, with a desire for more of Christ. They accept His invitation to commit to Him, leaving the world and its pleasures and wisdom behind, embracing Christ and His wisdom. They enter into a relationship with Christ to know Him more, not just knowing about Him.

In the Holy Place, we know God for ourselves. We try the Word out to see it working for us. I have many experiences of this. This is where we progress from knowing the God of the Bible to knowing our God personally. This is where I know the God of Zawadi (my God). Do you know your God? People in this place are semi-comatose to self, making God semi-active in them. This is a deliverance phase from the enemy's stronghold and mind-set. This is both the body and soul rescue from the enemy, delivered from the enemy's stronghold and mind-set. This is the "character change phase." People here have a name change from "children of the world" to "God's children," but they are still working on their character in partnership with the Holy Spirit's in order to live like children of God.

Here is where we learn to walk with my friend the Holy Spirit. Have you been where I was? When I once trusted in myself to stand, I fell. Just like when a little child learns to walk, and the parent sees an obstacle ahead, he reaches out to hold the child's hand, and the first thing the child does is . . . Yes, you got it! The child snatches their hand from the parent's hold, and they move away shrugging their shoulders. The parent then verbally warns the child of the danger of falling over the obstacle ahead, but the child trusts in their skill so much . . . that they fall on the same obstacle which the parent had warned them about.

That is what I did in the past when I trusted in my flesh, which many of us still do when learning to walk with the Holy Spirit. My friend the Holy Spirit teaches us to walk in God's ways, and after a few steps with Him, we think we are pros! We trust in our flesh . . . until we fall. May God help us not to trust in our flesh, but to put our trust in God's leadership and guidance. If this is you now, get up in Jesus' name, reach out for the Holy Spirit's hand, and learn from this mess like I did. Now I have a message, and you can have one too! MESS plus AGE (meaning maturity) equals MESSAGE. Help us, Holy Spirit, to trust in your guiding hand and never snatch it away in Jesus' name! Amen.

In this place, the soul is rescued, and our minds are changed into the mind of Christ as we read and meditate on the Word of God. Daily deliverance and cleansing are done here by the Word of God. People in this realm learn to guard their minds with God's Word. This is where my friend the Holy Spirit introduces the full armor of God and its proper use. We learn how to protect our minds from the evil arrows of darkness by proper use of the helmet of salvation.

Philippians 4:6–8 (NLT) says, "Don't worry about anything; instead, pray about everything. Tell God what you need, and thank him for all he has done. Then you will experience God's peace, which exceeds anything we can understand. His peace will guard your hearts and minds as you live in Christ Jesus. And now, dear brothers and sisters, one final thing. Fix your thoughts on what is true, and honorable, and right, and pure, and lovely, and admirable. Think about things that are excellent and worthy of praise."

The light or truth in this place is the lamp of the Word of God. The word of Faith; what we hope for according to God's Word but have not seen it yet, is our truth. The lamp gives light in this place. Like David said in Psalm 119:105, thy word is a lamp unto my feet and a light unto my path. The lamp lights up our pathway and only comes on when oil is present; otherwise, it stays off. The lamp represents the Word of God. The oil represents the revelation anointing of the Holy Spirit. The lamp without the oil is darkness. Many people read the Bible, even Satanists, or other antichrist religions, but they do not understand it because it is a hidden code treasure of heaven. Only the Holy Spirit can access the code; therefore, without Him, people will continue living in darkness.

Jesus had to unlock this code several times when the disciples did not understand His teaching. Jesus, by the Holy Spirit, opened their minds to understanding in Luke 24:45-53 "Then he opened their minds, that they might understand the Scriptures." Also after resurrection, Jesus was speaking with His disciples but they did not know it was Him so He opened their eyes, unveiling them, so they may see Him in Luke 24:31 "Their eyes were opened, and they recognized him, and he vanished out of their sight." Jesus quoted the prophet Isaiah in Mark 4:10-12 "When he was alone, those who were around him with the twelve asked him about the parables. He said to them, "To you is given the mystery of God's Kingdom, but to those who are outside, all things are done in parables, that 'seeing they may see, and not perceive; and hearing they may hear, and not understand; lest perhaps they should turn again, and their sins should be forgiven them.'"'"

Is. 6:9 "He said, "Go, and tell this people, 'You hear indeed, but don't understand; and you see indeed, but don't perceive.'"

That is why the disciples were told by Christ not to start their ministry with only the lamp. They had to wait for the oil, or they would be walking in darkness and be destroyed. Imagine buying a lamp without buying oil, and being confident that the lamp will light up for you when you need the light! You and someone without the lamp would be in the same situation. You would both be in darkness! You however, would have the upper hand because all you need is the oil and fire to enjoy the light. For believers to shine God's light into this dark world, the baptism of the Holy Spirit and fire is a must! Unbelievers have no lamp. Beginning believers have the lamp, when they accept Christ in their lives as Lord and Savior.

Three steps every successful Christian must have

1. Get the Lamp (Jesus Christ, the Word of God sent to us): Acknowledge that you are a sinner in need of a Savior, and accept Christ as your Lord and Savior. God will not give oil to people without a lamp because there is nowhere to pour the oil. They have no capacity. No lamp, no oil. No Jesus, no Holy Spirit.
2. Get the Oil (Holy Spirit Revelation): Be baptized with the Holy Spirit by asking the Father for Him through the name of the Son, Jesus Christ. With capacity to hold oil, now we can ask to be filled with oil. The Holy Spirit.

3. Get the Fire (Holy Spirit Power): The Holy Spirit anointing for Kingdom business which is your God-given assignment. No oil, no fire. No Holy Spirit, no anointing, or power of God. Without the oil, God cannot give us fire because the fire alone cannot light the lamp. The oil is what keeps the fire burning.

The oil is refilled by the intimate relationship with God the Holy Spirit. Living under His guidance and continual leadership is what keeps the oil flowing in our lives. Without this intimacy, the lamp cannot not get lit because the fire is lit by the Holy Spirit's fire (power). God's power does not come from man's work. It is all God's fire, by His Spirit. Making the Holy Spirit your friend is the key to succeeding as a child of God and an ambassador of Christ.

God hates strange fires. Man-made gimmicks that are very common in today's religion. There are great consequences for kindling your own fire, trying to imitate God.

"Behold, all you who kindle a fire, who adorn yourselves with torches around yourselves; walk in the flame of your fire, and among the torches that you have kindled. You will have this from my hand: You will lie down in sorrow." (Isaiah 50:11)

"Nadab and Abihu, the sons of Aaron, each took his censer, and put fire in it, and laid incense on it, and offered strange fire before Yahweh, which he had not commanded them. Fire came out from before Yahweh, and devoured them, and they died before Yahweh. Then Moses said to Aaron, "This is what Yahweh spoke of, saying, 'I will show myself holy to those who come near me, and before all the people I will be glorified.'" Aaron held his peace. [10] You are to make a distinction between the holy and the common, and between the unclean and the clean." (Leviticus 10:1-3, 10)

God's Word is useless without my friend the Holy Spirit. The devil read the Word but never had the revelation of it. He did not understand the consequences of killing Jesus because if had, he would have done all in his power to prevent Christ's death. Heaven's intelligence is extremely high tech! The human and spirit mind cannot comprehend it unless it is revealed to us by God the Holy Spirit.

No wonder after Jesus was baptized with the Holy Spirit, His Word shone a great light among many until His death, because access to the secret truths of heaven was granted to Him through the Holy Spirit. Do you want this access? The Holy Spirit is the secret. The Holy Spirit cannot be contended with. That is why the safekeeping of heaven's secrets, gifts, and treasures has been entrusted to Him for distribution. My friend searches deeper in man and knows the deep things of God. He knows every one's spiritual level, maturity, and capacity. He knows what we can be entrusted with and what we cannot handle. He distributes Kingdom wealth and gifts in great wisdom.

People in the Holy Place live by the daily bread provided by God (manna). This is the Logos (written) Word realm. During temptation, Christ used this weapon effectively. He proved to Satan that although Satan knew the written scripture, revelation of its truth only came from the Holy Spirit. Satan knew the written scripture well; however, he lacked the revelation of it. If Satan had this power of revelation, he would not have crucified Christ because this is what brought about his ultimate defeat. As much as scripture had prophesied about this plan, Satan did not get the revelation which only comes from the Holy Spirit.

Paul was very clear when he exposed the devil's limitation

to heaven's secrets. 1 Corinthians 2:7–9 says, "But we speak God's wisdom in a mystery, the wisdom that has been hidden, which God foreordained before the worlds for our glory, which none of the rulers of this world has known. For had they known it, they wouldn't have crucified the Lord of glory. But as it is written, "Things which an eye didn't see, and an ear didn't hear, which didn't enter into the heart of man, these God has prepared for those who love him."

We have established that the lamp, God's Word, comes alive and is activated only with the oil, the Holy Spirit's revelation. Otherwise, it is useless. Remember, quoting God's Word is not enough, because even the devil has it memorized and quotes it. He knows it so well that he can confuse you and misquote it to trick you like he tried to do to Christ in the wilderness. The difference is that Christ had the oil and fire which activated the lamp, and when Christ quoted it to the devil, the light came on and put away the darkness. The light of the Word exposed the devil so much that he fled from Christ. Dare to have God the Holy Spirit illuminate the lamp you have.

When I asked for God for the Holy Spirit, the Bible became alive to me. The Word came alive as I called it, as mentored by the Holy Spirit my friend. After my husband received the baptism of the Holy Spirit, he experienced the same thing. Beloved, revelation power is found in the oil, the Holy Spirit, and without Him, the lamp is dysfunctional. Without Him, there is no revelation of the Word, leading many to fall back out to the outer court, which eventually will lead to death.

In the Holy Place, people get to discover and begin fulfilling their God-given task. However, if they remain at this level, they may have to hand over to those who are willing to die completely to self for God to go deeper in them just like

Moses and Elijah had to hand off to Joshua and Elisha due to disobedience on Moses' part and fear of man on Elijah's. The Holy Place is the earthly equivalent of the living room. Those who follow the Helper, the Holy Spirit of God, enter here. The blood of Christ, the Word of God, and angelic protection are found here.

In this phase, God is just leasing our bodies, His temple, with an intention to own. We allow God to use us in the hope of owning us. He allows us some access into the Kingdom as long as we can get authorization from His Word and access by His Spirit. The more revelation we have of His Word, the more access we possess. The less we know and have the revelation of, the less we possess. God has an investment here according to our hunger and thirst after Him. Faith's provision is found here. Daily manna, water from the rock . . . We trust in God for our daily spiritual provision.

Extraordinary things happen in this realm from the revelation of knowledge. The lamp and bread of the Word of God are used to provide and illuminate a believer's life causing the extraordinary manifestation of favor and blessings. Death can creep here if not attacked by the sword of the Spirit. The Word of God is the truth in this place through the oil of the Spirit. It is also the food in this place. Christ is broken down for us in pieces by the Holy Spirit. Christ reveals Himself to us, and we taste His goodness. This deepens our relationship with Him causing a desire and hunger for more.

The holy Place is the "learning phase," where we learn God's ways and Kingdom living. This is our spiritual wilderness and training ground, where we learn how to obey God and incorporate the Ten Commandments into our lives as a lifestyle to please God. This is a phase where the Ten Commandments came into play with the children of Israel. The commands were meant to lead and guide the Israelites into holiness and a God-fearing lifestyle. They were meant to undo their slave and idol worship mentality and ways, replacing them with a God mentality and ways. The wilderness journey was to teach them and test them in these skills so that they can live holy in the Promised Land. This wilderness training of God's Word was a prerequisite to entering God's rest, to ruling and reigning with Christ. We all know that slaves do not rule kingdoms. Therefore, this is a place where kings are made.

This is also the realm where the applied blood of Jesus is activated. We cannot take a shower with our clothes on. We must take off our clothes and use the water and soap provided in order to be clean. In this place, we must make a choice to undress, which spiritually means getting real with ourselves and our filth, allowing God the Holy Spirit to fix and expose the filthy areas in our lives, teaching us to apply the blood of the Lamb of God for cleansing and deliverance.

We consciously decide to get real and deeply place our hands into the blood of Jesus and apply it in our lives for deeper cleansing and authority. This action is what saves us from death. When we apply the blood of Jesus and the Word of God in the different areas of our lives, deliverance power is activated. This is what takes away our slave mentality and replaces it with Kingdom and kingship mentality.

The application of God's Word in our lives is what justifies us, saves us, and makes us righteous. The application of the blood of the lamb on the doorposts of the Israelites was what saved them from the angel of death.

Exodus 12:13 says, "The blood shall be to you for a token on the houses where you are: and when I see the blood, I will pass over you, and there shall no plague be on you to destroy you, when I strike the land of Egypt." Being a doer of the Word and not just a hearer brings life. (James 1:22–25)

If you fell in a pool of mud, and then you undressed and got into a pool of clean water, and I provided you with a washcloth and soap, and you used it for bathing, how clean will you be? Will you have evidence of falling in the mud? Not at all. You would be very clean, as if you never fell in the mud in the first place. That is the power of purposeful application of the blood of Jesus in our lives. The power of deliberate application of God's Word in our lives, allowing it to cleanse and purify us, justifying us, leaves no evidence of sin in our lives.

The Holy Place is a medium-sized area because a few people make it here to live. Just like the children of Israel all got delivered from the Egyptians and crossed the Red Sea together, but many of them died in the wilderness. Few people from the exodus made it to where they could only see the Promised Land, including their leader Moses. This is because he never died to self. He still had anger issues. He had anger in Egypt when he killed the Egyptian soldier, and he had anger in the wilderness when he broke the Ten Commandments, and God made him write it all over again. Thinking that he may have learned his lesson before getting into the Promised Land, God instructed him to touch the rock for water to quench the thirst of the Israelites. He allowed the rebellion of the Israelites to get to him, and in anger, he hit the rock instead of touching the rock as God had commanded him.

The devil, in triumph, even fought for Moses' body as a trophy of victory over him. I'm sure he celebrated Moses' downfall saying . . . "The so-called deliverer who needed deliverance himself dies as a slave." Leaders, let us be careful not to pray for others and leave ourselves out in darkness. We must follow Christ's example when He prayed in John 17. He prayed first for Himself, then His disciples, then whoever will believe in Him. My friend the Holy Spirit must lead us, and we will have the right priorities.

It is sad that leaders get too busy leading that they do not work out their salvation with fear and trembling. As Paul said, we must crucify the flesh daily so that after preaching and leading others, we do not get disqualified as Moses did. Moses took God's grace for granted, and God withheld it from him. Just when God was getting ready to move him deeper and began showing him greater things, including His glory, Moses fell short of God's glory again. When God withheld His grace, no matter what Moses said, God never changed His mind. This is a very dangerous place to be. We get here when we take God's grace for granted, using it as a license to keep repeating the same sin.

> Then I pleaded with the Lord at that time, saying: 'O Lord God, You have begun to show Your servant Your greatness and Your mighty hand, for what god is there in heaven or on earth who can do anything like Your works and Your mighty deeds? I pray, let me cross over and see the good land beyond the Jordan, those pleasant mountains, and Lebanon.' "But the Lord was angry with me on your account, and would not listen to me. So the Lord said to me: 'Enough of that! Speak no more to Me of this matter. Go up to the top of Pisgah, and lift your eyes toward the west, the north, the south, and the east; behold it with your eyes, for you shall not cross over this Jordan. But command Joshua, and

encourage him and strengthen him; for he shall go over before this people, and he shall cause them to inherit the land which you will see.' (Deuteronomy 3:23–28, NKJV)

Many believers in the Holy Place realm are by-the-book givers or meet-the-requirement givers. They are in the late teenage and young adult stage of maturity in Christianity. They are people pleasers, still learning to be God pleasers. They are still limited by people's opinion of them. They still do things to fit in and be accepted by others. What people think of them is still important to them. They are afraid to stand alone for the truth sometimes. They do what is written in God's Word to try to please God and sometimes please others.

Christians here have different maturity levels according to how much Word they practice. Some are God pleasers who mostly care about what God thinks most of the time. They are people and semi-God pleasers. They give just what is required of them as it is written in God's Word to meet the requirements. They are unprofitable servants for they only do what is required of them. They do not go above and beyond what is required. (Luke 17:7–10) Some believers go above and beyond; sometimes, not all the time.

This is the same position that the rich young ruler was in Matthew 19:16–22. He had perfected the law as was required of him, but when he was asked to dive deeper, which had not been written in the law, he turned Christ's offer down. The proposal of being Christ's bride was rejected because, at this stage, people are still limited to the light of the lamp and the bread, which is the written Word of God. The lamp gives light, but it is not as bright as the glory light. The rich young ruler was not ready for the glory light. He accepted the written Word but not the spoken Word. He settled for this level.

People at this level have an "ours" mentality. They still own some rights and shares here. They think, "Some of what I have is mine, and some is God's. I own more of what is mine; that is, 85 percent, and God owns 10 percent of tithe and some offerings, about 5 percent, which totals 15 percent. I will give to Him what He requires in His word." Sometimes they pay bills and take care of their needs before giving to God so they give left overs instead of giving to God first. Some still struggle with prioritization.

Christ is revealed as the way and truth in this realm. We know Christ as the only way, and the Word of God as our only source of truth. Believers here judge everything according to God's Word. They run everything through this test and do not make decisions based on their own understanding but on God's understanding.

When we go to school, we go in with our own understanding, but after we are taught, we acquire a different understanding which causes us to succeed in life and in what we do in our careers. Likewise, the Word of God transforms us and renews our minds. Do you have God's understanding, or are you still leaning on your own? The twelve disciples entered this realm while all others deserted Christ. (See John 6:63–69.) They decided to lose their minds for the mind of Christ, while the others wanted to keep their minds and reject the mind of Christ.

The Holy Spirit convicts us of righteousness in this place. He gives us revelation on how to live according to the Word of God, allowing it to change us by pruning and purging the evil in us, making us righteous as we learn to obey and live by faith. This faith is then credited to us as righteousness. This is where midfloor Christians are. They have a better view than first-floor Christians but are still limited in their view. It costs a lot more to be here. There is still room for growth; therefore, they still have a roof over their head. The enemy will throw attacks at them but is afraid of them because they possess the defensive weapon, the sword of the Spirit, which is the Word of God.

The reason why King Solomon was successful and possessed a lot of wisdom was because He enjoyed God's Word and used it to solve problems. Look at the story of the two women who lived together with two babies and one slept on her baby, and he died. The woman whose baby died stole the other woman's baby while she slept and exchanged it for her dead baby. This is how the devil switches out our blessings for dead works because we sleep too much instead of seeking God, protecting what He has blessed us with and being led by the Holy Spirit.

Because the women were fighting over the one child claiming that it belonged to them, king Solomon asked for a sword to cut up the living child so He could give each half to the women. The sword here represents the Word of God because it helped make the decision and reveal who the birth mother was. The birth mother begged the king to give her child to the other woman instead of killing him. She could not bear to see the pain and death of her beloved child. On the other hand, the evil woman wanted the child cut in half so the other woman would suffer loss, just as she had. Beloved, the Word of God will distinguish between the real truth and the counterfeit. It will expose evil and protect the righteous. It will destroy wickedness and give justice and boldness to the righteous who are led by it. It is the source of truth. (See 1 Kings 3:16–28.)

Remember how the Israelites won the war in the wilderness? When Moses had to lift his staff up for them to win?

When we are fighting against the enemy, we cannot afford to put down the staff, which is the Word of God. We must hold it up as a defensive and offensive weapon. We must keep our faith up regardless of how tired we are. We must encourage each other to hold on to our faith in God's Word in order to succeed because the war in this place is a war of faith. The Lord only steps in when we activate His Word by faith.

> So Joshua did what Moses had commanded and fought the army of Amalek. Meanwhile, Moses, Aaron, and Hur climbed to the top of a nearby hill. As long as Moses held up the staff in his hand, the Israelites had the advantage. But whenever he dropped his hand, the Amalekites gained the advantage. Moses' arms soon became so tired he could no longer hold them up. So Aaron and Hur found a stone for him to sit on. Then they stood on each side of Moses, holding up his hands. So his hands held steady until sunset. (Exodus 17:10–12, NLT)

People in this realm cannot take a break from using God's Word and expect someone else to use it for them. Moses had to hold the staff himself for victory over the enemy. They never took turns to hold it with Aaron or Hur. These two only encouraged him. They helped to hold him up but never once touched the staff for him. No one can hold your staff for you, but they can lift you up in encouragement. Never let go of your staff because we must work out our salvation with fear and trembling. We do not work it out for another.

To lose weight and gain muscle mass, you must go to the gym yourself. My son is a track and field runner, and I tease him, telling him to take my body and run for me. He usually laughs and tells me it would be too heavy for him. He loves to run, so he is handsomely lean. On the other hand, running is torture for me, but I love to walk. The results are not interchangeable; they are very personal. Trevor trains daily, and that is why he looks the way he does. I do not do as much training as he does, so my body does not look anything close to his. I, however, admire him and wish I were as lean as he is.

Similarly, many people envy spiritually lean people, but they are too lazy to work out their spirits to look as good. They want the results, but they are not willing to pay the price for it. I am disciplined in my diet because my son's results are not mine. If his results were mine, I would lack the discipline. I would live an unhealthy lifestyle and rely on his success to keep me lean. God will not allow us to have a relationship with Him on behalf of someone else. He wants a personal relationship with each of us. Beloved, let us stop riding on someone else's salvation and work out our own. I once told my sons that there would come a point in their lives, like it did mine, when they seek God for themselves. They will not rely on their mother's or father's, grandparent's or great-grandparent's God. They will desire God for themselves and work out their salvation with a personal God.

War in this place is fought through faith in the written Word of God. The applied blood of Jesus is my defense and offense. It defends me from the enemy and attacks my enemies. Jesus defeated Satan when He was in His "wilderness phase" using the sword of the Spirit, which is the Word of God. (See Temptation of Jesus in Luke 4:1–13.)

When we take a break from God's Word, the enemy gains the upper hand. For example, Elijah never entered God's rest on earth because He entertained the spirit of fear from Jezebel. He allowed the spirit of fear to take him from the highest dimension of fearless faith, which he once operated in, and demoted him, where he then began living by sight and not by faith. He believed a lie that Jezebel was mightier than God who had killed all of Jezebel's idol worship priests—the God who answered him by fire, the God who stopped the rain and gave rain again. He fell too low to see God or communicate with Him. Yes, it is possible for someone who is highly anointed to fall very low. That is why we must follow Christ, not people. Paul told his congregation to follow him only if he is following Christ. If he strayed away, they should not continue to follow blindly. My friend the Holy Spirit is there to lead us because He never waivers. He is God.

Because Elijah fell too low, God could not trust him again. He had fallen short of the glory of God. However, God was merciful enough to get him back to the Holy Place. Because Elijah had fallen too far for God to stoop that low, in the outer courts, God sent an angel to get Elijah back on his feet, to a level where he could hear God again and communicate with Him. The angel fed Elijah and prepared him for a forty-day fast so he could rise above his flesh again because he was too fleshy for God. Elijah needed to come up to a level where God could speak to him, and he would hear God because where he was, he had lost heaven's network. Heaven could see and hear him, but he couldn't see or hear from heaven.

After the forty-day fast, God spoke to Elijah, asking him where he was and what he was doing because he had lost ground in the spirit realm. God questioned Elijah's position, not location. Are you in the place where Elijah was? Did you use to operate in great power and revelation? Have you fallen too low? There is hope! Pray and fast and get back your spiritual network so you can hear God and be restored. God told Elijah, just like He told Moses, that his work was over, and he had to hand off to his successor. Elijah was told to go and anoint his successor Elisha, who would get into the next level, the highest level of rest in God. Elisha got double the anointing that was upon Elijah, which Elijah missed due to fear and mistrust in God.

1 Kings 19:9 says, He came to a cave there, and camped there; and behold, Yahweh's word came to him, and he said to him, "What are you doing here, Elijah?"

God will never lack a person to take your place. Some people are ready to allow God to use them for His glory in whatever capacity He wishes. Are you one of them? Or are you going to be replaced? (See 1 Kings 19.)

The Holy Place is a place of full faith and reliance on the Holy Spirit in order to know what to do and where to go. It is a place where the light is the Word of God revealed to us by God the Holy Spirit. This is a place where the only thing we feed on is the written Word of God. It is a place of constant consultation with God through His Word while relying on the Holy Spirit for revelation. Many believers do not live here yet. They just visit this place once in a while when it is convenient. When storms rage, they go out to look for the natural light, their familiar ways . . . palm readers, fortune-tellers, horoscopes, and other ungodly solutions to solve their problems. They go back to living by sight and not by faith.

The Holy Place is where the hungry dwell. The table of showbread is located here, symbolizing Christ, the bread of life. He is the Word of God without whom we will spiritually starve to death. In this place, we get to know Christ intimately as we get to taste His goodness and faithfulness. People who are not hungry cannot enter in this place. This is where Christ taught people saying that they must eat His body and drink His blood, and all who had followed Him turned around and left Him because they thought that this lesson was too deep for them. (John 6:60)

Christ asked them to go deeper in Him, taking their love relationship into a whole new level, but they were not ready to leave all the other things behind. Just like when dating, and a man asks a woman to go to the next level of commitment, but the woman is not yet ready to settle or belong to someone. She still wants her freedom to hang out with other men without limitations or guilt. Many Christians have a hard time committing to Christ because they do not want to leave their bad behavior or friends behind. They do not want to be out of place or unpopular by being sold out to Christ. I know this to be true because when I accepted the invitation to go deeper in a relationship with Christ, I lost my friends, and many were jealous of me, calling me "over spiritual," including my husband. That is why the Holy Place is not a popular place to be. There is a price to pay. Jesus experienced this. His disciples did too, and all who are sold out to Him will experience it.

How can we trust God when our situation is dead and buried, but Christ says it is just asleep? How do you believe in God when He speaks life into your dead situation while you already buried it and moved on? How do you believe in God and look foolish to everyone else? Many Christians want to know Christ only when they are eating and drinking physical food, but not when they are eating and drinking spiritually and suffering for doing good. They do not want to fast and pray, eating the bread of life alone (the Word of God) for some time in order to know this bread (Christ) more.

They live a selfish life to please themselves, but when they get in trouble or are in need, they call on Christ, and they expect Him to drop everything and run to their rescue. These selfish Christians want a relationship with Christ only when He is meeting their needs, but they do not want to meet His needs. This is not relating; it is using. I will therefore make up a word and call it a "using-ship," not a relationship. Are you in a using-ship or a relationship with Christ?

If a lady refuses to be committed in a relationship to a man, if she is in trouble, is the man obligated to bail her out? Doesn't he move on to the lady who will commit to him, and then, he invests his time, money, and resources on the woman who has chosen to leave all for him? Why then blame God if He is not at your beck and call? Living in the Holy Place calls for a commitment to Christ by faith. It is this kind of faith that is credited to us as righteousness. This place is a place of complete trust and reliance on God's vision . . . the lamp of His Word, not the natural light. What God says is the source of truth.

If I am in a committed relationship with a man, and I am in need while another lady who had refused this commitment gets in trouble and needs his help too, who do you think he will respond to and use his resources on to rescue? Me, of course! He will pick up my call before he picks up an unknown caller's call. He will come running to my rescue because I am his. He is invested in me emotionally and in many other ways that it benefits him to come to my rescue.

What does it benefit the Kingdom to come to your rescue? Before any country sends troops on a rescue mission, they have to validate the importance of the people being rescued in relationship to the country. Why would they use their resources on people who have not pledged their allegiance to them? It is a waste of Kingdom resources because the Kingdom needs to rescue its own first in order to grow and be a successful kingdom. If they rescue people from a different kingdom, they have a lot to lose because they will benefit the other kingdom. That is the same as the Kingdom of God. Some scriptures confirming this fact in God's Kingdom are:

"Because he has set his love on me, therefore I will deliver him. I will set him on high, because he has known my name. He will call on me, and I will answer him. I will be with him in trouble. I will deliver him, and honor him. I will satisfy him with long life, and show him my salvation." (Psalm 91:14–15; emphasis added)

Psalm 34:7–9 "Yahweh's angel encamps around those who fear him, and delivers them. Oh taste and see that Yahweh is good. Blessed is the man who takes refuge in him. Oh fear Yahweh, you his saints, for there is no lack with those who fear him."

James 5:16b, NLT says, "The earnest prayer of a righteous person has great power and produces wonderful results."

God will rescue Holy Place dwellers before He rescues outer court dwellers. Just like a mother hen will rescue the chicks closest to her before she even attempts to rescue the ones farther out. She feels sad when the eagle snatches her young chick, but she cannot risk the lives of the others for the one wandering chick. The closer you are to God, the faster your rescue is, and the harder it is for the devil to attack you. He can't get through God to you. The safest place to be is hidden with Christ in God as in Colossians 3:3.

HOLY OF HOLIES CHRISTIANS

Deeper than the Holy Place is the Holy of Holies. This is the highest dimension in God, where we meet God the Father, who is the light in this place. There is no sun or moon and no lamp. The glory of God the Father is the light in the Holy of Holies. The High Priests were the only ones in the past who were permitted to enter into this place once a year on the Day of Atonement, to offer the blood of the sacrifice and incense which they sprinkled on the mercy seat where God sat.

There is a great difference between the shed blood, the applied blood, and the sprinkled blood. The shed blood is for whosoever believes. It is available for acceptance and cleanses us from sin. The applied blood requires our purposeful action in application and marks us for redemption, while the sprinkled blood speaks and prays grace for us. It marks us for eternity as brides. The dimensions of the Holy of Holies were way smaller than the Holy Place because fewer Christians make it to this dimension.

The Holy of Holies is the place of rest. This is where we meet the Father. This is where Christ Himself takes us. No one comes to the Father except through Christ. This is where Christ said that no one has seen or knows the Father except the Son and whomever the Son chooses to reveal the Father to.

Luke 10:22 states, "Turning to the disciples, he said, 'All things have been delivered to me by my Father. No one knows who the Son is, except the Father, and who the Father is, except the Son, and he to whomever the Son desires to reveal him.'"

For us to meet the Father, we must be chosen as brides. When you get to a part of the relationship where a man wants you to meet his father, at least in the real modest days, he must have proposed to you and wants to marry you. The first time my father-in-law heard of me from my husband was when my husband introduced me to him as his bride. His dad never knew me when I met my husband, or when we dated. He only knew me when my husband told him he had found a wife he wants to marry.

Has Christ found a bride in you? Has He introduced you to His Dad as His bride? That is when you enter into rest because the Father now takes it upon Himself to cater to you as He gets the wedding ceremony ready. You are now under His personal protection and treated as the Son is treated because you now belong to Him as His child. God takes Jesus seriously. Christ doesn't introduce just anyone as His bride. He is very careful. Recall in His story about the wedding supper, where He speaks about His bride and friends of the bridegroom. Which will you be? A guest or a bride? The choice is yours.

We all don't get the same price or sitting. The Father decides. Even the disciples were told that. Ours is to work out our salvation with fear and trembling. We are to hunger and thirst after righteousness so we may be filled. Jesus promises rewards for those who give up their lives for Him as He did for them. He promises different rewards like when He spoke to the churches in Revelations chapter 2 and 3. Here in the Holy of Holies, God the Father through His Spirit reveals the hidden things and deep secrets to those with this deep intimacy. Just as a husband pours himself into His wife during deep intimacy, God pours Himself into those who are deeply intimate with Him in this place.

The Father's glory illuminates your life and your entire being here. In this place of rest, the Father is the one dancing and rejoicing over you with singing as He holds you in His arms.

You danced and worshipped Him on your way here, so now it is His turn. He is the one doing the work on you, pouring Himself into you, releasing His favor and blessings and more dominion and authority over you. You now enter His rest here in the spirit, and He works on your behalf. This is where the greatest supernatural miracles occur. The Father rejoices that we are finally His! He is ecstatic, and He breaks out into a dance.

Zephaniah 3:17 says, "Yahweh, your God, is among you, a mighty one who will save. He will rejoice over you with joy. He will calm you in his love. He will rejoice over you with singing."

This is the greatest dimension in God. It is so deep that only the High Priest was allowed to access this place once a year. The High Priest was afraid of being struck dead here if he was unacceptable to God. There was a rope with a bell that was tied on the High Priest's ankle so that if he dies, the others could pull him out, for no one was allowed to access this place but once a year, as the chosen High Priest only. The High Priests went into this dimension by casting lots, not voluntarily. It was a dangerous place to be. This was when God spoke to them through angels like the time the angel Gabriel announced the birth of John the Baptist to his father Zechariah, who was the chosen High Priest that year.

> One day Zechariah was serving God in the Temple, for his order was on duty that week. As was the custom of the priests, he was chosen by lot to enter the sanctuary of the Lord and burn incense. While the incense was being burned, a great crowd stood outside, praying. While Zechariah was in the sanctuary, an angel of

the Lord appeared to him, standing to the right of the incense altar. Zechariah was shaken and overwhelmed with fear when he saw him. But the angel said, "Don't be afraid, Zechariah! God has heard your prayer. Your wife, Elizabeth, will give you a son, and you are to name him John." (Luke 1:8–13, NLT)

"and he shall put the incense on the fire before Yahweh, that the cloud of the incense may cover the mercy seat that is on the testimony, so that he will not die." (Leviticus 16:13)

"Engagement and Marriage Phase." Here, we dive all in and are completely hidden with Christ in God, hidden in His embrace and all He is. We are his brides, engaged, and one with Him. Here, we know God in His fullness. We accept His marriage proposal and get engaged. (See Hebrews 8:9–11; Jeremiah 31:32–34.) People who dwell here successfully fulfill their God-given task. Just like Christ, Paul, Peter, and John, the disciple of Christ, who wrote the book of Revelation. As much as others tried to kill John, he could not die. They exiled him to the island of Patmos where he fulfilled his purpose successfully. No one can kill your destiny in this realm.

People in this realm know when their work is almost over because they are one with God. Peter knew when his end was near. 2 Peter 1:14–15 (NLT) says, "For our Lord Jesus Christ has shown me that I must soon leave this earthly life, so I will work hard to make sure you always remember these things after I am gone."

Paul knew when his race was over.

2 Timothy 4:7–8 says, "I have fought the good fight. I have finished the course. I have kept the faith. From now on, there is stored up for me the crown of righteousness, which the Lord,

the righteous judge, will give to me on that day; and not to me only, but also to all those who have loved his appearing."

Christ knew when His time to die had come.

Luke 18:31–33 says, He took the twelve aside, and said to them, "Behold, we are going up to Jerusalem, and all the things that are written through the prophets concerning the Son of Man will be completed. For he will be delivered up to the Gentiles, will be mocked, treated shamefully, and spit on. They will scourge and kill him. On the third day, he will rise again."

The crowd could not prematurely kill Christ.

Luke 4:28–30 (AMP) says, "As they heard these things [about God's grace to these two Gentiles], the people in the synagogue were filled with a great rage; and they got up and drove Him out of the city, and led Him to the crest of the hill on which their city had been built, in order to hurl Him down the cliff. But passing [miraculously] through the crowd, He went on His way."

Christians living here are entirely dead to self, making God fully active in them. They are in the "resting phase," basking in God's glory, ruling and reigning. Their body, soul, and spirit are completely rescued from the enemy. This is the "Spirit Change Phase." The Spirit is finally rescued because God takes it over and lives through the body of the believer, manifesting through the soul, and filling our spirits with Himself. The enemy cannot snatch us from God's hand once we get here. It is too late for him.

John 10:26–30 says, "But you don't believe, because you are not of my sheep, as I told you. My sheep hear my voice, and I know them, and they follow me. I give eternal life to them. They will never perish, and no one will snatch them out of my hand. My Father, who has given them to me, is greater than all. No one is able to snatch them out of my Father's hand. I and the Father are one."

The light or truth in this place is the glory of God. Who God is; His faithfulness and Holiness is our truth. The glory of God is not dependent upon anyone because God's glory is eternal. This glory light never goes out; it is not limited to any surface area. It lights up infinitely and extensively with no limits. This is the perfection of spiritual sight, the perfect light.

The Holy of Holies is the earthly equivalent of the bedroom. Only one whom the Holy Spirit approves of and prepares as the bride of Christ enters here. The Father Himself is their protection because in Him is the fullness of all that Christ paid for. No one can penetrate or peek through this protection where Christ is also hidden, and we are hidden with Christ in God because we died and no longer live but Christ who lives in us. (Colossians 3:3) "For you died, and your life is hidden with Christ in God."

This is where all believers should dwell. The Promised Land, where we live a Kingdom lifestyle, completely sold out to the King, entering into His rest. In this phase, God is the homeowner of our bodies which is His temple. God completely owns us. He, therefore, fully invests His Kingdom in us as He pours Himself in us, revealing His deep secrets, what His plans and thoughts are in the now. As a homeowner, He can fully invest in us.

Divine provision is found here as well. Overflowing, unlimited, extravagant, and gigantic provision of resources for God's Kingdom and growth flows in this realm. It is the supernatural, miraculous realm, where Aaron's dead rod budded and was placed in the Holy of Holies. (Hebrews 9:3–4) This is where the dead are raised to life. Nothing dies in this realm. Death has no chance here—life rules.

Christians here rely on God revealing His deepest secrets to them, resulting in oneness. People here live by the **now** Word of God revealed to them by the Holy Spirit. Man shall not live by bread alone, (which is the written Word alone), but by every Word that proceeds from the mouth of God (the fresh new Manna, bread from God). The Holy of Holies is the Rhema (spoken) Word realm.

During temptation, Christ used the Word of God as His weapon effectively. He went deeper and proved to Satan and us the limitation which Satan possesses. Satan can tap into the written Word, as much as he lacks the revelation of it, but he has zero access to the Rhema Word of God. Satan has no idea what God is thinking or planning. He has no understanding of God's language, (heavenly supernatural tongues) and God's communication with His children.

Satan cannot stop us in this realm because He cannot see us or perceive our move. This is the God realm. No inferior beings can access this realm. This is a realm where giants fall and children of God possess their large properties and wealth. This is the realm where God mocks the giants by making them fall into the hands of His children. It is a very humiliating and deadly position for the kingdom of darkness, and that is why the devil works overtime for believers not to get into this dimension. This is a no-come-back zone for the enemy. They are wiped out completely.

The sprinkled blood is found in this dimension. Here, the blood now speaks on my behalf. I do not do anything here with the blood because it is in me; it runs in my veins. I am one with Christ, and the blood is now speaking the inheritance and legal rights I have because I now belong to Christ. Whatever He has is mine; whatever He paid for, I receive it. I am in Him, and He in me, and we are in the Father. The blood's vocabulary is greater than any human words or angelic tongues can describe. The blood speaks volumes and the deep wealth and wisdom of God. Hebrews 12:24 says, "to Jesus, the mediator of a new covenant, and to the blood of sprinkling that speaks better than that of Abel."

This is the part where you are now clean and dry and oiled with fresh fragrance on you, clean and presentable with new and fresh clothes. You are a whole new person, and anyone who gets close to you compliments your great aroma, your neat, clean, and beautiful white robe of righteousness. All others see is God's perfection in you. God gives you a new garment. The old garment that has been washed cannot make it here.

The body, Spirit, and soul of Christ and His robe of righteousness are acquired in this realm. Just like the prodigal son when he came home, his robe was taken off, he was cleansed, and a new robe was given to him symbolizing restoration back to right standing, authority, and kingship. Here, we are now promoted to be kings with Christ, seated on the throne with Him, with no evidence or trace of ever belonging to the world. Nothing to tell Christ and us apart. We are one.

This is a very small area because only one person can get in here at a time. It is a very rare place to be. Only a handful dwell here, not a crowd. Only the Holy Spirit and Christ can lead you into this place where you meet the Father and enter into His rest. In the case of the Israelites, only Caleb and Joshua out of the millions who began the journey of salvation and went through the same wilderness journey were able to fully yield and submit themselves to God and enter into the rest God had promised them. The Promised Land.

Only dead-to-self people enter here. You cannot live, have your own opinion, thoughts, and/or suggestions here. This is a God-rule zone. No suggestions, questions, excuses, or opinions are permitted here. If you have any, you are still alive, and you cannot enter this realm. This is where you rest from thinking and figuring things out and working out your own way, and let God do the work. In this place, the bridegroom pours Himself into His bride, releasing His seed in her.

This is the realm of extravagant givers. They are mature and selfless. They are not limited by people's opinion over them. They care only about what God thinks of them and do not regard anyone over God, not even their own family. They are purely God pleasers. When we get here, we give Christ everything because we have a clear understanding that everything we have was given to us by God. Therefore, God owns it all. We do not only tithe and give limited offerings; we give God 100 percent and allow him to allocate it as He desires.

We do not give because someone asked us to give. We inquire of God and give as instructed by the owner, Christ. He is specific about the amount and the place to give. We do not argue or reason with Him, even if He instructs us to give all that we have in our possession, just like He did the rich young ruler. We understand that we are good stewards of God's Kingdom, and because of this, God entrusts us with His Kingdom.

People at this level have a "Yours" mentality. They believe that, "All I have is Yours, God! I am a profitable servant, a good steward of God's estate and resources. What an honor it is to serve Christ in this capacity!" Christ is revealed as the way, the truth, and the life in this place. We get to know Christ as the only life. Our life is not our own. It belongs to God. Our bodies are His. He lives through us in His fullness. He decides what to do and when to do it, what to say and when to say it, where to go, and we just yield to Him because we are totally dead to self and possessed by God.

Believers here have lost their minds for the mind of Christ. They have no human interpretation of anything. They are back in Eden where all they knew was holiness and righteous fellowship with God the Father. They do not have the wisdom of this world anymore. They possess the full wisdom of God because God lives in them. We see this manifested in Christ and Paul. These believers tap into the deep secrets of God. While Christ was on earth, He took three of His disciples, Peter, James, and John, into this glory realm as we see in Matthew 17:5, Mark 9:7, Luke 9:35, and Matthew 3:17.

2 Peter 1:16–18 (NLT) says, "For we were not making up clever stories when we told you about the powerful coming of our Lord Jesus Christ. We saw his majestic splendor with our own eyes when he received honor and glory from God the Father. The voice from the majestic glory of God said to him, "This is my dearly loved Son, who brings me great joy." We ourselves heard that voice from heaven when we were with him on the holy mountain."

The Holy Spirit gives us the ability to rule and reign with Christ, making the right judgment as we sit on the throne with Christ, seeing things through his eyes.

Isaiah 11:3–5 says, "His delight will be in the fear of Yahweh. He will not judge by the sight of his eyes, neither decide by the hearing of his ears; but with righteousness he will judge the poor, and decide with equity for the humble of the earth. He will strike the earth with the rod of his mouth; and with the breath of his lips he will kill the wicked. Righteousness will be the belt of his waist, and faithfulness the belt of his waist."

These are highest level Christians, roof-top Christians with the highest view and no roof or closing over them. They are limitless! No limitations exist in this realm or dimension. It is an open heaven dimension. It costs everything to live here. Christ, His disciples, and Paul lived here. They predicted their death, knew their mission, and successfully lived it. They were completely sold out to the Kingdom and its cause. No persecution or trial made them fall back.

They mastered their attitude and allowed the Holy Spirit to guide and lead them into the Father's rest fully. Nothing mattered more to them than Kingdom growth and victory, pleasing the King even unto death. This is where we need to be, completely sold out, that the devil and his demons know us by name and tremble because of the authority we operate in. When they see us, they see the Father. (See Acts 19:11–17.)

War in this dimension is fought differently. The sprinkled blood acquits me and judges my enemies. For the Israelites, it was the Commander of the Lord's army. Supernatural victory was due to the Commander of the Lord's army leading them into strategic war. This dimension introduces heaven's army for war. We now have spiritual eyesight on spiritual war where we have the upper hand because we see what the enemy is doing from the third heaven, and attack him as he is still unaware of what we are planning to do.

Joshua 5:13–15 says, "Now when Joshua was near Jericho, he looked up and saw a man standing in front of him with a drawn sword in his hand. Joshua went up to him and asked, "Are you for us or for our enemies?" "Neither," he replied, "but as commander of the army of the Lord I have now come." Then

Joshua fell facedown to the ground in reverence, and asked him, "What message does my Lord have for his servant?" The commander of the Lord's army replied, "Take off your sandals, for the place where you are standing is holy." And Joshua did so."

After this, Joshua received instructions on how to fight the battle using supernatural techniques and strategies, number seven which is the number of rest (on the seventh day God rested; Genesis 2:2–3). "On the seventh day God finished his work which he had done; and he rested on the seventh day from all his work which he had done. God blessed the seventh day, and made it holy, because he rested in it from all his work of creation which he had done."

He repeats it three times, which is a seal of completion and perfection (seven priests, seventh day, seven times), to seal their entering into rest. This is the same process we see God commanding Aaron to follow when purifying the Holy of Holies, the Tabernacle, and altar . . . Sprinkling blood seven times in these three areas. He repeated the seven times of sprinkling of the blood three times. (See Leviticus 16:14–20.)

Have you entered into rest? Do you have this seal of completion upon your life? The Holy Spirit is the third witness of Christ and is the seal of perfection. When we are fully yielded to Him that He totally owns our bodies, He leads us to Christ, our bridegroom, and to our Father God. This is the rest in which we can never get to without my friend the Holy Spirit of God.

The Three Dimensions in God
Summary table

OUTER COURTS CHRISTIANS	INNER COURTS CHRISTIANS	HOLY OF HOLIES CHRISTIANS
Relationship	**Relationship**	**Relationship**
This is the introduction phase. Here people meet and greet Christ. They are acquainted with Him, but do not want to commit to a relationship as yet. People living here settle for 'knowing about Him' instead of having a desire to know Christ personally.	This is the dating and courtship phase. People launch a bit deeper here, as they desire more of Christ and accept His invitation to commit to Him. People living here enter into a relationship with Him from knowing about Him to knowing Him.	This is the engagement and marriage Phase. People here dive all in and are completely hidden in Christ in God, hidden in His embrace and all He is. People living here are his brides, engaged, and one with Him. They are in to know God in His fullness.
Growth	**Growth**	**Growth**
This is the lowest single level in God. Scarcely any growth.	This place has multiple levels or stages of growth in God. Still limited in growth.	This is the highest level in God while on earth in a human body. The growth here has no limits.

OUTER COURTS CHRISTIANS	INNER COURTS CHRISTIANS	HOLY OF HOLIES CHRISTIANS
Purpose People who *dwell* here do not get to discover their God-given task. People who dwell here are alive to self, making God inactive in them.	**Purpose** People who *dwell* here get to discover and begin fulfilling their God given task but do not complete it successfully. People who *dwell* here are semi-comatose to self, making God semi-active in them	**Purpose** People who *dwell* here get to successfully fulfill their God-given task. People who dwell here are entirely dead to self, making God fully active in them.
Phase This is the rescue phase where the body (temple) is rescued from enemy, moving people from the kingdom of darkness to the Kingdom of light. This is the name change Phase	**Phase** This is the deliverance phase from enemy's stronghold and mind set. This is both the body and soul rescue from the enemy, the making stage. This is the character change Phase	**Phase** This is the resting phase where the body, soul, and spirit are all rescued from the enemy. Resting and basking in God's glory, ruling and reigning. This is the spirit change Phase

OUTER COURTS CHRISTIANS	INNER COURTS CHRISTIANS	HOLY OF HOLIES CHRISTIANS
Light	**Light**	**Light**
Here, the light or truth in this place is the natural Sunlight, facts, seen or historic evidence. These people live by sight, not by faith.	Here, the light or truth in this place is the lamp, (word of God), which lights up by the oil, (Holy Spirit), producing fire which consumes evil in us and breaks down God's word, (cooking the food) making it easier for our spirits to digest. These people live by faith not by sight. Here we see God the Father in the fire, God the Son as the lamp (word), and God the Holy Spirit as the Oil.	Here, the light or truth in this place is the Glory of God. Who God is; His faithfulness and Holiness are our truth. This is the perfection of sight, the fullness of the perfect light and truth in Christ in God. Here dwells God the Father, Son and the Holy Spirit. The Holy Trinity lights this place and operates in people here as in John 14:23.

OUTER COURTS CHRISTIANS	INNER COURTS CHRISTIANS	HOLY OF HOLIES CHRISTIANS
Earthly equivalence…	Earthly equivalence…	Earthly equivalence…
Of the compound. Anyone who acknowledges Christ can come here. Whosoever believes in Christ and His sacrifice, (John 3:16 begins here). There is the gatekeeper i.e. angelic, and Blood protection found here.	Of the living room. Those who follow the helper, the Holy Spirit of God, enter here. The Blood of Christ, Word, and fire of God and angelic protection are found here.	Of the bedroom. Only one whom the Holy Spirit approves of and the Bride groom, Christ, invites enters here. The Father Himself is their covering and protection.
Enrollment phase	**Learning phase**	**Lifestyle phase**
Danger!! <u>Do not dwell</u> here	Warning!! <u>Do not dwell</u> here	Attention!! Please <u>dwell</u> here
Accepting Christ as Lord and Savior. Start the Journey, Crossing the Red Sea.	Learning God's ways and Kingdom living. Wilderness and training ground. Learning obedience from what we suffer.	Living a Kingdom lifestyle, sold out to the King. Bride of Christ entering the Promised Land, Eden, entering into God's rest.

OUTER COURTS CHRISTIANS	INNER COURTS CHRISTIANS	HOLY OF HOLIES CHRISTIANS
Ownership In this phase, God is just a renter of our bodies, His temple. We tell God what He can and cannot do with us. We limit God and His will for us. God does not invest in us here because we are high risk investment.	**Ownership** In this phase, God is just leasing with an intention to own our bodies, His temple. We allow God to use us conditionally (knowingly or unknowingly) in hope of owning us. God partially invests in us. We are a mixture of lower high risk and low risk investment depending on our level.	**Ownership** In this phase God is the Homeowner of our bodies, His temple. God completely owns us. He therefore fully invests His Kingdom in us. We are very profitable Kingdom investment.
Realm This is a realm of taking back what the enemy stole from us. Our freedom. The enemy is arrested and has to give up their wealth to us for God's Kingdom. Like Israelites got gold from the Egyptians.	**Realm** This is a realm of supernatural provision. Faith's provision. Daily manna, water from the rock, trusting in God for His daily provision.	**Realm** This is a realm of divine provision. Dispossessing our enemies totally. Overflowing unlimited, extravagant, and gigantic provision of resources for God's Kingdom and growth.

OUTER COURTS CHRISTIANS	INNER COURTS CHRISTIANS	HOLY OF HOLIES CHRISTIANS
Entry	Revelation	Miraculous
This is the entry way into the supernatural, but living here produces an ordinary life realm. No signs and wonders, from God through us. Signs and wonders from God to rescue us but we live just ordinary life. People believe in what they see (death) more than what God sees (life) in this realm. Death can rule if we remain here.	This is the revelation realm. The Lamp and bread of the Word of God is used to provide and illuminate a believer's life causing extra-ordinary manifestation of favor and blessings. God works through His Word in and through us so we do signs and wonders. Death can creep here if not attacked by the Sword of the Spirit.	This is the miraculous realm, where Aaron's dead rod budded and was placed in the Holy of Holies (Hebrews 9:3-4). This is where the dead are raised to life. Nothing dies in this realm. God operates in the fullness of who He is with unusual miracles, signs and wonders, and provision. Death has no chance here. Life rules.

OUTER COURTS CHRISTIANS	INNER COURTS CHRISTIANS	HOLY OF HOLIES CHRISTIANS
Prayer People in this place don't know how to pray. They pray a miss. They ask God to do things He has already done. They ask selfishly. E.g. They ask God to protect them even when they are living in sin. They do not know the scripture that says; "Yahweh's angel encamps around those who fear him, and delivers them."	**Prayer** The people in the Inner place are learning to pray here. They read the scripture that promises safety and they will claim it by living in the fear of God to activate their protection. These people are at different levels of prayer. This is a multi-level realm.	**Prayer** Those in the holy of Holies do not have to worry because a dead man is not afraid or worried about their safety. Nothing can kill them or harm them as they are no longer alive. God deals with their safety personally.
Religion Here we rely on People's interpretation of scripture resulting in many **religions.**	**Relationship** Here we rely on the Holy Spirit's revelation of God's written Word resulting in **relationship.** People living by bread provided by God, Manna. This is the **logos, (written) Word** realm.	**Oneness** Here we rely on God revealing His deepest secrets resulting in **oneness.** People living by the **now Word** of God revealed to us by the Holy Spirit. This is the **rhema, (spoken) Word** realm.

OUTER COURTS CHRISTIANS	INNER COURTS CHRISTIANS	HOLY OF HOLIES CHRISTIANS
The Shed Blood of Christ	**The Applied Blood of Christ**	**The Sprinkled Blood of Christ**
Here, the shed blood has cleansing power. It is waiting for my acceptance, I do not make the sacrifice nor do I work at all here. All I need to do is to accept that the Blood was shed for me, and sign up for cleansing. This Blood gives me hope that I can be saved and protected if I accept this sacrifice.	Here I get to deep my hand and apply the Blood in my life for deeper cleansing and authority. This action is what saves me from death. When I apply the Blood of Jesus and apply the Word of God in the different areas in my life, deliverance power is activated.	Here the Blood now speaks on my behalf. I do not do anything here with the Blood because it is in me, it runs in my veins, I am one with Christ and the Blood is now speaking oneness.
Very Large Area This is a **large area** because many people make it here and remain here.	**Medium Sized Area** This is a **medium sized area because** a few people make it here and remain.	**Very Small Area** This is a **very small area** because only one person can get in here at a time. A very rare place to be where only a handful dwell.

OUTER COURTS CHRISTIANS	INNER COURTS CHRISTIANS	HOLY OF HOLIES CHRISTIANS
Giving Stingy and Emotional Givers These Christians are like in the toddler stage. They are concerned with what they desire and want. **These are self and people pleasers and** have a **"mine!" mentality.** 0% belongs to God.	**Giving** Meet the Requirement Givers. These Christians are like in the late teenage and young adult stage. They are people pleasers; still learning to be God pleasers, therefore they are still partly limited by people's opinion of them. **These are people and Semi-God pleasers** who have an **"ours" mentality.** 1% - 99% belongs to God.	**Giving** Extravagant Givers These Christians are like in the over forty, mature adults who are selfless and are not limited by people's opinion over them. They care only about what God thinks of them. They do not regard anyone over God, not even their own family. **These are purely God pleasers.** People in this level have a **"Yours" mentality.** 100% belongs to God.

OUTER COURTS CHRISTIANS	INNER COURTS CHRISTIANS	HOLY OF HOLIES CHRISTIANS
Christ is revealed as the Way We know Christ as the **only Way** to the Father. The journey begins here.	**Christ is revealed as the Way and Truth** We know Christ as the **only way and truth**. The word of God is our source of truth here. The journey continues.	**Christ is revealed as the Way, the Truth and the Life** We know Christ as the **only way, truth and life**. Our life is not our own, it belongs to God. The journey climaxes.
The Holy Spirit… Leads us to repentance so we turn to God.	**The Holy Spirit…** Leads us into righteousness. By giving us revelation and insight on living according to the word of God, in righteousness.	**The Holy Spirit…** Gives us the ability to rule and reign with Christ, making right judgment as we sit on the throne with Christ seeing things through his eyes.

OUTER COURTS CHRISTIANS	INNER COURTS CHRISTIANS	HOLY OF HOLIES CHRISTIANS
First Floor Christians These Christians are Christians with no view. It doesn't cost much to live here. There is a low ceiling height on this floor representing extreme limitation.	**Mid Floor Christians** These Christians have a better view than first floor Christians but are still limited in their view. It costs a lot more to be here. There is still room for growth therefore they still have a roof over their head.	**Highest Level Christians** These Christians are roof-top Christians with the highest view and no roof or closing over them. They are limitless! No limitations exist in this realm or dimension; it is an open heaven dimension. It costs everything to live here.
WAR **(God fights: Stand Still and See the Salvation of God)** In this dimension, God fights the initial war to rescue us from the enemy's hold by sacrificing His only Son. _**The shed Blood is my salvation.**_ It saves me and destroys my enemies.	**WAR** **(You fight with God's help using God's Word)** The war in this dimension is fought through faith in the written Word of God. The Sword of the Spirit. _**The applied Blood is my defense.**_ It defends me and attacks my enemies.	**WAR** **(Supernatural victory: The Commander of the Lord's Army leads into strategic war)** War in this dimension is fought differently. _**The sprinkled Blood acquits me.**_ It acquits me and judges my enemies. I bask in God's victory.

CHAPTER 3

KNOWING GOD THROUGH MY FRIEND THE HOLY SPIRIT

TOGETHER AS ONE body, Christ reconciled both groups to God by means of his death on the cross, and our hostility toward each other was put to death. He brought this Good News of peace to you Gentiles who were far away from him, and peace to the Jews who were near. Now all of us can come to the Father THROUGH THE SAME HOLY SPIRIT because of what Christ has done for us. Ephesians 2:16-18 (NLT; Emphasis added)

This scripture clearly states that the only way we can know God is by accepting Christ as our Lord and Savior, and then asking for and receiving the Holy Spirit who will lead us to the Father through Christ. Without Christ we cannot come to the Father. Without Christ, we cannot receive the Holy Spirit, and without the Holy Spirit we cannot know Christ intimately. Without knowing Christ we cannot go to the Father for it is Christ who leads us to the Father. We therefore MUST have my friend, the Holy Spirit to lead us to Christ who leads us to the Father.

Knowing Christ and the Father is only possible through God the Holy Spirit. Who do people say Jesus is? What about you? Whom do you say Christ is? Some say He was just a prophet and that God has no Son. Others say He was just a good man historically because His existence and works were proven. But whom do you say He is? Do you KNOW HIM? Or do you only KNOW ABOUT HIM? The demons also know about Him and tremble.

> When Jesus came to the region of Caesarea Philippi, he asked his disciples, "Who do people say the Son of Man is?" They replied, "Some say John the Baptist; others say Elijah; and still others, Jeremiah or one of the prophets." "But what about you?" he asked. "Who do you say I am?" Simon Peter answered, "You are the messiah, the Son of the living God." Jesus replied, "Blessed are you, Simon son of Jonah, for THIS WAS NOT REVEALED TO YOU BY FLESH AND BLOOD, BUT BY MY FATHER IN HEAVEN. And I tell you that you are Peter, and on this rock I will build my church, and the gates of Hades will not overcome it. I will give you the keys of the kingdom of heaven; whatever you bind on earth will be bound in heaven, and whatever you loose

on earth will be loosed in heaven." Then he ordered his disciples not to tell anyone that he was the Messiah. (Matthew 16:13-20; emphasis added)

There are three lessons from these scriptures:

1. Man cannot know Christ on His own.

For three years or so, the disciples walked with Jesus, learned from Him, saw the miracles He performed, and many other things, but they still did not know Him. Is it possible to spend all day every day and live with someone for three years and yet not know them? How many times have you heard of what someone did that you thought you knew well, and you realize that you really did not know them as well as you thought? You only knew about them. This is because the real person is their spirit. Only God can reveal the real person to you. That is why we must pray for God to show us the hearts of those we are in a relationship with because they can be physically legal, in that they look and sound trustworthy, but in reality, they are spiritually illegal. i.e., they could be living in disobedience and rebellion against God, and leading us astray or toward danger regardless of what title they hold, just like Jonah, the prophet of God, did and he endangered all who were on the ship with him.

As we see in the scripture we just read, people said that Jesus was who He was not. Some said He was John the Baptist; others called Him Elijah; and still others, Jeremiah or one of the prophets. Why do you suppose they did this? They did this because human beings have a limited view of the future, and they can only compare you with their past or their experiences.

God, however, calls us from our future and what He created us to be. That is why it is very crucial for every person to find out who God calls them. Look at the example today, where people name their children after animals, weather, past experiences, present feeling or situation, or after other people. No human being is qualified to name you other than your creator. God knows who He created you to be, and He longs to see you live in this fullness. God the Holy Spirit knows who you really are as He was there creating you. He saw what was put in you during creation, which is why He is the ONLY qualified Kingdom mentor.

2. Only God the Father, through the Holy Spirit, can reveal His Son Jesus to us in a personal way.

As we read in the scripture, Jesus never bothered to address or comment on how wrong the people were in saying who He was. Why do you think that is? He was the creator in Genesis, so He knows the limitations of man. He doesn't worry about people's perception of Him. He then went on to ask the next question, which was more personal. When you ask someone what people think about you, they most likely will be quick to respond because they are not responsible for other people's thoughts or perceptions of you. But when you ask them what *they* think of you, it gets very personal. In this case, you are trying to know what is inside their heart. This is protected information. Many people are not quick to answer this question because they want to be politically correct; i.e., say the right thing in the right way.

We see this evident in the disciples of Jesus. When Jesus asked the first question, everyone was happy to respond to it.

They all replied to it telling of the rumors they had heard. Does this sound familiar? However, when Christ asked the second question, only one person, Simon Peter, responded. Jesus then blessed Simon son of Jonah, the one who answered fearlessly and made him aware that he had tapped into the supernatural and touched the heart of the Father; and God the Father by His Spirit revealed His Son Jesus Christ to Simon.

From the scripture we read in Matthew 16, Jesus told Peter: "for this was not revealed to you by flesh and blood, but by my Father in heaven." What does this mean? Why was Jesus quick to respond in this way and give God the Father credit instead of Peter for knowing who He was? It is crucial to hear what Christ is saying here. He was saying that no man on earth can ever reveal Him to us, only the Father can do that through His Spirit. The disciples walked, talked, and dined with Christ and still did not know Him. He couldn't reveal Himself to them either. He said clearly that His testimony of Himself was valid to Him because He knew who He was: Jesus answered them, "Even if I testify about myself, my testimony is true, for I know where I came from, and where I am going; but you don't know where I came from, or where I am going." (John 8:14)

As much as Jesus' testimony of Himself was right, it was not valid if He testified about Himself. This was according to the Law God gave to Moses in Deuteronomy 19:15, "One witness shall not rise up against a man for any iniquity, or for any sin, in any sin that he sins. At the mouth of two witnesses, or at the mouth of three witnesses, shall a matter be established."

"If I testify about myself, my witness is not valid. It is another who testifies about me. I know that the testimony which he testifies about me is true." (John 5:31–32)

"It's also written in your law that the testimony of two

people is valid. I am one who testifies about myself, and the Father who sent me testifies about me." (John 8:17–18)

Knowing someone is "heart knowledge"; intimacy (the selfless giving of all of yourself without holding back to another). Knowing about someone is "head knowledge"; intellect (educated knowledge). Christ is not after intellectual knowledge; He is after intimacy. You can be brilliant and educated, yet you can't keep a marriage. Marriage is sustained by intimacy. How many highly educated people do you know that are divorced? How many uneducated people are happily married? Intimacy comes from knowing someone, not knowing *about* someone. There is a significant difference.

3. Knowing Christ causes a name change and a revelation of your assignment on earth.

The reason for your creation is revealed through your intimacy with God. Why did Jesus not change all the other disciples' names as He did Peter? Because He had only been revealed to Peter by His Father. Knowing Christ is a personal encounter, not a crowd encounter. It is a personal relationship. God the Father could have revealed Christ to all of them, and they would have chorused the answer, but He didn't. He could have chosen anyone else, but He didn't. Why? Is God biased? Is He a respecter of persons? Absolutely not! God feeds the hungry. He will not force you to eat or shove His revelation into your Spirit. He is not a desperate God. We must hunger and thirst desperately after Him.

Peter was the one disciple who was always hungry. He was the first one to ask questions, the first one to answer or act even when he was wrong. He was like one would be called in

Swahili, *kimbelembele*. This is a term used to describe someone who is overly eager to learn and is not afraid to be wrong and volunteers for everything even if it means making a fool of themselves. Peter confessed his lack of faith openly; he asked Jesus to call him deeper in Him to walk on water like Him, and he was the one who vowed not to deny Jesus.

Peter was the one who cut off the soldier's ear in attempt to protect Jesus from being arrested. Peter was the "dramatic one." He did not do this in an attempt to bring attention to himself; rather, it was as a result of his hunger and thirst after Christ. Some people are just loud as a show-off, but not Peter. He was seriously curious and hungry to know Christ. He was so hungry in this new life of being with Christ that His spirit was open to understanding. God's revelation is pulled from heaven to earth by one thing: HUNGER! When I became hungry for God and started seeking Him hungrily with all my heart, He revealed Christ to me. I even asked Him to send me Christ that I may see Him, and He did. Jesus said in Matthew 5:6, "Blessed are those who hunger and thirst after righteousness, for they shall be filled."

Have you ever tried feeding children who are not hungry? It is very frustrating because as much as you have cooked and however tasty the food is, the children will waste it. How about when you feed hungry children? Oh, how rewarding it is to see them all scramble and eat hungrily, filling their plates and going for seconds and thirds. I loved feeding my second son because he ate more and enjoyed any food I made. He enjoys eating. He was always open for food, ate his brother's leftovers and *still* had room for more! He made cooking fun for me.

In the same way, God enjoys feeding His hungry children. He has so much tasty spiritual food and revelation that can supply all His hungry children. I, therefore, pray always to stay hungry and thirsty so God may continually feed me without limitations. The way I do this is by sharing with those in need as He gives me the food, then I go for more, and He continually feeds me to keep the overflow channel open. Just like a river that allows water to flow through it and feeds it into many other streams, I allow God the Father through Christ, by the Holy Spirit, to feed me and feed many more through me. Are you hungry? Or do you stay so full that you cannot receive from God?

Simon's name was changed to Peter, meaning "rock." He was named after his assignment, to be a "rock." He had not yet manifested as a rock when Christ named him, but Christ revealed to Him that he was created to be a rock in God's Kingdom. He was told that as a rock, Christ would build His church using Peter, and no power of hell would ever be able to prevail against him. Also, he was entrusted with the keys of the Kingdom of heaven, that whatever he disallows on earth will be disallowed in heaven too, and whatever he allows on earth, heaven will allow. This was a living will Jesus was writing for him at that time. Just like a father would take his son and promise him land and wealth when he leaves earth.

God has granted us the intelligence we need to live this life in the fullness of who He is. Jesus told His disciples that it was for their benefit that He leaves them so that He can send them a Helper, my friend the Holy Spirit, who would live IN them and would always be WITH them, helping them, teaching, and counseling them. No matter where they were, God the Holy Spirit would be present with them. They did not need to be in the same location as they had to be when Jesus was with them to be with God. This is because the Holy Spirit is not limited to time, space, place, or distance, which was the limiting factor for Jesus when He lived on earth in the flesh. God the Holy Spirit is everywhere at the same time. He is the witness of Christ and the one who manifests the Word. My friend does not speak of His own accord; instead, He speaks what He hears from God the Father. God the Father's will is God the Son's will and God the Holy Spirit's will.

> I still have many things to say to you, but you cannot bear them now. However, when He, the Spirit of truth, has come, He will guide you into all truth; for He will not speak on His own authority, but whatever He hears He will speak; and He will tell you things to come. He will glorify Me, for He will take of what is Mine and declare it to you. All things that the Father has are Mine. Therefore I said that He will take of Mine and declare it to you. (John 16:12–15, NKJV)

After we receive God the Holy Spirit in us, He then leads us to fully knowing Christ Jesus, the Word, and when we obey and keep the Word, the Father loves us and can now come and live in us with the Word, who is Christ. Jesus answered him, "If a man loves me, he will keep my word. My Father will love him, and WE WILL COME TO HIM AND MAKE OUR HOME WITH HIM." (John 14:23, caps added)

This means that without the Word—Christ—we can never get to the Father, and without the Holy Spirit, we can never get to know the Word, who is Christ. How do we hear and allow Christ into our hearts? Only through God the Holy Spirit's conviction. I know Christ longs to come into our hearts to live because He says this in the book of Revelation to His church.

This is because many of us in the church have become lukewarm and have fallen away chasing the cares of this life instead of seeking the Kingdom and Christ's righteousness.

> Write this letter to the angel of THE CHURCH in Laodicea. This is the message from the one who is the Amen—the faithful and true witness, the beginning of God's new creation: "I know all the things you do, that you are neither hot nor cold. I wish that you were one or the other! But since you are like lukewarm water, neither hot nor cold, I will spit you out of my mouth! You say, 'I am rich. I have everything I want. I don't need a thing!' And you don't realize that you are wretched and miserable and poor and blind and naked. So I advise you to buy gold from me—gold that has been purified by fire. Then you will be rich. Also buy white garments from me so you will not be shamed by your nakedness, and ointment for your eyes so you will be able to see. I correct and discipline everyone I love. So be diligent and turn from your indifference. "Look! I stand at the door and knock. If you hear my voice and open the door, I will come in, and we will share a meal together as friends. Those who are victorious will sit with me on my throne, just as I was victorious and sat with my Father on his throne. "Anyone with ears to hear MUST LISTEN TO THE SPIRIT AND UNDERSTAND WHAT HE IS SAYING TO THE CHURCHES." (Revelation 3:14–22, NLT; emphasis added)

Jesus makes it clear that we cannot live holy if we do not yield to the leadership of God the Holy Spirit. . The church must listen and understand the instructions and teachings of God the Holy Spirit. He urged the churches to listen and obey the Holy Spirit. Christ says He has been LOCKED OUT OF THE CHURCH. He "supposedly" owns the church, but the church has rejected Him. He is now standing outside, knocking at the door so that the church may let Him back in. He is NOT knocking on the door of the world, because He was never invited by the world to begin with. The church invited him, but the church is lazy in working out their salvation with fear and trembling and has become lukewarm.

Christ cannot stay in a lukewarm environment because He is very hot and passionate about His church. We put Him out of our lives by being lukewarm. It is better to say no to Him than to say yes and not be sold out to Him. How would you feel if you loved someone very deeply, but the person you love doesn't love you back the same? They just like you but not love you. This is what we do to Christ. He loved us even unto death, the most humiliating death on the cross. He was tortured and beaten so badly that they dehumanized Him. We must love Him back even unto death—death of our selfish ambitions and ideas—and give our lives to Him, so He may live through us.

"Just as there were many who were appalled at him his appearance was so disfigured beyond that of any human being and his form marred beyond human likeness." (Isaiah 52:14, NIV)

As the church, we MUST listen to what the Holy Spirit is saying, so that we may know and correct our wrong and be victorious like Christ. In doing so, we shall sit on His throne with Him just like He listened to the Holy Spirit, was victorious, and now sits on the throne with His Father. Jesus said to him, "I am the way, the truth, and the life. No one comes to the

Father, except through me. If you had known me, you would have known my Father also . . ." (John 14:6–7a)

"Don't you believe that I am in the Father, and the Father in me? The words that I tell you, I speak not from myself; but the Father who lives in me does his works." (John 14:10)

The Word, Christ, was conceived by the Holy Spirit, and the Holy Spirit inspired those who wrote the Word of God because the Holy Spirit knows the Word, Christ, like no one else! Without the Holy Spirit, we are orphaned! We have no Father. These are not my words but the words of Christ Himself.

"I will not leave you orphans. I will come to you." (John 14:18)

How was Christ going to come to us? Through God the Holy Spirit. Christ went and prayed to the Father to release God the Holy Spirit to us so we can know Christ, and He can live in us, and the Father can come in us too. Thus, we will have a Father and not be orphaned. God the Holy Spirit is, therefore, the channel or prerequisite to knowing Christ personally and intimately and of having a Father who lives in us.

The Holy Spirit is a channel of communication between God and man. He is the voice of God to us. Without my friend, we cannot hear God or know His will. We can never please God or see God without holiness from His Holy Spirit. My friend is the power of God in His Word. He makes God's Word come alive in us. Without Him, people read the Bible without understanding, revelation, or experiencing change. With Him revealing God's Word to us, the Word of God becomes sharper than a double-edged sword and cleanses us from the inside out.

CHAPTER 4

THE FRUIT AND GIFTS OF MY FRIEND THE HOLY SPIRIT

The Fruit of the Holy Spirit . . .

But I say, walk by the Spirit, and you won't fulfill the lust of the flesh. For the flesh lusts against the Spirit, and the Spirit against the flesh; and these are contrary to one another, that you may not do the things that you desire. But if you are led by the Spirit, you are not under the law. Now the deeds of the flesh are obvious, which are: adultery, sexual immorality, uncleanness, lustfulness, idolatry, sorcery, hatred, strife, jealousies, outbursts of anger, rivalries, divisions, heresies, envy, murders, drunkenness, orgies, and things like these; of which I forewarn you, even as I also forewarned you, that those who practice such things will not inherit God's Kingdom. But the fruit of the Spirit is love, joy, peace, patience, kindness, goodness, faith, gentleness, and self-control. Against such things there is no law. Those who belong to Christ have crucified the flesh with its passions and lusts. If we live by the Spirit, let's also walk by the Spirit. Let's not become conceited, provoking one another, and envying one another. (Gal. 5:16–26)

The Holy Spirit has a fruit that has nine great God qualities. When we receive from Him, He grows these qualities in us. Just like a tree produces fruit, we produce fruit as we grow in Him. An orange tree produces oranges, not lemons or bananas. If the Holy Spirit lives in you, you will produce His fruit which the flesh or the sinful nature cannot produce on its own. This fruit contains . . . unconditional love, joy, peace, patience, kindness, goodness, faithfulness, humility (gentleness), and self-control. Is this what others see in us and feel through us? An orange tree consistently produces oranges—nothing else! A mango tree produces mangoes—not lemons.

Love must be in action and not just in words. John 3:16 is active love. "For God so loved the world that He gave His only begotten son . . ." He loved and then followed it with the act of giving that which cost Him all He had—his best. Challenge yourself, and instead of telling someone you love them, show them by action. God never said, "I love you, world!" and then stopped at that. He showed the world His love by sacrificing His only begotten Son. We too must follow His example. Love is a verb . . . a "doing" word.

The Holy Spirit has the fruit of joy and peace in the midst of the storm, not only when things are good. He gives us patience in the most trying times. Sometimes, we get so impatient and unkind to people that if we had an opportunity to minister Christ to them, we would fail miserably. This is because our actions toward them did not display us as Christlike. We lacked the fruit of patience, which is followed by kindness. It is hard to be kind to mean people, but once the fruit grows in you, it is gratifying. Your kindness despite their selfish attitude will lead them to repentance, but if you are harsh with them, you are no different than they are. We must have goodness and faithfulness in all we do and say, so that the goodness and faithfulness of Christ may be evident through us. We must possess humility and self-control regardless of the situations we face. These character traits represent what is in Christ. It is easy to win souls for Christ when we are like Him because people will desire what we have. Jesus gave us the best way to know what spirit is in a person. He said we shall know them by their fruits.

> Beware of false prophets, who come to you in sheep's clothing, but inwardly are ravening wolves. By their fruits, you will know them. Do you gather grapes from thorns, or figs from thistles? Even so, every good tree produces good fruit; but the corrupt tree produces evil fruit. A good tree can't produce evil fruit, neither can a corrupt tree produce good fruit. Every tree that doesn't grow good fruit is cut down, and thrown into the fire. Therefore, by their fruits you will know them. (Matt. 7:15–20)

This is so with those led by the Spirit of God. The oranges in an orange tree appear when the tree is mature enough to produce fruit. As we spend time with God the Holy Spirit, we grow and mature in Christ, and we produce good fruit. May we continually allow the Holy Spirit to lead us so we can be like Christ whom we were predestined to be like.

"For whom He foreknew, He also predestined to be conformed to the image of His Son, that He might be the firstborn among many brethren." (Rom. 8:29, NKJV)

"But we all, with unveiled face, beholding as in a mirror the glory of the Lord, are being transformed into the same image from glory to glory, just as by the Spirit of the Lord." (2 Cor. 3:18, NKJV)

"And do not be conformed to this world, but be transformed by the renewing of your mind, that you may prove what is that good and acceptable and perfect will of God." (Rom. 12:2, NKJV)

We renew our mind daily with the Word of God, replacing the ungodly thoughts with God's Word and obeying Him. We must be led by the Holy Spirit continually because, without Him, we cannot have the revelation of God's Word, which has the transforming power. Reading the Bible or hearing the Word of God without divine revelation is like reading or listening to just another novel or book. The Word of God is the power of God.

"By the word of the Lord were the heavens made; and all the host of them by the breath of his mouth." (Ps. 33:6, KJV)

How do we keep our fruit growing?

As we read earlier . . .

"Blessed is the man who doesn't walk in the counsel of the wicked, nor stand on the path of sinners, nor sit in the seat of scoffers; but his delight is in Yahweh's law. On his law he meditates day and night. He will be like a tree planted by the streams of water, that produces its fruit in its season, whose leaf also does not wither. Whatever he does shall prosper." (Ps. 1:1–3)

We keep growing by consciously choosing to live according to God's Word by His grace through His Spirit. The scripture above requires a conscious decision and choice not to do evil or associate with evil company. We must delight in God's Word, not just reading and going through the motions.

We must work out our salvation with fear and trembling as in Philippians 2:12. I like what David also said in Psalm 39:1 & 4. He said that he would watch closely what he does and speaks so that he may not fall into sin. David was wise enough to ask God to remind him that his days are numbered so he may live like a stranger and visitor on earth. Living wisely. This is my prayer daily. Sometimes when you decide to live right, temptations will come your way to make you fall. However, you must always ask God to help you not to give in to temptation. If we give in, we must immediately repent and forgive ourselves, being careful not to repeat the same mistake. We learn from our mistakes and in humility, help others not to make the same mistakes.

We bear lasting fruit by relying on God the Holy Spirit to lead us into all truths; by trusting in the Word of God, memorizing scripture (hiding God's Word in our hearts like King David did), obeying God's Word, and being doers of the Word and not just hearers because the fruit comes in doing, not hearing. Our actions are our fruit. Like David said, "How can a young man keep his way pure? By living according to your word. With my whole heart, I have sought you. Don't let me wander from your commandments. I have hidden your word in my heart that I might not sin against you." (Ps. 119:9–11).

The Gifts of the Holy Spirit...

The Holy Spirit of God has gifts that Jesus paid for, and He now distributes to the children of God as He sees fit. Gifts are given out for the Kingdom's growth, benefit, and profit. Unlike fruit, gifts are for the benefit of growing the Church of Jesus Christ, while fruit is for individual growth and maturity. This means that gifts of the Spirit do not qualify you for heaven, but the fruit of the Spirit, on the other hand, does. In short, fruit is for you to eat and grow into the image and likeness of God, while gifts are meant to build the church. It is possible for you to grow the church and not yourself and eventually be destroyed. Gifts display God's power over the kingdom of darkness.

The seventy returned with joy, saying, "Lord, even the demons are subject to us in your name!" He said to them, "I saw Satan having fallen like lightning from heaven. Behold, I give you authority to tread on serpents and scorpions, and over all the power of the enemy. Nothing will in any way hurt you. Nevertheless, don't rejoice in this, that the spirits are subject to you, but rejoice that your names are written in heaven." (Luke 10:17–20)

"Not everyone who says to me, 'Lord, Lord,' will enter into the Kingdom of Heaven; but he who does the will of my Father who is in heaven. Many will tell me in that day, 'Lord, Lord, didn't we prophesy in your name, in your name cast out demons, and in your name do many mighty works?' Then I will tell them, 'I never knew you. Depart from me, you who work iniquity.'" (Matthew 7:21–23)

Jesus meant that we can cast out demons in His name and heal the sick, even raise the dead, and still go to hell. Why?

Because His gifts are for the benefit of the Kingdom, not a guarantee of heaven. Just as one would work in a company and bring many profits to the company using company resources, if they mess up due to a lack of integrity and character, they will be fired even though they had brought much profit to the company. This is because the company is bigger than the individual. If we don't work on our character (fruit of the Holy Spirit), our gifts will draw many to the Kingdom but we will be destroyed. The Kingdom of God is much greater than we are. We must represent the Kingdom of God in integrity. God is not interested in us performing mighty works, because the mighty works are His doing. Did you hear that? The works are *His* doing, not ours! We have no glory to share in this and no reward to get from performing miracles. However, there is a reward for bearing lasting fruit of the Holy Spirit.

God is more interested in our character than in our service. In our fruit more than the gift. Character is work done by the individual on themselves. It begins when we point our finger at ourselves, not at others. Taking the log out of our own eye instead of trying to remove a speck from someone else's eye, while we are going blind due to the thick log in our eye like Christ said in Matthew 7:5. Character is developed out of love for God and the reverence and fear of Him. Gifts are never given just out of love. God is love, and just because He is love and He loves you does not mean He will provide you with gifts.

Therefore, do not measure God's love by the gifts He distributes through His Holy Spirit. God's love was displayed by the greatest sacrifice ever made. His only begotten Son died up on the cross, for all who will believe and receive Him. Not everyone who gives you a gift loves you. They may do it because of a season or occasion, but it doesn't mean they care about you. You also do the same, especially if it is gift exchange time. You give the gift, not knowing who will get your gift. Or when you are invited by a friend to accompany them to a wedding or birthday party, you buy a gift without knowing the people who will receive your gift personally.

There are times we give gifts because we love the person, just like God loves us and gave us His Son and His Spirit. But sometimes, we give out of the obligation of the season or occasion. Some people will give a homeless person a gift of a meal, clothing, or shelter because they love God and people. Some people give gifts to charities because they care, and some because they don't want to pay too much on their taxes. Others give to be recognized and create a name for themselves. Clearly, love is not a measure or requirement for receiving any gift.

In the same way, not everyone who gets the gift loves the gift giver. Not everyone you give gifts to loves you or cares about you. In the same way, not many people who receive the gifts of the Spirit love God. The gifts are given without repentance or conditions. It is at the will and discretion of the Holy Spirit. This is where it gets tricky. Because people mostly live by sight and not by faith, they tend to believe in and follow people who have gifts (do signs and wonders) than those with righteous character.

They go to evildoers like those who practice witchcraft, palm readers, magicians, and many others, including false prophets who perform signs for them to marvel at. Non-believers will come to a miracle service because of the signs and wonders that may occur there. That is why the Pharisees asked for Jesus to show them a sign, and Thomas doubted Jesus' resurrection until he saw and touched Jesus. That is why, without faith, it is impossible to please God.

"Then certain of the scribes and Pharisees answered, "Teacher, we want to see a sign from you." But he answered them, "An evil and adulterous generation seeks after a sign, but no sign will be given it but the sign of Jonah the prophet. For as Jonah was three days and three nights in the belly of the whale, so will the Son of Man be three days and three nights in the heart of the earth." (Matthew 12:38-40)

The Holy Spirit has gifts which He gives as He wills for the edification of the church of Jesus Christ. You can never buy or earn these gifts. The Holy Spirit distributes them at His discretion. These gifts came forth through Jesus Christ's victory over the enemy when He gave us back our dominion. We can desire and pray for these gifts, but that's it—just like people place gifts under a Christmas tree with no obligation or work required on the receiver of the gift. The gift giver does not have to give the gifts, but he or she chooses to do it and chooses whom to give the gifts to. Likewise, gifts are given by the Holy Spirit to whomever He chooses, and the receiver does not have to do any work or perform any rituals to receive the gift. It is actually a sin to try to obtain these gifts through any other means. Many have been initiated into the occult because of this.

Many of us are quick to desire the gifts but are not willing to pay the price needed to use these gifts faithfully. Unlike gifts that are given freely, fruits of the Spirit need work to produce them. Without the fruit of the Holy Spirit, which produce in us the character of Jesus Christ, the gifts will be perverted. We need godly character to successfully carry out the gifts of God in our lives for the benefit of the Kingdom. It is the Holy Spirit who works in us to make us willing to do and carry out God's will. Only by the Holy Spirit can we put to death the deeds of the flesh so we can live in reverent fear of the LORD.

"So then, my beloved, even as you have always obeyed, not only in my presence, but now much more in my absence, work out your own salvation with fear and trembling. For it is God who works in you both to will and to work, for his good pleasure." (Phil. 2:12–13)

"For if you live after the flesh, you must die; but if by the Spirit you put to death the deeds of the body, you will live." (Rom. 8:13)

Just as a farmer has to work hard at cultivating the land and taking care of the crops so that they bear healthy fruits, we too must work out our salvation with fear and trembling. We must continually rely on the Holy Spirit, crucify our flesh, and offer our bodies daily as a living sacrifice, holy and pleasing to God, which is the true act of worship (Rom. 12:1). Fruit takes time to grow into you, but gifts are instant. Gifts do not depend on works like fruits do (cultivating, watering, weeding, and pruning); instead, they are dependent on the gift giver and his timing. The Holy Spirit may come on a person because He wants to prophecy, give him or her the gift, and then leave. He doesn't do this because the person is perfect. Remember, He made the donkey to speak, so He can use anything.

Having gifts without the fruit is very destructive. It is like giving an eight-year-old child a car to drive, assuming the child can drive the vehicle safely. The child will drive it like he or she plays video games—recklessly! The car would be a danger to the child and others.

That is why the Holy Spirit in every believer wants them to have all His fruits. He distributes gifts according to our maturity level too. The Holy Spirit sees the heart and what fruit you have and gives gifts at His discretion. Just as parents will withhold some of their property from their children until they are mature enough to handle it safely, God also knows what His children can handle. He will not give you something that will destroy you and others. Gifts are best used under the complete guidance and continual leadership of the Holy Spirit!

"But I say that so long as the heir is a child, he is no different from a bondservant, though he is lord of all; but is under guardians and stewards until the day appointed by the father." (Gal. 4:1–2)

CHAPTER 5

THE WORK OF MY FRIEND THE HOLY SPIRIT

✓ **My friend is a seal and deposit God gave us, guaranteeing our inheritance.**

"For as many as are led by the Spirit of God, these are children of God." (Rom. 8:14)

"in whom you also, having heard the word of the truth, the Good News of your salvation—in whom, having also believed, you were sealed with the promised Holy Spirit, who is a pledge of our inheritance, to the redemption of God's own possession, to the praise of his glory." (Eph. 1:13–14)

When we are sealed, we belong to God, and no one can touch us because only God, our owner, can break the seal. Without the seal, we are exposed to defeat because the Holy Spirit is not there to protect and preserve us.

- ✓ **My friend is the witness of Christ.**

No one knows you more than your spirit. Likewise, no one knows God more than His Spirit. The Holy Spirit teaches us about Christ and confirms His Word with signs and wonders being a great witness of Christ and the finished work of the cross.

"For who among men knows the things of a man, except the spirit of the man, which is in him? Even so, no one knows the things of God, except God's Spirit." (1 Cor. 2:11)

See also 1 John 5:5–8

- ✓ **My friend gives boldness and strength.**

The Holy Spirit gives boldness to witness to others about Christ in our actions and our words. If the world sees Christ in us by our unconditional love for one another, they will hunger for Him. But if they do not see a difference, they will not desire Him. The Holy Spirit is God in us; He displays God to the world through obedient sons and daughters of God.

My friend sees and knows all that happens in the spirit world or realm. He reveals to us what our spiritual enemies are up to. We remain undefeated as long as He lives in us, and we obey Him. This gives us boldness in knowing that we are unbeatable when God the Holy Spirit leads us. "The wicked flee when no one pursues; but the righteous are as bold as a lion." (Proverbs 28:1)

Righteousness and holiness are only achievable by my friend's help. Righteousness makes you bold, fearless, with nothing to hide. Paul and the disciples were always asking for boldness from God to continue doing their God-given assignment. We are a Kingdom at war, and its "warriors don't negotiate; they take authority!" as someone once said. It takes God to have the boldness to take authority in the spiritual realm and have it manifest in the earthly realm. That is why we have to have God the Holy Spirit.

"The Spirit of the Lord came powerfully upon him so that he tore the lion apart with his bare hands as he might have torn a young goat. But he told neither his father nor his mother what he had done." (Judges 14:6)

> They said to him, "We've come to tie you up and hand you over to the Philistines." Samson said, "Swear to me that you won't kill me yourselves." "Agreed," they answered. "We will only tie you up and hand you over to them. We will not kill you." So they bound him with two new ropes and led him up from the rock. As he approached Lehi, the Philistines came toward him shouting. The Spirit of the Lord came powerfully upon him. The ropes on his arms became like charred flax, and the bindings dropped from his hands. Finding a fresh jawbone of a donkey, he grabbed it and struck down a thousand men. (Judges 15:12–15)

✓ **My friend is the hand of God.**

He gave Elijah strength to outrun the king's chariots.

"In a little while, the sky grew black with clouds and wind, and there was a great rain. Ahab rode, and went to Jezreel. Yahweh's hand was on Elijah; and he tucked his cloak into his belt and ran before Ahab to the entrance of Jezreel." (1 Kings 18:45–46)

"Now, Lord, look at their threats, and grant to your servants to speak your word with all boldness, while you stretch out your hand to heal; and that signs and wonders may be done through the name of your holy Servant Jesus." (Acts 4:29–31)

"Now when they saw the boldness of Peter and John, and had perceived that they were unlearned and ignorant men, they marveled. They recognized that they had been with Jesus." (Acts 4:13)

"Therefore, they stayed there a long time, speaking boldly in the Lord, who testified to the word of his grace, granting signs and wonders to be done by their hands." (Acts 14:3)

"Yes, and you will be brought before governors and kings for my sake, for a testimony to them and to the nations. But when they deliver you up, don't be anxious how or what you will say, for it will be given you in that hour what you will say. For it is not you who speak, but the Spirit of your Father who speaks in you." (Matthews 10:18–20)

✓ **My friend is the ever-present teacher and life coach.**

The Holy Spirit helps us to complete God the Father's work on earth. He did it in Christ, and that is why Christ said it was better that He goes away that we may get the Helper, the Holy Spirit. Jesus wants us to have the same exact Teacher, Counselor, Life Coach, and Guide that He had. No one has an excuse of not living victoriously like Christ. We are more than conquerors because Christ has already conquered.

God the Father sent God the Holy Spirit to stay in Christ, to teach Him and remind Him throughout His assignment on earth so that He could be successful in His God-given task. If you don't get the importance of God the Holy Spirit, I pray that the veil in your spirit will be removed and destroyed so that you may desire and ask for the Holy Spirit whom Christ has promised His bride.

In life, one cannot get too far without a life coach and without remembering the lessons they have been taught. When we are born, our coaches are our parents. When we go to school, our teachers add on to our life coaching. The more we advance and grow, the more life coaches we have. It goes on when we go to work; we find a mentor who trains us and helps us to advance. In church, the preacher helps coach us. We encounter many other mentors and life coaches at different stages in life. At every level we are in, there is someone whom we all look up to or learn from, knowingly or unknowingly. It could be a book you read, a movie you watched, a lesson you heard, etc.

No matter how many notes the disciples of Jesus took while they were with Him, they could not remember all the words Jesus spoke or instructed them to do while they were together. The disciples had approximately twenty-six thousand, two hundred and eighty hours with Him, and every word He spoke was EXTREMELY IMPORTANT AND VALID. There was no word worth deleting, erasing, or forgetting. Jesus never spoke an idle word. In fact, Christ said that He spoke what He heard His Father speak and did what He saw His Father do. (John 12:49–50) He did this by the power of the Holy Spirit. There are many things Jesus said and did that were never recorded because there would not be room enough for all the books on earth if all His words were written. John attests to this when he said: "There are also many other things which Jesus did, which if they would all be written, I suppose that even the world itself wouldn't have room for the books that would be written." (John 21:25)

How then can we know all that Jesus did and said and

observe all His commands successfully? How do we live a productive and fruitful life, staying on target like Christ did? How do we know all that was taught by Christ over two thousand years ago? How is it that we are held responsible for knowing the will of the Father for our lives and do it? This is only possible through the leadership and mentorship of God the Father, through God the Holy Spirit.

"For it is God who works in you BOTH TO WILL AND TO WORK FOR HIS GOOD PLEASURE." (Philippians 2:13; emphasis added)

God the Holy Spirit works in us and people see the transformation on the outside. He transforms us and gives us the desire and ability to obey and please God. In turn, others witness this change by our kind words of wisdom and actions, for God's pleasure. This in turn draws many to Christ, which brings glory to God.

"For if you live after the flesh, you must die; BUT IF BY THE SPIRIT YOU PUT TO DEATH THE DEEDS OF THE BODY, YOU WILL LIVE. FOR AS MANY AS ARE LED BY THE SPIRIT OF GOD, THESE ARE CHILDREN OF GOD." (Romans 8:13–14; emphasis added)

Only the Holy Spirit can help you kill the flesh and its evil desires. You cannot do it by your might or "good works." Your spirit can only be led, changed, and made holy by the help of the Spirit of God. You cannot succeed as long as the flesh is leading the spirit because they are opposites and desire different things. The flesh and the spirit are always at war with each other. God knows this, and that is why He sent a mentor for our spirits.

God is a Spirit, and because we were created in His image and likeness, we should know that we are spirits dressed in a bodysuit. We are first spirits, and then a body was created for us to wear because we had to live on earth. The body is an earth suit. When people go to space, they wear a space suit. When people live on earth, they wear an earth or bodysuit made from the earth. Even Christ had to wear a body to live on earth.

"It is the spirit who gives life. The flesh profits nothing. The words that I speak to you are spirit, and are life." (John 6:63)

> For the mind of the flesh is death, but the mind of the Spirit is life and peace; because the mind of the flesh is hostile towards God; for it is not subject to God's law, neither indeed can it be. Those who are in the flesh can't please God. But you are not in the flesh but in the Spirit, if it is so that the Spirit of God dwells in you. But if any man doesn't have the Spirit of Christ, he is not his. If Christ is in you, the body is dead because of sin, but the spirit is alive because of righteousness. (Romans 8:6–10)

> I tell you, keep asking, and it will be given you. Keep seeking, and you will find. Keep knocking, and it will be opened to you. For everyone who asks receives. He who seeks finds. To him who knocks it will be opened. "Which of you fathers, if your son asks for bread, will give him a stone? Or if he asks for a fish, he won't give him a snake instead of a fish, will he? Or if he asks for an egg, he won't give him a scorpion, will he? If you then, being evil, know how to give good gifts to your children, how much more will your heavenly Father give the Holy Spirit to those who ask him? (Luke 11:9–13)

Christ came and lived in a world where the dominion God gave to Adam and Eve was still with the devil. Christ, by the Holy Spirit, made it unto death, got back our stolen dominion, and gave it to us. He descended and ascended and brought the gifts to us. (Eph. 4:7–12) Jesus disarmed the principalities and powers; they have no authority over us. We now have authority over them in His name.

"wiping out the handwriting in ordinances which was against us; and he has taken it out of the way, nailing it to the cross; having stripped the principalities and the powers, he made a show of them openly, triumphing over them in it." (Col. 2:14–15)

"But very truly I tell you, it is for your good that I am going away. Unless I go away, the Advocate will not come to you; but if I go, I will send him to you" (John 16:7, NIV).

Jesus tells His disciples in Luke 24:49, NIV, "I am going to send you what my Father has promised; but stay in the city until you have been clothed with power from on high."

Jesus also commanded the disciples to baptize in the name of the Father, the Son, and the Holy Spirit. This also shows the importance of baptism after receiving salvation.

> Then Jesus came to them and said, "All authority in heaven and on earth has been given to me. Therefore go and make disciples of all nations, baptizing them in the name of the Father and of the Son and of the Holy Spirit, and teaching them to obey everything I have commanded you. And surely I am with you always, to the very end of the age." (Matt. 28:18–20, NIV)

The Holy Spirit Is the Power of God . . .

Jesus was spoken of by John the Baptist as One who baptizes with the Holy Spirit and fire.

"I baptize with water those who repent of their sins and turn to God. But someone is coming soon who is greater than I am—so much greater that I'm not worthy even to be his slave and carry his sandals. He will baptize you with the Holy Spirit and with fire." (Matt. 3:11, NLT)

"Being assembled together with them, he commanded them, "Don't depart from Jerusalem, but wait for the promise of the Father, which you heard from me. For John indeed baptized in water, but you will be baptized in the Holy Spirit not many days from now." (Acts 1:4–5)

"But you will receive power when the Holy Spirit comes upon you. And you will be my witnesses, telling people about me everywhere—in Jerusalem, throughout Judea, in Samaria, and to the ends of the earth." (Acts 1:8, NLT)

Jesus never started His ministry until He was baptized with the Holy Spirit. He would not even have been conceived were it not for the Holy Spirit. The Holy Spirit led Jesus through His God-given task even when it was very hard. He led Him through temptations, strengthened Him, reminded Him what to say and when to say it, made Him wiser than His teachers, and gave Him boldness so that others marveled at His teaching. They said that Jesus taught as one with authority. Therefore, Jesus warned His disciples against preaching and being His witness before they were baptized with the Holy Spirit because the Holy Spirit is His true witness. (See Luke 24:49.)

✓ **My friend reveals Jesus Christ.**

Without the Holy Spirit, we cannot know Jesus intimately, and without the intimate knowledge and relationship with Christ, we cannot know the Father. Jesus said to His disciples in Luke 10:21–23, after He had sent the seventy followers, and they had performed miracles and were glad that the demons obeyed them in Jesus' name, that they should not be happy because demons obey them, but rather, they should be excited that their name is written in the book of life. This shows that demons can obey you in Jesus' name, but still, you can go to hell. Remember, He said not all who call Him Lord will enter the Kingdom of heaven but only those who do the will of His Father in heaven. (Matt. 7:21)

Just like a son does not take every girlfriend he has to his parents and introduce the girl as his bride, Jesus will only introduce His intimate friends, His brides, to His Dad. I pray to be one of them. Why do I say this? Jesus said it in Matthew 22 when He gave the parable of the wedding feast. He said the Kingdom of God is like this parable. When the wedding was ready, the servants were sent to call in the invited guests, but the guests were unwilling, so strangers and all others were invited. However, one of the guests refused to wear the wedding garment (salvation). He was thrown out in the outer darkness. So if the wedding supper is prepared, and there are guests and friends of the bridegroom, then there must be a bride. John the Baptist said that he must decrease as Christ increases because Christ Jesus was the bridegroom, and the friend of the bridegroom, John the Baptist, was happy for the bridegroom to be joined with his bride. (John 3:29–36)

> In that same hour Jesus rejoiced in the Holy Spirit, and said, "I thank you, O Father, Lord of heaven and earth, that you have hidden these things from the wise and understanding, and revealed them to little children. Yes, Father, for so it was well-pleasing in your sight." Turning to the disciples, he said, "All things have been delivered to me by my Father. No one knows who the Son is, except the Father, and who the Father is, except the Son, and he to whomever the Son desires to reveal him." Turning to the disciples, he said privately, "Blessed are the eyes which see the things that you see." (Luke 10:21–23)

The Holy Spirit purifies us (God's Temple) for God to dwell in.

A new homeowner likes to have their house cleaned and new furniture delivered for an exciting new beginning, according to their preference. When you receive Christ as your Lord and Savior, God the Holy Spirit helps you to clean up your house. You must fill it with the Word of God by reading, meditating, memorizing, and living according to His Word. If the Word of God does not occupy your heart (the house), demons worse than the ones you had before salvation and deliverance will come back in easily. You will be tempted, and you will fall into temptation if you do not have the Word of God in you. The Word of God is the sword of the Spirit that destroys the enemy.

When an unclean spirit has gone out of a man, he passes through waterless places, seeking rest, and doesn't find it. Then he says, 'I will return into my house from which I came out,' and when he has come back, he finds it empty, swept, and put in order. Then he goes and takes with himself seven other spirits more evil than he is, and they enter in and dwell there. The last state of that man becomes worse than the first. Even so will it be also to this evil generation. (Matt. 12:43–45)

We need the blood of the Lamb to cleanse us as we allow Christ into our hearts. We need the Word of God to wash, fill us, and renew our minds as we follow Christ. We then testify of God's goodness and deliverance as we live for Him. When we are completely sold out to Christ, we have nothing in this world to lose. We gain eternal life because this is what we live for.

"They overcame him because of the Lamb's blood, and because of the word of their testimony. They didn't love their life, even to death." (Rev. 12:11)

✓ **My friend keeps us from sinning.**

"So now there is no condemnation for those who belong to Christ Jesus. And because you belong to him, the power of the life-giving Spirit has freed you from the power of sin that leads to death. He did this so that the just requirement of the law would be fully satisfied for us, who no longer follow our sinful nature but instead follow the Spirit." (Romans 8:1–2 & 4, NLT)

The Holy Spirit sets us free by giving us power over sin when we follow His leading and direction. Sin cannot rule over those who yield entirely and trust fully in the Holy Spirit. We must consult Him at all times.

✓ **My friend will teach you all things.**

When I say that my friend will teach you ALL things—I mean ALL things. He is much more than amazing. He will reveal Jesus so vividly to you. He will teach you about the Father. He will reveal and explain to you your assignment, and not only that, but He will also help you to fulfill it to perfection beyond your comprehension. He is doing the same with me.

The Holy Spirit teaches us all things. He is all-knowing, which makes Him the most excellent instructor in heaven and on earth. He knows your language, and He knows how you understand things, and so His lessons are customized for you. He not only does that, but He opens your mind to understand His teaching. He also reminds you of the information you learned when you need to remember it, that you may put it into action. He teaches you at that particular time what you need to do and say, in any situation. He is always speaking and has a GREAT sense of humor.

My friend taught me how to cook dishes I had tried cooking over and over but to no avail. He has taught me subjects in school that I needed to understand more and how to relate to people—my husband, my children, friends, and enemies. He has taught me how to know who is talking to me in discerning of spirits. He teaches me everything. Whatever subject you can think of, He knows it.

"But the Helper, the Holy Spirit, whom the Father will send in My name, He will teach you all things, and bring to your remembrance all things that I said to you." (John 14:26, NKJV)

"You gave also your good Spirit to instruct them, and didn't withhold your manna from their mouth, and gave them water for their thirst." (Nehemiah 9:20)

"Teach me to do your will, for you are my God. Your Spirit is good. Lead me in the land of uprightness." (Psalm 143:10)

"But there is a spirit in man, and the breath of the Almighty gives them understanding." (Job 32:8)

✓ **My friend helps us to pray effective prayers.**

I share my experiences on this in a later chapter.

Likewise the Spirit also helps in our weaknesses. For we don't know what we should pray for as we ought, but the Spirit Himself makes intercession for us with groanings which cannot be uttered. Now He who searches the hearts knows what the mind of the Spirit is, because He makes intercession for the saints according to the will of God. (Rom. 8:26–27)

The Holy Spirit teaches us all things and reminds us of what Jesus said to us. After Jesus was baptized, the Holy Spirit led Him into the wilderness to be tempted by the devil. Just as someone works out in the gym to have stronger muscles, our spiritual muscles must be trained through temptations, but God walks us through it. You can't graduate if you don't get tested on what you have been taught; this is true in the physical and spiritual world.

The Holy Spirit led Jesus into the wilderness to be tempted but did not leave Him alone. He was there with Christ, reminding Him what scripture to quote back to defeat the devil. He did this with me too in an experience I will share with you later in the book. The Word of God is the sword of the Spirit. Without the Word of God, we can never be victorious over the enemy. Read the temptation of Jesus in Matthew 4:1–11.

- ✓ **My friend helps us through temptation like He did Christ.**

"Then Jesus, being filled with the Holy Spirit, returned from the Jordan and was led by the Spirit into the wilderness, being tempted for forty days by the devil. And in those days He ate nothing, and afterward, when they had ended, He was hungry." (Luke 4:1–2)

That was when the devil took an opportunity like a thief does. He attacks us at our weakest time. The devil has three temptations he uses at all times to make us sin and fall short of God's glory. When we fall short of God's glory, it means that God can't live in and operate successfully on earth in a defiled temple or body. Adam and Eve fell for the devil's trick, but Jesus overcame him by the sword of the Spirit, which is God's Word. How about you? Do you study God's Word enough to help you in times of need? We know that the enemy comes to steal, kill, and destroy as in John 10:10, "The thief only comes to steal, kill, and destroy. I came that they may have life, and may have it abundantly."

This tells you that with each temptation, the devil has something he wants to steal from you. These three things are worth everything we have. God has given us these things to live a victorious Christian life, and the devil knows it! What are these priceless things the enemy is so interested in stealing from us? We shall look at them one by one with every temptation.

- Temptation 1. Luke 4:3–4

"Then the devil said to him, "If you are the Son of God, tell this stone to become a loaf of bread." But Jesus told him, "No! The Scriptures say, 'People do not live by bread alone.'""
1 Treasure to be stolen is *Your identity*.
Do you know who you are in Christ? Who does God say you are? If you know this, you will speak it back to the enemy when he lies to you about your identity. Remember, your identity comes from Christ. Do not accept any name or image that is not of God. Many fall for this and look for their identity in man, their spouses, parents, teachers, bosses, etc.

- Temptation 2. Luke 4:6–8 (NLT)

"I will give you the glory of these kingdoms and authority over them," the devil said, "because they are mine to give to anyone I please. I will give it all to you if you will worship me." Jesus replied, "The Scriptures say, 'You must worship the Lord your God and serve only him.'"
2 Treasure to be stolen is *Your dominion, authority, and glory*
Dominion, authority and glory are found when we worship Yahweh alone as God. Do you know what you own and have authority over? Do you know your inheritance in Christ? What He paid for? For example, your healing, deliverance, and peace? Power, dominion, and authority over all kingdoms of the earth and darkness? You must remain loyal to God and

worship Him alone to rule and reign with Him.

- Temptation 3. Luke 4:9–12 (NLT)

"Then the devil took him to Jerusalem, to the highest point of the Temple, and said, "If you are the Son of God, jump off! For the Scriptures say, 'He will order his angels to protect and guard you. And they will hold you up with their hands so you won't even hurt your foot on a stone.'" Jesus responded, "The Scriptures also say, 'You must not test the Lord your God.'"
 # 3 Treasure to be stolen is Your trust in God's ability.

Do you believe that God is an all-able, all-powerful, almighty God? Do you need Him to prove that He is God or that He loves you more than what He already did for us through Christ on Calvary? Wasn't this more than enough proof of His amazing, extravagant love? Never doubt God's love or care for you, no matter what is going on around you. He cares so much about you and wants to see you succeed. He does not respond to doubts, He responds to faith. Christ knew who His Father was and how loved He was that He did not have to make His Father prove His love for Him.

Do you find yourself in doubt of God's love for you? No one should! God is love, and there can be no separation of love from Him. He is love Himself. The devil is a liar, and he does his best to discredit God's love because it is perfect and unconditional. God the Father sacrificed His Son's life for sinners! Scripture says in Romans 5:8, while we were yet sinners, Christ died for us. Read the scripture and find out what God says about you. How He cares about you, how He cannot get you out of His sight, how often He thinks about you. Read Psalm 139:1–8. Then see again in Jeremiah 29:11 what good plans He has for you.

"When the devil had finished tempting Jesus, he left him until the next **opportunity** came." (Luke 4:13, NLT emphasis added)

The devil is an opportunist. He keeps repeating the same three concepts of "identity crisis," not knowing who you are in Christ. Rank crisis . . . not knowing your authority and position in God. Remember that we are seated with Christ in the heavenly places. And finally planting in us doubts in God's identity . . . Making God too small in your eyes because some things didn't go your way. Don't give in; don't give the enemy an opportune time. Be yielded and entirely filled to overflowing with the Holy Spirit.

Needless to say, Jesus was victorious over the enemy. Hallelujah! Thank God for the Holy Spirit, who teaches us and leads us to triumph in Christ Jesus!

CHAPTER 6

MY FRIEND THE WILL EXECUTOR

Isaiah breaks down what Christ paid for that we may be free from the devil's grip and bondage of sin.

Surely He has borne our griefs And carried our sorrows; Yet we esteemed Him stricken, Smitten by God, and afflicted. But He was wounded for our transgressions, He was bruised for our iniquities; The chastisement for our peace was upon Him, And by His stripes we are healed. (Isaiah 53:4–5, NKJV)

Jesus Christ . . .

1. He paid for our griefs
2. He paid for our sorrows and pain
3. He paid for our sin when He was wounded
4. He paid for our wickedness and generational sins when

He was bruised/crushed
5. He paid for our peace when He was chastised; no more guilt and shame from sin
6. He paid for our healing by His stripes

Beloved, if you are born again and still suffer the above brutality which Christ paid for, you are deceived. It is like Bob (just to mention a name as an example) working as a janitor in a company which he owns, but he does not know that he owns the company. When Bob's father passed away from old age, he left Bob a lot of wealth; but because of Bob's ignorance and busy schedule, he has not had a chance to read the will which his father left him. Bob's father left him great wealth so that Bob would never have to work a day in his life again. However, Bob is too busy with his three jobs and a family that he has no time to meet with the will executor to read his father's will, claim it, and possess what is his.

If Bob continues to ignore the executor and never reads the will which his father left him, he will die a poor man, and he will never have time to spend and enjoy his riches with his family. However, if Bob puts his busyness of life aside and makes time to meet with the will executor and reads the will, he will be set free from his bondage. He will be a wealthy man, able to raise his family, and have time for his wife and children. He will also be a channel of blessing to many others.

This is what the church of Jesus Christ is suffering from. We are too busy to ask for the Holy Spirit, who is our Father's will executor, and too busy to read God's Word (His will). We are too busy to find out what God the Father has given us through Christ and what we are required to do to possess it all. That is why we are still in bondage and slaves to the one we are supposed to be masters of. Have you ever wondered how it is possible that Christ came from heaven to earth, suffered greatly, died, rose from the dead on the third day, and gave us all dominion and power over the enemy; yet people's lives remain the same as if His great sacrifice never happened?

They live as if salvation, deliverance, redemption, healing, prosperity, and all the promises which Christ paid for are void. The devil is a liar! Stop your busy works and turn back to God. Stop making friendships, entertainment, and other cares of this world your god. Arise and get knowledge of what belongs to you in Christ Jesus through our Helper, God the Holy Spirit. Ask for Him and then study God's will in His Word, and possess all that you are entitled to. Let us stop making the sacrifice that God made through His Son of no value.

God does not make such great sacrifices for nothing! Find out all that belongs to you and possess it all because it is not short of being like Christ on earth. We should be walking in the same authority and power which Christ walked in while on earth. We should be performing great signs and wonders for the sake of the Kingdom of God, destroying and dispossessing the kingdom of darkness and doing greater things than Christ did as He promised in John 14:12. "Most certainly I tell you, he who believes in me, the works that I do, he will do also; and he will do greater works than these, because I am going to my Father." (John 14:12)

God the Holy Spirit is the executor of the will we possess through Christ Jesus. We cannot know what we have in Christ apart from revelation from God the Holy Spirit. When Jesus died and rose again, He left us a will and went to heaven. Before someone dies, he or she writes a will and entrusts the will to a will executor, whose work is to secure the property and make sure that the people who are named on the WILL are entitled to receive ALL that was left for them.

Examples:

- JOHN 3:16 reveals to us those entitled to the WILL OF EVERLASTING LIFE . . . WHOSOEVER BELIEVES IN GOD'S SON, JESUS CHRIST.

"For God so loved the world, that he gave his one and only Son, that whoever believes in him should not perish, but have eternal life." (John 3:16)

- Psalm 91 has the Will for divine protection and favor, and it is for . . .

"whoever dwells in the presence of the Most High God."

- Psalm 34:7's Will for protection from God's angel is for . . .

"Those who fear God."
"Yahweh's angel encamps around those who fear him, and delivers them." (Psalm 34:7)

What is a WILL and when is a WILL executed?

According to http://legal-dictionary.thefreedictionary.com/Execution+of+Wills:

A will is . . . "A document in which a person specifies the method to be applied in the management and distribution of his estate after his death. A will is a legal instrument that permits a person, the testator, to make decisions on how his estate will be managed and distributed after his death."

Hebrews 9:15–17 confirms and explains Christ as the testator and because of His confirmed death and resurrection, the Will He left us is legally in effect.

"That is why he is the one who mediates a new covenant between God and people, so that all who are called can receive the eternal inheritance God has promised them. For Christ died to set them free from the penalty of the sins they had committed under that first covenant. Now when someone leaves a will, it is necessary to prove that the person who made it is dead. *The will goes into effect only after the person's death.* While the person who made it is still alive, the will cannot be put into effect." (Hebrews 9:15–17, NLT; italics added)

Now that Jesus died and rose again and ascended unto the Father, who is His designated Will executor on earth? In a will, there is the executor of the will whose definition of duties according to http://legal-dictionary.thefreedictionary.com/executor, are . . . "The person appointed to administer the estate of a person who has died leaving a will which nominates that person. Unless there is a valid objection, the judge will appoint the person named in the will to be executor. The executor must ensure that the person's desires expressed in the will are carried out. Practical responsibilities include gathering up and protecting the assets of the estate, obtaining information in regard to all beneficiaries named in the will and any other potential heirs, collecting and arranging for payment of debts of the estate, approving or disapproving creditor's claims, making sure estate taxes are calculated, forms filed, and tax payments made, and in all ways assist the attorney for the estate (which the executor can select)."

Christ's will executor is God the Holy Spirit whom the judge, God the Father, has appointed. My friend knows Christ's will and all that He has left us. He reveals to us the perfect will of God, what God created us to do; what He put in us during creation, and how to rule successfully over the part of the Kingdom which God has entrusted us with. Only God the Holy Spirit can do this. Christ appointed the Holy Spirit to execute His will; God the Father, who is the judge, has appointed the Holy Spirit for this task. Let us look at a few scriptures to support this.

"But the Helper, the Holy Spirit, whom the Father will send in My name, He will teach you all things, and bring to your remembrance all things that I said to you." (John 14:26, NKJV)

"And we are His witnesses to these things, and so also is the Holy Spirit whom God has given to those who obey Him." (Acts 5:32, NKJV)

"He will glorify and honor Me, because He (the Holy Spirit) will take from what is Mine and will disclose it to you. All things that the Father has are Mine. Because of this I said that He [the Spirit] will take from what is Mine and will reveal it to you." (John 16:14–15, AMP)

What is prophecy?

According to Merriam-Webster.com dictionary, "Prophecy" is . . . "The function or vocation of a prophet; specifically: The inspired declaration of divine will and purpose, a prediction of something to come."

"For no prophecy ever came by the will of man: but holy men of God spoke, being moved by the Holy Spirit." (2 Peter 1:21)

When the Holy Spirit came upon the people who believed in Christ Jesus, they started speaking in a heavenly language, and they also prophesied. This means they spoke and accessed heaven and the WILL of the Father, which is the same as that of the Son. They then spoke it out loud and declared the divine WILL and purpose of God, predicting the future. See how God the Holy Spirit works as the WILL executor? He is the channel of communication from heaven to earth, and earth to heaven. My friend the Holy Spirit is the only revealer of God's perfect WILL to man. Jesus said to His disciples that He had so much more to tell them, but they could not bear it all within that short time, but He promised that when the Holy Spirit comes, He will teach them all things and remind them what Christ said to them.

The Holy Spirit will reveal the Word of God to us and give us more from heaven that has not been written in the Bible. This is because there is so much more to God and His promises that if the books were written, the whole earth would be overflowing with books. The wisdom of God is unsearchable! Only God the Holy Spirit can contain it all. Just as a Kindle tablet holds many books in one device, so does the Holy Spirit carry God's WILL, WORD, and WISDOM in Him. Many times, He has taught me scripture before I even read it! I knew it, and later on, found out that it was actually written in the Bible. Yes, He authored the Bible, so He knows all that is written in it. We must receive Him if we are to live in the fullness of the Will of God, which was made possible by the great sacrifice made by Christ Jesus, our LORD and Savior.

THE ABSENCE OF THE HOLY SPIRIT CAUSES PARALYSIS IN THE CHURCH.

The Holy Spirit is the action or hand of God. He manifests God's Word. Without my friend, creation would not have been manifested, and Christ would not have been conceived. Women and the Holy Spirit have the same title—Helper. Without a woman's egg, conception would not occur, and the seeds of a man would not be beneficial alone. Without Eve, Adam would be the only one on earth. Seed without water and/or soil to help it grow is useless. A woman receives seed from a man, and it is joined to hers to give life. She nurtures and grows it into a human being. The water and soil take the seed and develop it into a plant, fruit, or vegetables fit for consumption. The woman gives life to the man's seed. "Now the Lord God said, "It is not good (beneficial) for the man to be alone; I will make him a helper [one who balances him—a counterpart who is] suitable and complementary for him." (Genesis 2:18, AMP)

The church of Jesus Christ without the Holy Spirit is not beneficial. This is because the Holy Spirit takes the Word from the Father and manifests the Word on earth. Jesus Himself, being the Son and the Word of God, did not have any miracles recorded before He was baptized with the Holy Spirit. The Word of God never benefits anyone without the revelation power of the Holy Spirit. The devil knows the Word but has no revelation of it because if he did, he would not have crucified Christ our Lord. He would have known that the death would lead to resurrection and ultimate victory over sin and death, over him and his power.

God the Father performed the baptism of the Holy Spirit on Christ. John the Baptist could not baptize anyone with the

Holy Spirit; he only baptized in water unto repentance.

"I indeed baptize you with water unto repentance, but He who is coming after me is mightier than I, whose sandals I am not worthy to carry. *He will baptize you with the Holy Spirit and fire.*" (Matthew 3:11, NKJV; italics added)

It is also evident in the scripture we read earlier in Acts 19:1–6. The believers did not receive the Holy Spirit with the baptism of John the Baptist; instead, they received Him after they accepted Jesus Christ as their LORD; and they were then counted worthy of the inheritance and Will that Jesus paid for. After they received the Holy Spirit, they broke into the action of speaking in other tongues and prophecy. They then had direct access to heaven and the promises of God in Christ.

> The first book I wrote, Theophilus, concerned all that Jesus began BOTH TO DO AND TO TEACH, until the day in which he was received up, after he had given commandment through the Holy Spirit to the apostles whom he had chosen. To these he also showed himself alive after he suffered, by many proofs, appearing to them over a period of forty days, and speaking about God's Kingdom. Being assembled together with them, he commanded them, "Don't depart from Jerusalem, but wait for the promise of the Father, which you heard from me. For John indeed baptized in water, but you will be baptized in the Holy Spirit not many days from now. (Acts 1:1–5; emphasis added)

In today's church, many people have ignored the instruction Jesus gave His disciples. Once you accept Him as your LORD and Savior, you must also ask to be baptized with the

Holy Spirit and His fire. Do not go out witnessing or doing God's work without the Holy Spirit. Going without the Holy Spirit is like enrolling in the military and then deploying yourself without the support, intelligence, and help of the country you went to represent. You will be out on your own without the information needed to fight effectively. You will be blind, not knowing your enemy's position or weapons because you have no communication with the country you are protecting. This deployment would be a suicide mission. You would basically be fighting on your own. Are you like the children of Israel, on a spiritual suicide mission because they ignored the Spirit of God and in doing so, they forfeited their transformation and renewing of the mind which led to their destruction?

The Holy Spirit baptized Jesus and then led Him into the wilderness to be tempted by the devil. This is the first time we hear of the Holy Spirit's guidance and leadership in Christ's public ministry. Christ faithfully followed this divine guidance and leadership of the Holy Spirit. Then the Holy Spirit told Him what to say with every temptation, and He was victorious. That was why Jesus told His disciples not to worry about what to say when they were being tested because the Holy Spirit will teach you at that time what to say. (Luke 12:11–12)

After the wilderness test, which was, I believe, meant to see how well Jesus would follow the instruction and leading of the Holy Spirit, Jesus began His ministry. He was now entrusted with the Kingdom to the public. Just like one would take a car for a test drive to be sure all is working before owning it, the Holy Spirit was testing out Christ's ability to hear and follow directions for the tough ride ahead. The Holy Spirit determines your promotion in the Kingdom of God. He teaches you as He lives in you when you accept Christ and receive His baptism, you become His legal body to use for the Kingdom of God.

"Jesus returned *in the power of the Spirit* into Galilee, and news about him spread through all the surrounding area. He taught in their synagogues, being glorified by all." (Luke 4:14–15; emphasis added)

"For God's Kingdom is not in word, but in power." (1 Corinthians 4:20)

If Jesus, being the Son of God, did not start His ministry without the baptism of the Holy Spirit, and His disciples did not begin their ministry without the baptism of the Holy Spirit as instructed by Christ, who are we to go about Christ's ministry without the baptism of the Holy Spirit? I warn you and speak to you as Christ told His disciples: "And now I will send the Holy Spirit, just as my Father promised. But stay here in the city until the Holy Spirit comes and fills you with power from heaven." (Luke 24:49, NLT)

There is no power without the Holy Spirit. There is no manifestation of God's glory without the Holy Spirit. There is no knowledge of Christ and God the Father without the Holy Spirit. We are supposed to be carriers of God's glory. We lost the glory after Adam sinned in the Garden of Eden. The devil was jealous of us being the carriers of God's glory because he used to be the carrier of it until pride demoted him. When the devil, at creation, saw God creating man from dirt and not from precious stones like the devil was made of, and then he saw God placing His perfect glory in this earthen vessel, Satan was appalled! His mission from then on was to make humans fall short of God's glory, just like he fell short of it. Satan was successful in this mission back in the Garden of Eden, but thanks be to God for His perfect plan of redemption through His Son Jesus Christ, by the help of the Holy Spirit! We can now live free of sin!

"for all have sinned, and fall short of the glory of God; being justified freely by his grace through the redemption that is in Christ Jesus." (Romans 3:23–24)

We can never succeed without the Holy Spirit of God. There is no shortcut in the Kingdom of God. Just like you cannot be successful in an executive position without proper education and training, we cannot be entrusted with the Kingdom of God without the training from the Holy Spirit. Why? Because the Holy Spirit is the wisdom of God. He makes us think like God and opens our eyes to see through God's eyes. He is the one who gives assignments, degrees, and promotions in God's Kingdom. Gifts and fruits of the Spirit only come from Him.

We can never be like Christ without the Holy Spirit. We can never have the power of God without Him because He is the power of God. Life in Christ is impossible without my friend. Why do you think the devil works overtime to make the Holy Spirit look bad and be misunderstood? Because the Holy Spirit is the key to the Kingdom's power! Without Him, the Kingdom of God has no power on earth. In the Old Testament, enemies were destroyed when the Holy Spirit showed up on a person whom God had anointed like David, Samson, Gideon, Elijah, and many others. Jesus said . . . "But if I *by the Spirit of God cast out demons*, then God's Kingdom has come upon you." (Matthew 12:28; emphasis added)

When you receive the baptism of the Holy Spirit and fire, you will destroy the kingdom of darkness. Jesus never troubled the kingdom of darkness when He was born of the Holy Spirit. He tormented the kingdom of darkness after He was baptized with the Holy Spirit. That is why He was the only one who could do great miracles because the Father baptized Him alone with the Holy Spirit. No one gives their enemy or an immature child a gun to use because they will destroy themselves and others as well. Likewise, God will not give the overflow of His Spirit to His enemies, those living in sin; or immature sons and daughters, those who take the grace of God as a license to sin.

God baptizes His mature sons and daughters who ask for the Holy Spirit for the Kingdom's sake. These are ones like Christ, who received the infilling of the Holy Spirit at salvation, and they cooperated with the Holy Spirit who has matured them for their salvation and Kingdom use. The baptism, like with Christ and His disciples, made them ready to impart to others through the Holy Spirit's power and fire. The Holy Spirit gives gifts to these mature sons and daughters. He never gave Christ the power until He proved mature and responsible and one who could be entrusted with the Kingdom. These gifts of the Holy Spirit are the power bombs in God's Kingdom to destroy the works of darkness as they build and gain more Kingdom territory for Christ. As your instructor and destiny Helper, the Holy Spirit will give you more Kingdom jurisdiction depending on your spiritual growth and maturity.

The devil is afraid of the Holy Spirit because the Holy Spirit gave him the greatest shock and surprise of his entire life. The devil knew Christ was powerless without the Holy Spirit. The Holy Spirit led Jesus to the wilderness because without the Holy Spirit, Jesus would not have defeated the devil in the wilderness. The Holy Spirit had taught Christ self-control, which helped Him remain sinless when He was betrayed, tortured, and crucified. The devil celebrated Christ's death because there was no display of God's power in the crucifixion and death. When one dies, they are powerless. Death has victory over them. Death came from sin, and sin came from the kingdom of darkness. But there is a power stronger than death, and that is the power of resurrection life in Christ through God the Holy Spirit. When Christ died, He gave up the Holy Spirit to the Father. After the appointed days that Christ was to remain in the grave were over, the Holy Spirit came back into the body of Christ with supernatural power, and He resurrected Christ. That is why the devil works the hardest for people not to receive Christ, and if they do, he keeps them from knowing the power of salvation, life, and holiness found in Christ through my friend the Holy Spirit. My friend is the power of God, the transformer of lives, and the glory of God, the one who helps us live in victory over sin and death!

Satan knows that the Holy Spirit drove out giants and gave the children of Israel the land of the giants. This meant that they got to possess humongous houses, farms, land, and gold and silver. Imagine a giant's gold and diamond ring! Everything was multiplied many times over because of two men who allowed the Holy Spirit to transform them and use them to lead the Israelites into the Promised Land. The same Spirit helps us to possess back all that the enemy has stolen from God's Kingdom and us. God says He loves justice and hates robbery. By His Spirit, God administers justice to His children, and the devil knows this, so the devil works hard to keep us from knowing and desiring our will executor, God the Holy Spirit. I love my friend the Holy Spirit the will executor.

CHAPTER 7

MY FRIEND THE BRIDE SEEKER, PREPARER, AND PERFECTOR

THE BRIDE OF Christ . . .

Who is the bride of Christ? The bride of Christ is the most intimate and highest rank a believer in Christ can ever have here on earth and in the life to come. It is not the working of miracles or the raising of the dead. It is not being a bishop, evangelist, apostle, or holding the highest title on earth. It is not being a pastor of the largest congregation on earth. It is none of these and more—it is being the bride of Christ, intimacy with Christ.

The bride of Christ is the one whom the bridegroom is coming for and the one for whom the wedding supper is being prepared. The bride completes Christ and the joy of the

Father. When a man on earth gets married to his bride, he feels complete. There is a celebration. Her status changes from Miss to Mrs. He becomes a husband and leader of the home. They get to another level of intimacy that only a husband and wife can get to. So it is with the bride of Christ. There is life and greater intimacy with Christ after this life, after the wedding. Just as life begins all over again the moment one gets married, life starts all over again in greater heights when the bridegroom comes for His bride for the wedding supper and when the wedding is done.

The bride of Christ is one who keeps herself pure without blemish and looks forward to each moment in preparation, anticipation, and readiness for her bridegroom. She will not compromise or let anyone take the place of her beloved; she will not allow her wedding garment to be soiled. She does not entertain anyone who causes her to veer from her vision of her groom and His desires. A bride of Christ is one who is sold out to Him and entirely led by the Holy Spirit of God. That is why the Word of God concludes with the bridegroom's coming in Revelation 22:17, "And *the Spirit and the bride* say, 'Come!' And let him who hears say, 'Come!' And let him who thirsts come. Whoever desires, let him take the water of life freely." (NKJV; italics added)

The Holy Spirit is the bride preparer. He gets the bride ready for her bridegroom, and they together invite the bridegroom back to get His bride. The bride is a mature son or daughter of God. Whatever inheritance the Father gives to the Son belongs to Him and His bride. The bride of Christ is one who does not only know about Christ but goes more in-depth into knowing Christ. We get to know Christ only by the revelation of Him through the Holy Spirit.

The Ten Virgins

Regarding the story of the ten virgins, the five wise ones knew their bridegroom while the five foolish ones knew *about* their bridegroom. The five were wise because they realized that even if the bridegroom took a long time to come, He would surely come at the right time. They did not rely on their timing of Him but on the Holy Spirit's timing of Him. Therefore, they not only carried oil to light their lamps, which represents salvation where Christ breathes the Holy Spirit in them, but they went the extra mile and brought extra oil which represents the baptism of the Holy Spirit and fire. They not only had the oil to light the lamp, they had extra oil to keep the lamp burning. The lamp symbolizes the Word of God that could only shine with the oil, which signifies the Holy Spirit's revelation of the Word. The Holy Spirit revealed to them who their bridegroom, Jesus Christ, was. The extra oil gave them understanding, power, wisdom, knowledge, might, council, and the fear of the Lord. This is what kept them going when the others ran out of the standard or basic oil needed to light the lamp for a while, not for the long haul.

The five wise ones were fully loaded with the oil without measure (the fullness of the Holy Spirit—the seven Spirits of God) like Christ. They, therefore, bore fruits that would last. These represent Christians who are hungry and thirsty after righteousness, who don't just want to meet the bare minimum to get to heaven, but they long and desire for deep intimacy and a lasting relationship with Christ. They come in with no reservations for Christ. They are completely sold out—not one foot in and another out. These are **Hot** Christians, pleasing to God.

The foolish ones were also virgins, but they did not know their bridegroom—they knew *about* him. They knew that he was coming, but they were not sensitive about His timing. They got ready according to their timetable. They had the Word (lamp) but not enough revelation (oil). They ignored the Holy Spirit, who is the revealer of their bridegroom, Jesus Christ. Remember, the psalmist in Psalm 119:105 said, "Thy Word is a lamp unto my feet and a light unto my path." These ones missed the bridegroom because they ran out of oil. They gave the bare minimum to receive him and never sought intimacy with their bridegroom. They ignored the extra oil, which is the baptism of the Holy Spirit, and it led to their rejection. They tried to get extra oil in the end, but it was too late. They had fruit but it did not last.

These represent the majority of Christians who are **lukewarm**. These Christians nauseate Christ. Without the Holy Spirit, the Word of God cannot be effective in your life. They lacked the seven Spirits of God; therefore, they had no wisdom, knowledge, understanding, power, might, council, or the fear of God. Which category do you fall in to? The wise or foolish virgins?

The Holy Spirit illuminates Christ and God the Father to the church. Without Him, God's Word is just like any other book. The devil knows the whole Bible. Some nonbelievers also know the Bible; however, they do not have the revelation of the Word. This is because it is only revealed to us by the Holy Spirit. By the baptism of the Holy Spirit, believers gain greater knowledge, wisdom, understanding, power, might, council, and the fear of God just like Christ!

The devil does not know the things of God, either. That is why he made the mistake of crucifying Jesus. Had he known the victory in the death and resurrection of Christ, he would not have played a part in the torture and crucifixion of Jesus. The devil knew all along the scriptures from the prophet Isaiah in chapter 53 on the suffering of the Savior and the victory behind it but did not have the revelation of this scripture. There is no way anyone can know God but by His Spirit. The Holy Spirit of God is God, and only God can reveal God to you. We saw earlier that the only two people who inherited the Promised Land from the people who originally came from Egypt were Joshua and Caleb. God said that the reason they inherited this promise was that they had a "different spirit." They knew God.

"Because all these men who have seen My glory and the signs which I did in Egypt and in the wilderness, and have put Me to the test now these ten times, and have not heeded My voice, they certainly shall not see the land of which I swore to their fathers, nor shall any of those who rejected Me see it. *But My servant Caleb, because he has a different spirit in him and has followed Me fully*, I will bring into the land where he went, and his descendants shall inherit it." (Num. 14:22–24; italics added)

Caleb and Joshua not only knew about God, but they knew their God. God is never satisfied with people knowing *about* Him or just believing that He exists. He needs people to seek after Him and know the reward of seeking Him.

"Without faith it is impossible to be well pleasing to him, for he who comes to God must believe that he exists, and that he is a rewarder of those who seek him." (Hebrews 11:6)

The devil and his demons know about God and believe in Him, and they even tremble. "You believe that there is one God. You do well. Even the demons believe—and tremble!" (James 2:19)

Knowing about a person is the initial stage of any relationship. No one in his right mind and judgment would want to get married to someone they only know about. Instead, they want to get married to someone they personally know. Christ is coming back to marry a bride who knows Him. Jesus values relationship, not religion. Religion is man-made not Christ-made. Christ did not teach us religion; instead, He taught us how to be in a relationship and in fellowship with God. He never came to establish a religion, because many religions existed at the time. He came to establish a relationship with us.

"Thus says the Lord: 'Let not the wise man glory in his wisdom, Let not the mighty man glory in his might, Nor let the rich man glory in his riches; *But let him who glories glory in this, That he understands and knows Me, that I am the Lord, exercising lovingkindness, judgment, and righteousness in the earth. For in these I delight,'* says the Lord." (Jer. 9:23–24, NKJV; italics added)

Do you know and understand God?

ABRAHAM AND GOD, A PICTURE OF WHAT WAS AND IS TO COME.

• Abraham's name means "a father of many nations"	• God is, the Father of many nations
• Abraham's second son, Isaac, was the child of the promise by whom the nation of Israel was born. (First son from another woman was Ishmael).	• God's second son, Jesus Christ is the Son in whom we have the promise of salvation. (First human son was Adam, Christ is considered the second Adam).

• God told Abraham to sacrifice his then only son Isaac, who was innocent. He agreed, and God provided a ram just before Abraham killed his son on the third day. This symbolized that Isaac had been sacrificed and then brought back to life by God's power.	• Jesus Christ, an innocent sacrifice, was sacrificed by God and brought back to life on the third day.
• Abraham sent his servant to look for a willing bride for his son Isaac.	• God sent the Holy Spirit to bring back a willing bride for His Son Jesus Christ.
• Abraham is known as the Father of faith.	• God is the Father of Faith

Hebrews 11:17–19 (NIV; emphasis added):

"By faith Abraham, when God tested him, offered Isaac as a sacrifice. He who had embraced the promises was about to sacrifice his one and only son, even though God had said to him, "It is through Isaac that your offspring will be reckoned." *Abraham reasoned that God could even raise the dead, and so in a manner of speaking he did receive Isaac back from death.*"

See Genesis 22 on Abraham's sacrifice.

Abraham was old, and well stricken in age. Yahweh had blessed Abraham in all things. Abraham said to his servant, the elder of his house, who ruled over all that he had, "Please put your hand under my thigh. I will make you swear by Yahweh, the God of heaven and the God of the earth, that you shall not take a wife for my son of the daughters of the Canaanites, among whom I live. But you shall go to my country, and to my relatives, and take a wife for my son Isaac." The servant said to him, "What if the woman isn't willing to follow me to this land? Must I bring your son again to the land you came from?" Abraham said to him, "Beware that you don't bring my son there again. Yahweh, the God of heaven, who took me from my father's house, and from the land of my birth, who spoke to me, and who swore to me, saying, 'I will give this land to your offspring.' He will send his angel before you, and you shall take a wife for my son from there. If the woman isn't willing to follow you, then you shall be clear from this oath to me. Only you shall not bring my son there again." The servant put his hand under the thigh of Abraham his master, and swore to him concerning this matter. The servant took ten camels, of his master's camels, and departed, having a variety of good things of his master's with him. He arose, and went to Mesopotamia, to the city of Nahor. (Genesis 24:1–10)

Before he had finished speaking, behold, Rebekah came out, who was born to Bethuel the son of Milcah, the wife of Nahor, Abraham's brother, with her pitcher on her shoulder. The young lady was very beautiful to look at, a virgin. No man had known her. She went down to the spring, filled her pitcher, and came up. The servant ran to meet her, and said, "Please give me a drink, a little water from your pitcher." She said, "Drink, my lord." She hurried, and let down her pitcher on her hand, and gave him drink. When she had done giving him drink, she said, "I will also draw for your camels, until they have done drinking." She hurried, and emptied her pitcher into the trough, and ran again to the well to draw, and drew for all his camels. (Gen 24:15–20)

Then Laban and Bethuel answered, "The thing proceeds from Yahweh. We can't speak to you bad or good. Behold, Rebekah is before you. Take her, and go, and let her be your master's son's wife, as Yahweh has spoken."" When Abraham's servant heard their words, he bowed himself down to the earth to Yahweh. The servant brought out jewels of silver, and jewels of gold, and clothing, and gave them to Rebekah. He also gave precious things to her brother and her mother. They ate and drank, he and the men who were with him, and stayed all night. They rose up in the morning, and he said, "Send me away to my master. (Gen 24:50–54)

"They said, "We will call the young lady, and ask her." They called Rebekah, and said to her, "Will you go with this man?" She said, **"I will go.""** (Gen 24:57–58; emphasis added)

Isaac went out to meditate in the field at the evening. He lifted up his eyes, and saw, and, behold, there were camels coming. Rebekah lifted up her eyes, and when she saw Isaac, she dismounted from the camel. She said to the servant, "Who is the man who is walking in the field to meet us?" The servant said, "It is my master." She took her veil, and covered herself. The servant told

Isaac all the things that he had done. Isaac brought her into his mother Sarah's tent, and took Rebekah, and she became his wife. He loved her. Isaac was comforted after his mother's death. (Gen 24:63–67)

We see that Abraham's servant, Eliezer, whose name is not mentioned here but was the one presumed to be Abraham's heir before Isaac was born, and His name means "my God is help," was in charge of all His master Abraham owned. Eliezer was a symbol of the Holy Spirit who is "God our Helper." Are you willing to go with Him to know *your* bridegroom?

After these things Yahweh's word came to Abram in a vision, saying, "Don't be afraid, Abram. I am your shield, your exceedingly great reward." Abram said, "Lord Yahweh, what will you give me, since I go childless, and he who will inherit my estate is Eliezer of Damascus?" Abram said, "Behold, to me you have given no children: and, behold, one born in my house is my heir." Behold, Yahweh's word came to him, saying, "This man will not be your heir, but he who will come out of your own body will be your heir." (Genesis 15:1–4)

Likewise, God the Holy Spirit is in charge of all God the Father owns. Rebekah served the servant and his camels. She not only served the servant but the animals, which were the property of the master. She was then given gifts because of her heart of service. Likewise, the Holy Spirit gives gifts according to His discretion to those who will accept to serve God as He leads according to God the Father and Son, and for those who will take care of what belongs to Him, His church. Just like the servant did not give gifts to random women at the well but only to the woman who offered to serve him and accept to be Isaac's bride, the Holy Spirit gives gifts to those who have agreed to serve God and be the brides of Christ. The servant asked Rebekah if she had room for him and all he had with him, and she said yes.

Do you have room for the Holy Spirit and all that He has so He can come in and spend the night? The scripture above says the servant spent *all night*. The Holy Spirit is willing to spend all night with you and in the morning take you to your bridegroom. Spending the night means He will come in the darkness of our hearts and souls and transform us so we may shine as bright as our bridegroom does who is brighter than the sun. Once the Holy Spirit comes in, He does away with the kingdom of darkness in us and brings us into the Kingdom of light. He doesn't just stop there. When we accept His invitation and baptism, He takes us on this journey to our Savior, Master, and Lord Jesus Christ, preparing us to meet our bridegroom for our wedding. This is just like in the Old Testament when Esther was prepared by the eunuch to be the bride for the king, and as the children of Israel were prepared to possess the Promised Land. Those with a different Spirit, led by my friend the Holy Spirit will be the brides of Christ and possess the Promised Land.

Rebekah was a willing bride. She was more than ready to leave all she knew behind. Rebekah left her family and friends without hesitation. Her family wanted to detain her for a few more days, but she refused and agreed to go to her bridegroom right away. The Holy Spirit does not want to wait for you to continue with your lifestyle away from Christ. Are you willing to leave your old life behind immediately to follow the Holy Spirit who will lead you to intimacy with Christ? How eager are you to have intimacy with Christ? Luke 14:26 says, "If anyone comes to me, and doesn't disregard his own father, mother, wife, children, brothers, and sisters, yes, and his own life also, he can't be my disciple."

My friend the Holy Spirit wants to seal us with the engagement of Christ with gifts and fruit that make us presentable brides of Christ. The servant gave Rebekah a ring for her nose and bracelets for her hands the minute she did what the servant desired, which was to serve him and his master's property. These gifts set her apart from all others. She became richer than she was when she came to the well. Then when she agreed to leave her family and go with the servant to her bridegroom, she got even more riches; jewels of silver, and jewels of gold, and clothing, a seal and deposit for what was about to come to her from being married to Isaac. Isaac owned all that his father owned, making her a coheir with Isaac. Notice that the servant clothed her with jewels and garments. He knew what Isaac liked, and what Isaac's father loves, so he clothed her with garments that are acceptable to the family she was about to belong to. In our case, the garment of righteousness in Christ Jesus.

The Holy Spirit is here to clothe us in jewels and garments from our Father's Kingdom of righteousness, just like our bridegroom likes it and our Father loves so that we can look like Him. In the same way, Jesus prayed to the Father to send us the Holy Spirit as a betrothal of us to Christ just like Abraham's servant was sent to get a bride for Isaac, and he gave her gifts as her betrothal and then took her to him. The Holy Spirit is here to get the bride for Christ. He begins His assignment by convicting people of sin, righteousness, and judgment, showing them the need for a savior.

"If you [really] love Me, you will keep and obey My commandments. And I will ask the Father, and He will give you another Helper (Comforter, Advocate, Intercessor—Counselor, Strengthener, Standby), to be with you forever—the Spirit of Truth, whom the world cannot receive [and take to its heart] because it does not see Him or know Him, but you know Him because He (the Holy Spirit) remains with you continually and will be in you." (John 14:15–17, AMP)

The Holy Spirit's primary purpose and the end result, therefore, is to:

1. Make us aware of our sin and the need for a savior.
2. Betroth us to Christ, reveal Christ to us so that we may move from knowing about Him to knowing Him intimately.
3. He prepares us, gives us gifts to serve our Lord, and leads us to Him to live with Him forever.

The Holy Spirit is the point of contact between Christ and us. We cannot know Jesus apart from Him. We can hear about Him like anyone can, but really knowing Him within us intimately takes the power of the Holy Spirit. We can never serve God successfully without His power and gifts which are only given by the Holy Spirit.

God will not force us to marry His Son Jesus, nor will Jesus force Himself on us. We must be the ones willing to be His brides by receiving God the Holy Spirit as our guide to our bridegroom. The Holy Spirit, just like Abraham's servant, leads us through the journey here on earth to get to our bridegroom who is with His Father. Isaac never left his Father's house to go look for his bride. His father, Abraham, had specific instructions not to take Isaac back to where he came from. Jesus has already been here on earth, and He is not coming back as a human being on earth to look for His own bride. God the Holy Spirit is the one sent to get and prepare the bride for Christ and will return with her to Him.

Jesus Christ is such a gentleman. He loved us freely and openly showed us love and affection by dying for us on the cross. He then gave us a choice to accept Him as our bridegroom. He already paid the bride price. Now it's up to us to receive Him in our hearts and be called by His name, just as the bride changes her name to her husband's name.

Christ says in Revelation 3:20 (NKJV): "Behold, I stand at the door and knock. If anyone hears my voice and opens the door, I will come in to him and dine with him, and he with Me."

Would Rebekah have known anything about Isaac and the wealth that awaited her from her bridegroom if Abraham's servant did not inform and lead her? Would she have known the way she should go to get to Isaac if she refused to go with the servant and insisted on going on her own like many of us do? If she had no way of knowing this apart from the servant informing and guiding her to her bridegroom, how much more do you think you can know about Christ without God the Holy Spirit's teaching, revelation, and guidance?

The Bible clearly states that finding and preparing the bride of Christ and making her ready for her bridegroom is the work of the Holy Spirit. If you reject the Holy Spirit, you reject Christ, your bridegroom. If you accept the Holy Spirit, you accept Christ and agree to learn and know your bridegroom intimately. You cannot have Jesus without the Holy Spirit because He is the sent Helper to help us and teach us all things about Jesus and the Kingdom, and to prepare us for Christ and the great wedding supper.

The Spirit and the bride say, "Come!" He who hears, let him say, "Come!" He who is thirsty, let him come. He who desires, let him take the water of life freely. (Revelation 22:17)

The Holy Spirit and the bride are the ones who invite the Lord Jesus Christ to come back for the bride just like when Abraham's servant returned with the bride, Isaac came to pick up his bride. Jesus came to make way for us to be accepted as His brides and children of God because He is God. The Holy Spirit's primary purpose and goal are to take back a prepared bride for Christ. We need Him to cleanse us, purify us, and to make us worthy of our Savior and bridegroom. He puts on us the jewels of purity, righteousness, holiness, love, and beautifies us for our King Jesus. It is so amazing that the Holy Spirit does not give up on us even when we give up on each other. He is the one who inspired the Word of God, and the one who reveals the Word to us, and then the Word cleanses us. The price that heaven paid was too costly for Christ to give up on us so quickly. The Holy Spirit knows this because He was very much a part of the redemption miracle from Christ's conception in Mary's womb to Christ's death and resurrection in Luke 1:35 and Romans 8:11.

If the Holy Spirit was this important for God's plan of redemption to take place, how much more critical is His role now in finalizing what He began? I cannot emphasize enough how much we need Him, so we can know Jesus. I also can't begin to explain to you the joy that the Holy Spirit feels in completing this work inside you. It is His great pleasure! He literally longs for this. Do not wait to be clean to come to Him. Just come to Christ like you are, then let the Holy Spirit cleanse you. Let Him make you the bride of Christ. Rebekah had first to accept to be Isaac's wife and not just that, but she also had to agree to follow the servant who knew where Isaac was for Isaac to marry her.

If Rebekah refused to follow the servant, though she desired to be Isaac's wife from what she heard about him, she would not have been successful in being his bride. She would have given up the privilege of being the wife of the son of the promise, Isaac. Isaac's dad specifically instructed the servant to go without Isaac, and if the woman refused to follow him, Isaac would not go back to the land to look for a wife. The lady who would accept to be Isaac's wife without meeting Isaac personally qualified to be his wife. She, however, had to trust and follow the servant's leadership and guidance in order to meet Isaac personally. She had to entirely rely on the servant to tell her about Isaac and to take her to him for a more intimate relationship and marriage.

THE EUNUCH
(See the book of Esther in the Old Testament)

The king favored Esther because she desired to find out what pleased the king instead of relying on her own beauty or wisdom. The king gave all the girls who came to the contest a eunuch to consult with and to assist them in their preparation to please the king. The king did this because even though the eunuch was biologically unproductive, he was kingdom productive. He knew what pleased the king and what the girls needed to do to win the king's favor and be chosen as the new queen.

Be very careful not to judge as man does because the person whom you despise or look down upon, one who looks "unproductive" in your eyes, might be the same person holding the secret to your breakthrough. They may not seem useful or productive in your eyes, but to God, they are qualified and productive; and if you're not careful, you will miss your blessing because of your judgment. Never despise the eunuchs in your life because they are there to direct you and lead you to your bridegroom.

Esther was the only one among all the girls who made use of her eunuch because she held the king in very high regard and valued his wisdom. She knew that the king doesn't just act without reason, and if the king gave them a eunuch, there was a perfect reason behind it. The eunuch was the key to their success. She, therefore, decided to give up her wishes and desires, her likes and wants for what the king desired and found pleasing. She chose to look at beauty from the king's perspective rather than her own or the other people's perspective. I can picture Esther asking the eunuch what the king loves and desires and learning keenly what pleased the king. She then would practice it until it became her new standard. With this kind of mind-set, Esther had won the contest before she even began competing.

I also picture the other girls asking for each other's opinion and approval and acting on what they thought to be pleasing in their eyes to entice the king. They utterly despised the king's chosen helper. They ignored the eunuch and looked for help from each other—ordinary citizens—instead of the eunuch who was a kingdom dweller. They got too busy with their own desires and likes; they were consumed with what made them look good in their own eyes and in the eyes of the others. They ignored the king's eunuch, who was the key to their success. They did not discern the secret behind the eunuch or his purpose. They had no value for the king and took his wisdom for granted. The eunuch looked unproductive in their eyes, so they despised the key to their destiny. With this mind-set, they had already lost the contest before they even began.

They did not want to let go of their traditions and that of other people to embrace the kingdom traditions. They wanted the kingdom life, wealth, and benefits but not the kingdom sacrifice. Unlike Esther, they wanted to reign with the king without giving up their own desires for the king's. Doesn't that sound like most Christians?

In the end, the girls took a year to prepare to be queen, but they were rejected by the king, while the king instantly chose Esther. God's favor is not fair. It is not how long you have been saved, preaching, or working in the kingdom that qualifies you to rule and reign with Jesus. It is your constant dying to self, living in obedience, sacrificing your desires for His, and your will for His to please Jehovah God. It is continually yielding to the leadership of the Holy Spirit (who would be like the eunuch in the story) that guarantees your selection into God's Kingdom. How much do *you* value and love God?

Our King of kings, Jehovah our God, has called many people to prepare to live in His Kingdom to please Him. He has given us a "eunuch figure"—the Holy Spirit—who is there to teach us everything the King wants and desires. He reveals to us our destiny because He was there during creation, and He saw all that the King put in us. The Holy Spirit knows all things. He has access to the King twenty-four hours a day, seven days a week. He is one with the King.

The Holy Spirit tells us what the King desires and shows

us things from the King's perspective. Just like the eunuch, He is available to you if you want His guidance and expertise, He does not impose on you. Those who listen and obey Him, who seek wisdom from Him on how to please the King, are the only ones who will be chosen as the King's brides. The rest will be rejected in the end. You may be in God's Kingdom, born again, in the palace preparing but doing it in your own wisdom and understanding or other people's wisdom, totally ignoring your eunuch, the Holy Spirit, who knows the heart of the Father. Just like a eunuch was seen as useless outside the kingdom, the world despises the Holy Spirit because they do not see or know Him.

In the end, because all have been called, if you do not seek for guidance and obey the Holy Spirit on how to please the King, you will be rejected. If we want to be chosen to live in God's Kingdom, we must put God's desires before our own desires. We must seek first the Kingdom of God and His righteousness and all these things shall be added unto us. (Matthew 6:33) If we do this, we will be like Esther. We will be favored and chosen as an heir in the Kingdom. But we will be doomed forever if we decide to look for all other things before seeking the Kingdom of God first and His righteousness.

If we, like the other girls, choose to seek the temporary pleasures of the flesh and of the world and then try to seek the king's approval, we will be rejected. It would have been better for us if we had not tasted being in the palace, to begin with. After rejection, the girls never went out to the public again. They became one of the king's concubines and were never invited to go to the king unless he was very pleased with them and summoned them by name which was almost impossible given the many concubines the kings had. They never got to be wives, have children or enjoy a family. Their value diminished, and their state was worse than when they began. Remember Matthew 22:14 . . . Many are called, but few are chosen.

> Before each young woman was taken to the king's bed, she was given the prescribed twelve months of beauty treatments—six months with oil of myrrh, followed by six months with special perfumes and ointments. When it was time for her to go to the king's palace, she was given her choice of whatever clothing or jewelry she wanted to take from the harem. That evening, she was taken to the king's private rooms, and the next morning she was brought to the second harem, where the king's wives lived. There she would be under the care of Shaashgaz, the king's eunuch in charge of the concubines. She would never go to the king again unless he had especially enjoyed her and requested her by name. Esther was the daughter of Abihail, who was Mordecai's uncle. (Mordecai had adopted his younger cousin Esther.) When it was Esther's turn to go to the king, <u>**she accepted the advice of Hegai, the eunuch in charge of the harem. She asked for nothing except what he suggested, and she was admired by everyone who saw her.**</u> Esther was taken to King Xerxes at the royal palace in early winter of the seventh year of his reign. ***And the king loved Esther more than any of the other young women. He was so delighted with her that he set the royal crown on her head and declared her queen instead of Vashti.*** (Esther 2:12–17, NLT; emphasis added)

Esther only did what the eunuch suggested. She accepted his advice fully and was declared queen on the spot. What a counselor! I want to be declared a bride of Christ on the spot and crowned a child of God! Do you? We must listen to, accept, and do only what the Holy Spirit advises us to do.

CHAPTER 8

SINS AGAINST MY FRIEND THE HOLY SPIRIT

THE HOLY SPIRIT is the most protected Godhead. The Bible warns us from sinning against God the Holy Spirit. Let us look at some of the sins against the Holy Spirit mentioned in God's Word.

- **My Friend Can Be Blasphemed.**

"Most certainly I tell you, all sins of the descendants of man will be forgiven, including their blasphemies with which they may blaspheme; but whoever may blaspheme against the Holy Spirit never has forgiveness, but is subject to eternal condemnation."—because they said, "He has an unclean spirit." (Mark 3:28–30).

Many people blaspheme the Holy Spirit when they

condemn His work in men and women and saying that they are the works of the evil spirits. If you are not sure which spirit is operating in a person, do not judge. You need to pray for the spirit of discernment which God will give to you graciously, rather than letting you sin against the Holy Spirit. Do not credit God's work to the devil. The price heaven paid is too costly for the enemy to take credit for it.

- **My Friend Can Be Grieved.**

"And do not grieve the Holy Spirit of God, by whom you were sealed for the day of redemption." (Eph. 4:30)

The Holy Spirit is grieved by rebellion and disobedience when we continue to practice sin even after He has warned us. The Holy Spirit is very patient. He can also be taken away from us. I grieved the Holy Spirit once in my very close walk with Him. He was very patient and warned me several times about something I was doing that would lead to my downfall, but I had more confidence in my flesh than I should have. As surely as the Holy Spirit had warned me, I fell and grieved Him, and He was taken away from me.

"But they rebelled and grieved His Holy Spirit; So He turned Himself against them as an enemy, And He fought against them." (Isa. 63:10)

God became their enemy when they grieved the Holy Spirit. It is a dangerous thing to have God as your enemy. This is described by the Israelites in the wilderness, who had a habit of disobedience and rebellion. The Holy Spirit is very patient and will help you through your mistakes. If you learn and turn away from them, He will use your mistakes to make you a better person, but if you practice sin, He will be taken away from you.

"Create in me a clean heart, O God. Renew a right spirit within me. Don't throw me from your presence, and don't take your Holy Spirit from me. Restore to me the joy of your salvation. Uphold me with a willing spirit." (Ps. 51:10–12)

This scripture was King David's prayer after he murdered one of his faithful soldiers, Uriah the Hittite, to cover up his sin of adultery against him. David took Uriah's wife, Bathsheba, when Uriah was in battle and impregnated her. He then sent for Uriah from battle so he could come home to sleep with his wife, but Uriah refused to be comfortable with his wife while his fellow soldiers were still in combat. David got him drunk, but Uriah slept outside the palace, not in his house. David, seeing that he would be found out, sent Uriah back to the battlefield with his own death note, instructing the commander of the army to assign Uriah a position in the heat of battle so he would be killed. After this was done, David was so grieved by this sin. He repented and prayed for forgiveness and for God not to take His Holy Spirit from him. He asked God to restore the joy of his salvation that he had lost to sin. When the Holy Spirit is taken away, you lose joy and peace that He gives. David was where I had been when I lost the Holy Spirit.

Many times we get into the same predicament, but if we confess our sins, God is faithful and just to forgive us and cleanse us from all unrighteousness. David knew this and had faith in God's grace.

- **My Friend Can Be Taken Away.** This is spiritual starvation, which may lead to spiritual death.

My friend . . . was taken away from me.

Once, years ago, the Holy Spirit warned me several times

of the danger of falling into sin while I was busy helping someone else. He said, "If the person you are trying to rescue from drowning was pulling you down into the water and fighting the rescue, you must leave them alone, or both of you will drown." He again said, "It is easier to be pulled down by someone who's in a low position than for you to pull them up." We are not God; only God changes people.

"But others save with fear, pulling them out of the fire, hating even the garment defiled by the flesh." (Jude 1:23)

I had confidence in myself and my flesh instead of taking precautions as the Holy Spirit had warned. I fell into sin against His temple, and my life was stained because I did it by my might and wisdom. When I grieved the Holy Spirit, and He was taken away from me, I was the most miserable person ever. This is because He was my best friend, my teacher, counselor, comforter, and source of wisdom. He was everything to me. He told me of things before they happened, helped me through the things I faced at that specific time, gave me words to speak when I had none, encouraged me, and revealed my destiny to me. I lost *everything* when I lost Him.

I learned my lesson really fast and very painfully because I used to and still do write songs only by the power of my friend the Holy Spirit. But when He left, I did not get any new songs. I prayed and confessed my sin, repented, turned back to God, and asked God to give me back His Spirit. I came to realize that no person or thing is worth me losing God the Holy Spirit for. My God the Holy Spirit was and is worth more than life itself.

For almost a whole year, from January to November, I never received any song from Him. Then in November, a song came, and that was how I knew that God had mercy on me and had given me back His Holy Spirit. The song was in the Swahili language saying, "Touch me once more, touch me once more, fill me with Your Holy Spirit, Lord, touch me once more, touch me once more." I was extremely excited, and from then on, I learned NEVER to grieve the Holy Spirit of God. Life is empty and unbearable without Him. No one is greater; nothing is better. I had rather lose it all than lose my best friend. Thank God for a very tough but unforgettable lesson. Living without hearing from God through His Spirit is like going deaf and blind all of a sudden after enjoying great eyesight and hearing.

I plead with you, don't grieve the Holy Spirit. He has feelings; He is sensitive and passionate. He transforms us into the image of Christ. That's why Jesus said you could blaspheme Jesus (the Son of God) all you want, but never do it to the Holy Spirit. Even the blood of Jesus cannot cleanse you from this unforgivable sin. I hope and pray that you enjoy and cherish God the Holy Spirit and don't wait to lose Him to know His value. Many people see the importance of someone or something only after they lose it. Learn from my mistake, because it is the worst feeling one would ever have. I tremble at the remembrance of that hopeless and helpless feeling I had.

David was a witness of King Saul not having the Spirit of God. King Saul's rebellion cost him the Holy Spirit, and as a result, an evil spirit would torture him from time to time. David, the shepherd boy, would play music for King Soul so that the evil spirit would stop tormenting him. David knew what it was like to have the Holy Spirit, and after he sinned, he could not imagine living without God the Holy Spirit in His life. He lost his joy and peace and pleaded to God to have Him back.

"Then Samuel took the horn of oil, and anointed him in the middle of his brothers. Then Yahweh's Spirit came mightily on David from that day forward. So Samuel rose up and went to Ramah. Now Yahweh's Spirit departed from Saul, and an evil spirit from Yahweh troubled him." (1 Sam. 16:13–14)

Samson, the strongest man ever, lost the Holy Spirit through disobedience.

When Delilah saw that he had told her all his heart, she sent and called for the lords of the Philistines, saying, "Come up this once, for he has told me all his heart." Then the lords of the Philistines came up to her, and brought the money in their hand. She made him sleep on her knees; and she called for a man, and shaved off the seven locks of his head; and she began to afflict him, and his strength went from him. She said, "The Philistines are upon you, Samson!" He awoke out of his sleep, and said, "I will go out as at other times, and shake myself free." *But he didn't know that Yahweh had departed from him.* (Judges 16:18–20, italics added)

Samson was destroyed for disobedience. He grieved the Holy Spirit, who was in him, by disclosing the secret of his strength to his enemies and having his hair cut off, which God had commanded him not to do.

If you have grieved the Holy Spirit, and He has been taken away, know that God is gracious and merciful. You must confess your sin, repent, and turn away from your sin and seek God again with passion until God gives Him back to you. Only God the Father can give you back His Spirit. He gave us His Son, but He never stopped at that. Because of His infinite love, God gave us His Holy Spirit as well. What a great God we serve! He sets us up to be fully equipped to succeed and live as children of God on earth. The same power and strength Christ had while on earth that helped Him through His God-given task is the same power you and I have to fulfill our God-given assignment. Glory to God and thank God for the Holy Spirit!

Some people may argue and say, Jesus said that the Holy Spirit would be with us forever in John 14:16. Yes, but Christ put a condition on this promise. If we keep sinning, do we assume that the Holy Spirit will continue to stay in us? As far as the Holy Spirit is concerned, God the Father and God the Son do not leave us, but we can leave them. As for the Holy Spirit, He does not leave. He is taken away by the Father and given back to us by the Father. This is seen during Saul's demotion as king.

"If you love me, keep my commandments. I will pray to the Father, and he will give you another Counselor, that he may be with you forever—the Spirit of truth, whom the world can't receive; for it doesn't see him, neither knows him. You know him, for he lives with you, and will be in you." (John 14:15–17)

We must love Christ through obedience and yielding to the Holy Spirit as our mentor. In doing so, the Holy Spirit will come and remain in us forever. But for those who rebel, the Holy Spirit cannot dwell in you and go with you to hell. He cannot strive with you as God said in Genesis 6:1–3 when sin abounded, and men wanted to lead themselves into their own lusts.

The Holy Spirit is a guarantee for those who are in Christ Jesus alone. Remember, He will not operate apart from the Word, and the Word will not work unless the Father speaks or sends the Word. If you insist on disobedience like I did, the Holy Spirit will be taken away from you. Realize that even in the Old Testament, the Holy Spirit did not remove Himself from the people. He did not leave them. He was taken away by the Father at His Word (the Son). The Holy Spirit did not speak; the Father spoke and said:

"When men began to multiply on the surface of the ground, and daughters were born to them, God's sons saw that men's daughters were beautiful, and they took any that they wanted for themselves as wives. Yahweh said, "My Spirit will not strive with man forever, because he also is flesh; so his days will be one hundred twenty years." (Genesis 6:1–3)

Notice that when the Spirit of God was taken away, the lifespan of man was decreased significantly. Before that, humans used to live very long. Methuselah lived the longest at 969 years—almost 1,000 years old! God cut down 849 years to only 120 years. See what disobedience yields? Death!

Genesis 5:27 says, "All the days of Methuselah were nine hundred sixty-nine years, then he died."

- **My Friend Cannot Be Deceived or Lied To.**

The Holy Spirit is God. No one can ever lie to God. God is all-knowing, omnipotent, omnipresent, and omniscient. He is the discerner of the hearts of people. He knows the intentions of our hearts. He created humans.

"Do not be deceived, God is not mocked; for whatever a man sows, that he will also reap." (Gal. 6:7)

It is a great deception to think that we can lie to God.

- **My Friend Can Be Quenched.**

"Do not quench the Spirit." (1 Thess. 5:19)
A Pastor Suffers the Consequences of Quenching My Friend
I was in a situation where the pastor in the church I attended quenched God the Holy Spirit during worship on a

Resurrection Sunday. It all began when God gave me a new song, and the Holy Spirit had been teaching me on worship. I recorded the music with my producer and asked the pastor's wife if I could share the song in worship at church. I told her that I was willing to wait until they had a chance for me to worship God. I said this because they usually permitted people to sing to the congregation. Some were genuine, others were performers. Being a worshiper, I desired to lead people into worship with the new song, allowing the Holy Spirit to move in the congregation.

She was excited and asked me to go and share with the praise and worship team at their Saturday meeting what the Holy Spirit had taught me on worship and then sing the song on Sunday, just before the pastor preached. I was extremely excited since I had rivers of living water bubbling in my belly, ready to flow. On the Wednesday of the same week, before Resurrection Sunday, I was doing my devotions and Bible study in my dining room when God the Holy Spirit spoke to me as clearly as He always did. He said, "I don't want you to lead worship just before the pastor comes. I want you to lead the worship in the main worship service."

I was shocked! I was not part of the praise and worship team, so how could I take over and lead worship? But I knew not to argue with Him, so I responded, "You know what a privilege and honor it is for me to get a chance to worship at all this soon, not counting, it is even harder and very special to get a chance to sing just before the preacher preaches. Nevertheless, I will do whatever you want me to do, but please, you tell this to the pastor's wife."

As soon as we finished this conversation with the Holy Spirit, my phone began vibrating on the couch in my living room, and I went to see who was texting me.

It was the pastor's wife saying, "Hi, I am sorry. I forgot that I had put someone else to sing just before the pastor preached, but I would like you to lead the main worship service on Sunday. It will be very powerful if the other person sings, and you lead the worship." You can just imagine what my reaction was! Yes, you are absolutely right! My jaw dropped, and I was amazed at how God worked so fast. God knew what my answer would be because He created me, and so He had already dealt with the pastor's wife.

I told the pastor's wife of the conversation I had a few minutes ago with the Holy Spirit, and she was shocked and excited.

I went and spoke to the worship team on Saturday and taught them the worship song. The worship team and I were amazed and marveled at the Holy Spirit and how He revealed God to us that day.

Then Resurrection Sunday came, and just as God had instructed me to lead worship, I obeyed and the Holy Spirit took over entirely. I was in the service, being led by God the Holy Spirit. But before I knew it, the pastor came out of his seat and started talking on the microphone over me. He signaled the sound team to cut my sound off and sent his wife up on the stage to stop me. Before I knew what was going on, the pastor's wife touched my shoulder, and when I looked at her, she snatched her hand so fast from my shoulder, moved back and looked down and could not look at me anymore. She acted as if she had seen a ghost. She was trembling. I knew that God had revealed something to her, and she realized what they had just done. Immediately, the Holy Spirit reminded me of a dream He had shown me a few weeks earlier concerning the church, and all that was happening in the dream just replayed at that moment.

In the dream, my husband and I were in church sitting in the congregation. The pastor and his wife were standing at the pulpit and were busy looking at some paperwork. Upon the altar, I saw that the dark red curtains were falling off entirely on one side. I rushed from my chair up to the altar and climbed up a chair so I could reach and fix the curtains before they fell off the whole altar. My husband came and helped me on the other side by holding up the curtain rod as I put back the curtain. The pastor and his wife were very busy looking at some paperwork and were oblivious to the fallen curtains at the altar. As I was busy putting the curtains back, God warned the pastor and his wife through my husband, who shouted out to them repeatedly, pointing at the curtains and what I was doing as he tried to get their attention three times saying; "*You cannot ignore this for the next level! You cannot ignore this for the next level! You cannot ignore this for the next level!*" Then I woke up from the dream.

In reality, at the service that day, the pastor attempted to stop the service, but the Holy Spirit made him repeat all the songs we had sung. The pastor later called the worship team leaders in a meeting and told them that I was demon possessed. My husband and I were so discouraged that Sunday when we went home that we went and took a nap. I asked God the Holy Spirit to encourage me. He asked me why I was discouraged. He said that the pastor and his wife never attacked me; they attacked Him. He asked me a simple question. "If someone comes to fight you, do they fight you or the clothes you are wearing? You are my outfit." He said, "They attacked me, not you. The pastor called me a demon, for I was in you. If you need encouragement, you know the principle: give, and it shall come back to you, in good measure, pressed down, shaken together, and running over. If you need encouragement, encourage someone else."

I went and got scripture from the Bible and sent it to all my phone contacts. In a few minutes, I received many encouraging texts back, and the text-messaging ministry was birthed out of the pain and need for encouragement. A ministry was birthed out of my misery. That ministry exists to this day, reaching many around the world. From this experience in church, I had been called overly spiritual by people in the church and by my "friends." Others thought I was demon possessed. My husband did not understand my friendship with God the Holy Spirit and the boldness in me to share God's message and to prophecy to the pastor and others I was sent to. He had felt bad for me and also felt embarrassed by the incident in church. My husband had said to me that day as we drove home, "That is why I told you not to speak in public."

I confidently said to him that I was willing to be ridiculed and persecuted for Christ's sake. I made it clear that I was willing to obey God even unto death. A few months later, the pastor called my husband and me to the side one Sunday after service. He was very broken and he apologized to us for his behavior that Resurrection Sunday.

He confessed and said that he realized he had quenched the Holy Spirit because he was a respecter of people. He went on to say that these same people whom he had feared and respected had now turned against him. The pastor explained that, on that Resurrection Sunday, he feared that his unsaved church members, who were his big supporters would get bored, so he came up and cut off the Holy Spirit. Thinking he was attacking me, he attacked God Himself. Some very prayerful intercessors left because they said that they had travailed in the Spirit for revival and the move of God, and when it finally happened . . . The pastor chased God away.

Needless to say, he ignored what God wanted to do, and he never got to the next level. He later lost his new church building, which was worth over a million dollars, as well as more than half of his church members. The pastor lost his influence to many because he did not value what God valued. He feared people and not God. Because he was not sensitive to God the Holy Spirit, he kicked God out of His own house but embraced people who did not care anything about God.

"No one can serve two masters. Either you will hate the one and love the other, or you will be devoted to the one and despise the other. You cannot serve both God and money." (Matt. 6:24 NIV)

We must all know that God is not a respecter of persons. He values and protects God the Holy Spirit. Let us love God enough to appreciate what He values and not fall into the sin of quenching, grieving, or blaspheming God the Holy Spirit.

Many years later after this incident, after praying for this church and pastor, we met him in another country doing outreach ministry. I pray that he learned from this experience and is now serving God with all his heart, following the leadership of God the Holy Spirit.

CHAPTER 9

MY FRIEND THE HOLY SPIRIT AND I

- **My friend teaches me how to pray.**

Healed of a severe headache.

ONE DAY, I woke up with a throbbing headache. I was scheduled to work that day, but the headache was so severe that my husband asked me to call off work. I had faith in God that He would heal me, and besides, it was too late to call off work. I prayed as I got ready for work, saying, "Father, in Jesus' name, thank you for waking me up this evening (I worked the night shift). I have a headache, and it hurts so badly, please—"

Before I could finish, my friend the Holy Spirit stopped me and said to me, "What are you saying?"

I asked Him, "What do you mean what I am I saying?"

He replied saying, "God knows about your headache, but the headache doesn't know about your God! Did David, while facing Goliath, pray and tell God about Goliath, or did he tell Goliath about his God? Did Shadrach, Meshach, and Abednego tell God about the king who wanted to throw them into the fiery furnace, that was heated seven times higher than normal, or did they tell King Nebuchadnezzar about their God? Jesus said if you speak to the mountain and tell it to move, by faith, it shall move! He never said you shall speak to Him about the mountain."

There you go! A great prayer lesson learned! Immediately, my prayer changed from a prayer of sympathy to a prayer of faith because God doesn't respond to anything but faith. I told the headache about my God, who is my healer, about the finished work of the cross, and my victory in Christ Jesus. I reminded the headache that by the stripes of Jesus Christ, I was healed over two thousand years ago, and my healing was not negotiable. By the time I got to work, the headache was gone and never returned!

I shared this with my patient and his family, who needed the same Word. Without the help of my friend the Holy Spirit, the headache would have succeeded in stealing my joy, peace, money, and patient care. My patient would have missed this Word from God when he needed it most. With God, we are more than conquerors because we have His Spirit, who helps us fight these battles. Let us embrace the Holy Spirit in us to teach us all things and remind us of things God has taught us. Hallelujah!

- **My friend reminds me in temptation.**

It was about 3:00 a.m. when the Holy Spirit woke me up to pray. As I prayed for a friend's mother who was a minister of the Gospel but was suffering from ESRD (End Stage Renal Disease) and was on dialysis, I heard demons threatening me, saying, "You better stop praying, because if you don't, we will do to you what we did to your mother."

I knew they had caused my dad's stroke because my mother is a minister of the Gospel, and she does deliverance ministry. The demons hate it, so they attacked my dad to distract her from her ministry. They were threatening to attack my husband in the same way they did my father. I ignored them, finished praying, and went to bed. I used to lie with my child, who was about two years old at the time because my husband traveled a lot as a businessman.

About thirty minutes into my sleep, the Holy Spirit said to me, "Turn around."

I had been lying on my abdomen, so I turned around and lay on my back. As soon as I turned, I looked up at the white ceiling in the dark room. Formless black demonic spirits were hovering from side to side that filled my ceiling. My first thought was that these demons had come to get me, but my baby was there, and I wished they had found me alone. Immediately, God the Holy Spirit reminded me of a scripture I had read a few weeks before. He asked me to proclaim that I am hidden in Christ in God!

This scripture amazed me with the fact that in Christ, I am protected in layers, and I am untouchable. If anyone were to come to get me, they would have to go through God the Father to get to God the Son to get to me, which is impossible to go through. It is like being the yolk of an egg inside a chicken. For anyone to get to you, they must catch the chicken, kill it, take the egg, break it, and then get the yolk. How hidden we truly are!

"If then you have been raised with Christ, seek the things that are above, where Christ is, seated at the right hand of God. Set your minds on things that are above, not on things that are on earth. For you have died, and *your life is hidden with Christ in God.*" (Col. 3:1–3, italics added)

I shouted from the scripture, "*I am hidden with Christ in God!*" and immediately, the demons vanished! I felt the protection and boldness come over me. I commanded the demons never to come back or even interrupt my sleep anymore. I slept as peaceful as a baby after that.

In the morning, the Holy Spirit gently asked me, "Do you know why they came?"

"No," I replied. "Why did they come?"

He gently responded, "Because when they threatened you, you did not speak back the Word of God like Jesus did in the wilderness when the devil tempted him. When you kept quiet, it showed that you accepted their threat and by so doing, you opened a door for them to attack you legally in the spirit. Remember how Jesus responded to every test in the wilderness? Jesus responded by quoting God's Word, and He won! The Word of God is the sword that destroys the enemy."

From that day, I learned my lesson. Whenever evil thoughts come—and by evil, I mean, thoughts not of God or ideas contrary to what God has said or promised—I fight back with God's Word. For example, when I feel fearful, or I get thoughts of fear, I know that fear is not from God, so I do what the Word of God says. "We use God's mighty weapons, not worldly weapons, to knock down the strongholds of human reasoning and to destroy false arguments. We destroy every proud obstacle that keeps people from knowing God. We capture their rebellious thoughts and teach them to obey Christ." (2 Corinthians 10:4–5, NLT)

I know that these thoughts of fear are not just thoughts, but strongholds, arguments, and high things that exalt themselves against the knowledge of God. I, therefore, get the weapon of our warfare, which is the Word of God, to counter the attacks of the enemy. "And take the helmet of salvation, and the sword of the Spirit, which is the word of God." (Ephesians 6:17). For the spirit of fear, I quote the scripture in 2 Timothy 1:7 and personalize it. I speak it to the spirit of fear that is trying to come in me, and I declare that "God has not given me a spirit of fear, but He has given me a spirit of power, a spirit of love, and a spirit of a sound mind. So I rebuke you, spirit of fear, now and expel you from me in Jesus' name!"

This scripture tells me what stronghold I am dealing with; it is a spirit called fear. Fear is a stronghold and it partners with the spirit of anxiety. Remember, the weapons of our warfare are not carnal but are mighty through God. Through the Word of God, I immediately get the victory over any evil spirit. Notice that power is a spirit, love is a spirit, and a sound mind is a spirit. Ask God to replace the evil spirit that causes mental instability with the spirit of power, love, and sound mind. Physical, mental, and spiritual health is a promise from God. Jesus paid for it. By His stripes we were healed.

"But He was wounded for our transgressions, He was crushed for our wickedness [our sin, our injustice, our wrongdoing]; the punishment [required] for our well-being fell on Him, and by His stripes (wounds) we are healed." (Isaiah 53:5, AMP)

Jesus paid for our well-being and healing! A sound mind

is paid for! Claim it, believe it, and receive it in His name! A lady I worked with had a fear of flying. She shared this with me, and I told her about fear being a spirit from the enemy. I explained to her that we defeat the enemy by the sword of the Spirit, which is the Word of God. I gave her the assignment of looking up in the Bible what God says about fear, which she did. She came back after a mini vacation, where she took a flight with her family. She took God at His Word and declared it. The scripture that worked for her was Isaiah 41:10, NLT: "Don't be afraid, for I am with you. Don't be discouraged, for I am your God. I will strengthen you and help you. I will hold you up with my victorious right hand."

The battlefield is in the mind. If you win it in your mind, then it is easier to win it in the physical because it has not entered your heart. Scripture says we must guard our hearts, for the heart is the wellspring of life. Just like you wouldn't sign for a package that is not yours. Likewise, we must cast down arguments and every high thing that exalts itself against the knowledge of God as it comes. Refuse to take anything that the enemy delivers to you. Jesus did not suffer for nothing. He paid all the debt we owed because of sin. We are free to live for God.

Beloved, read the Word of God and store up treasures in you, that God the Holy Spirit may remind you what you should say at the right time.

- **My friend gives me the gift of discernment of spirits.**

My husband's life is saved.

My husband worked as a businessman, driving our truck from state to state, while I went to nursing school and took care of our three precious boys. He was not comfortable on the road with someone else watching our children, and we both agreed it was best for our family that I stop working and raise our children. I was a director in an assisted living facility at the time, so I stopped working when our third baby was born. I was home alone with the children most of the time all week, and he would come home on the weekends. Sometimes he came back for a few days in the middle of the week, depending on his workload and the distance.

One morning, as I was doing dishes right before I went to school, I heard a voice. It was a still, calm voice that said, "Your husband is going to die today." If I did not have the Holy Spirit of God in me and His gift of discernment, I would have thought it was God telling me this before it happened to prepare me. However, with the help of the Holy Spirit, I knew it was Lucifer himself, not just his demons—and definitely not God, because God is not the author of confusion. He does not contradict His Word or promises. I knew what God had spoken about my husband's destiny. He promised us long lives, and I knew that my husband was God's voice to me as the head of our home. God spoke and still speaks to me through my husband, and I was not about to let it go. My husband was not going to die prematurely!

I immediately remembered what the Holy Spirit taught me, to speak back the Word of God to the enemy. I had nothing to fear with the Word of God and my Helper with me. I said to Lucifer out loud and sternly, "No! My husband will *not* die today, because he is God's voice to me, and God has promised us long lives. My husband has a great future ahead; therefore, NO! My husband will not die today, but he will live to tell the goodness of the LORD in the land of the living!"

I finished doing the dishes and left for school. That day, I tried reaching my husband on the phone several times but to no avail. Then at about 3:30 p.m., my phone rang. It was a call from a number I did not recognize. I picked it up, and it was my husband! I asked him what was going on, and he went on to explain that he had been walking for about five miles to get to a phone because his phone did not have any network.

He continued to explain that his truck had lost control and was now hanging off a cliff in the Tennessee mountains. He had called a tow truck company, whose crew had a difficult time trying to recover the truck. They could not get to it easily without compromising their safety and that of our truck. They suggested that the best option to recover the truck was to flip it on its side and pull it out. This would cause a significant loss on our part. My husband prayed for God's wisdom to recover our truck, and he told them to look for other ways to do it besides flipping it. Finally, after a long struggle, they recovered the truck safely. My husband was alive and safe, all glory to God! I told him about my conversation with the devil earlier that morning. He was shocked and very grateful that I did not agree with the enemy's plan.

When you trust in God and are led by His Holy Spirit, the enemy cannot do anything to you unless you permit him to. The enemy wanted to kill my husband and was in a sly way, asking for my approval. But because God the Holy Spirit is my Helper, and I read and listen to the spoken Word of God through spending time with Him, I did not fall for the evil trick. Jesus said that His sheep hear His voice, and a stranger they will not follow.

Most certainly, I tell you, one who doesn't enter by the door into the sheepfold, but climbs up some other way, the same is a thief and a robber. But one who enters in by the door is the shepherd of the sheep. The gatekeeper opens the gate for him, and the sheep listen to his voice. He calls his own sheep by name, and leads them out. Whenever he brings out his own sheep, he goes before them, and the sheep follow him, for they know his voice. They will by no means follow a stranger, but will flee from him; for they don't know the voice of strangers. (John 10:1–5)

- **My friend reveals to me the enemy's plan of a deadly accident on my family member.**

One day on my way from work as I drove to my son's race, I felt the urge to pray in tongues and not listen to music, audio book, or preaching in the car as I mostly did. I drove and prayed in tongues flowing in the spirit, when I felt strongly that there was a car accident planned on my family. I started thinking of my family members who were out driving at the time. I thought it was probably targeted on my son and me on the way back home from the race, but I also remembered that my husband was out of town travelling too. My other son was out running errands as well. I began praying against this evil scheme of darkness, and I hid us all in Christ in God, canceling all the evil plans of darkness.

I then received a song from the Holy Spirit on "Immanuel". Immanuel is God's name meaning "God with us."

"Look! The virgin will conceive a child! She will give birth to a son, and they will call him Immanuel, which means 'God is with us.'" (Matthew 1:23 NLT)

The song goes:

> "IMMANUEL, GOD WITH US, CLOSE TO US, NEVER AFAR, IMMANUEL, I'M NOT AFRAID I WALK WITH HIM, IMMANUEL."

I sang this song until it changed from '*I'm not afraid*' to '*I'm not alone*'. I was deeply and strongly assured in my spirit of Emmanuel's presence with my family at all times. I was received so much peace and contentment as I sang this song over and over again. After I was done praying and singing, while still on my way to my son's race about one and a half hours from home, my son who was running errands called me and said that he had been involved in an accident. I asked him how he was and if he had been injured. He reported no injuries. I was glad and relieved that he was the one calling me and not someone else reporting his accident.

I asked him if he had injured anyone else, and he said no. He said that he was all alone in the incident. The car was damaged, the windshield all shattered but my baby boy was unharmed. Immanuel was right there with him. The car damage looked worse than it really was. It took a few hours to fix it. The evil plan of darkness was for my son to have a roll over where he would have been injured and or killed, but Immanuel took control of the car that to this day we cannot explain how the car did not rollover, injure, or kill anyone apart from Immanuel's intervention.

My Friend, the Holy Spirit led me to tap into the heaven's network and download the evil plans of darkness so as to dismantle and destroy it. I now intimately know my Jesus as my family's Immanuel.

- **My friend gives me the Father's eyes.**

What God sees when He looks at humans.

One day in Kennesaw State University's parking lot in Georgia, U.S.A., I sat in my car with a lady I will call Grace (not her real name), and we were talking excitedly about the goodness of Jesus. As we spoke, I felt as if Jesus were there listening in, enjoying the conversation of His praises, when suddenly I was caught up in heaven. I was standing on the left side of God the Father, and HE shone so brightly that when I tried to turn my head to look at Him, my neck would not allow me to turn and look into the extremely, extravagantly bright light coming from Him. It was too strong for my natural eyes. Now I know what Paul meant when he wrote . . .

"which in its own times he will show, who is the blessed and only Ruler, the King of kings, and Lord of lords; who alone has immortality, dwelling in unapproachable light; whom no man has seen, nor can see: to whom be honor and eternal power. Amen." (1 Timothy 6:15–16)

In front of us stood many slender, beige-colored beings, some so small and tiny, some medium-sized, and some so tall that there was no end to them.

I said to God, "Father, what are we looking at?"

He responded, "This is what I see when I look at humans. These are their spirits. Do you see these that are tiny and malnourished? These are the spirits of men and women who don't read the Word of God, pray, obey, or grow in bearing fruit. You see these tall ones without any end? These are the obedient children who pray, seek God, read the Word of God, hear God's voice, and respond promptly in obedience. These people bear much fruit, and you don't see their end because there is no limit to the Spirit!"

Then immediately, as quickly as I left earth, I returned into my car. This happened so fast that Grace did not notice that I had been caught up in heaven in the spirit. It was so fast that our conversation was not interrupted at all.

"Wow! God has just given me His eyes to see!" I said to Grace and went on to tell her about my experience.

This is a great revelation and challenge to all people. It is true when God told the prophet Samuel in 1 Samuel 16:7 (NKJV), But the Lord said to Samuel, "Do not look at his appearance or at his physical stature, because I have refused him. For the Lord does not see as man sees; for man looks at the outward appearance, but the Lord looks at the heart."

What does God see in *you*? Are you malnourished or growing beyond limits? If God gave us His eyes to look at your spirit, what would we see? Let's seek God and invest in eternity. The body will soon die, but the spirit will live forever. We can, therefore, invest in the flesh, which leads to eternal death or invest in the spirit, which leads to eternal life. We have a free will. God already did His part by giving us life through His Son Jesus Christ. It is up to us to accept Him and live our lives in total obedience to Him. This should be our first priority in life, not in the temporary pleasures of sin. Like Jesus said in Mark 8:36, what would it profit us if we gained the whole world and lost our soul? Let us always be led by the Holy Spirit of God, and we shall be victorious!

Remember, we are spirits in a body and not the other way round. We were spirits first, and then God prepared a body for us to do His will. When you look at yourself in the mirror, what you see is your outfit; the person wearing your body is the *real* you, your spirit. Just as you are not the clothes you wear, you are not the body you wear. When people speak with you, they don't talk to your clothes; they speak to the person wearing the clothes. Likewise, God does not speak to our body. He speaks to the one wearing the body, the spirit that you are. Jesus said in John 4:24 that God is Spirit, and they who worship Him MUST worship Him in spirit and in truth. When you remove your clothes, those clothes cannot move or function independently; your clothes only move and go places when you wear them.

Likewise, our body can never function without the spirit. When the spirit of a person leaves him or her, the body dies. It falls down and cannot rise again. Unfortunately, this truth has been hidden to many by the enemy, and we see many people taking care of their outward appearance and neglecting their spirits. They feed the desires of their body and flesh and ignore what truly keeps them alive, their spirits. That is why Jesus said, "Woe to you, scribes and Pharisees, hypocrites! For you cleanse the outside of the cup and dish, but inside they are full of extortion and self-indulgence. Blind Pharisee, first cleanse the inside of the cup and dish, that the outside of them may be clean also. Woe to you, scribes and Pharisees, hypocrites! For you are like whitewashed tombs, which indeed appear beautiful outwardly, but inside are full of dead men's bones and all uncleanness. Even so you also outwardly appear righteous to men, but inside you are full of hypocrisy and lawlessness." (Matt. 23:25–29, NKJV)

- **My friend is a Spirit of warfare.**

He teaches me spiritual warfare.

One night I had a dream that was so real in the spirit. In this dream, my Helper, the Holy Spirit, was disclosing to me what the enemy was doing in the spirit. I dreamt that I was asleep but suddenly woken up by a loud, deafening sound of my home security system alarm. I went out of the bedroom and to the hallway. Coming toward my bedroom was an extremely tall lady carrying a small basket with some flyers in it. She was heading straight to my bedroom, where my husband lay. I stopped her outside in the hall and asked her who she was and what she was doing in my house. She said she was going to give my husband something, and that she had entered my house because "I found your door closed but not LOCKED." As tall as she was, I found myself fighting her with a strategy that I could not have known on my own. With the knowledge and strength of the Holy Spirit, He fought her through me. I twisted her arm behind her, hit the back of her knee with my knee, which forced her to kneel in a submissive position; then I beat her up and threw her down the stairs and out of the door. She tried to resist but was defeated miserably! Upon her leaving, she injected the palm of my hand with something very painful as she was on the ground beaten.

Upon waking up the following morning, I felt my muscles very sore! I asked my husband why I felt sore all over as if I had worked out. Then I remembered that it was all from the warfare in the dream. It manifested in my physical body! I then knew that I had a war to fight for my marriage. Sure enough, it was a tough and painful one to the point of my marriage being on life support. I remember twelve years into our marriage, on Halloween day, we sat around a table and were going to get divorced, but God turned it around to the beginning of life and change in our marriage. By God's grace, we made it through it all and emerged stronger and better from the pain we suffered. We have learned obedience like Christ did, from the things we suffered. (Hebrews 5:8)

During the time I waged war for my marriage, the Holy Spirit instructed me when to pray, how to pray, and when to attack instead of praying. He is a strategist when it comes to war. I obeyed Him, and He did it for me! He can and will do the same for you.

The Holy Spirit revealed to me that my marriage was suffering and struggling because I had it in my hands. He said that the enemy was messing with it because he could get to it. As I was in my living room praying, it felt so real that I had my marriage in my hands. The Holy Spirit said to me that as long as I had my marriage in my hands, the devil can and will steal it from me. But if I place it in God's hands, he can never take it from God. He instructed me to close my marriage door, and this time, lock it and give the key to Jesus. I immediately repented and lifted my hands with my marriage on them and in tears, cried to God, asking Him to please take my marriage. I went on asking Him desperately to take it because I was tired of the enemy messing around with it. I was tired and exhausted! Fighting for this marriage for twelve-plus years and still, the days that we are miserable outweighed our good days. Everything you can think of had gone wrong in our marriage. Our love for our children is what kept us together and fighting to keep our marriage.

As I stood there in my living room in Georgia, hands held

up high as if carrying some massive package with the heavy weight of my marriage on it, with tears streaming down my cheeks, I surrendered my marriage to God and begged Him to take it. Suddenly and unexpectedly, my hands dropped from the lifted position. My prayers were suddenly cut short! The sudden drop of my hands made me realize how heavy my marriage weighed on me. However, the heavy load had been lifted! That was when I realized that marriage in my hands was a real load! I had carried a hefty package all my married life, and I was tired and wore out!

In disbelief and amazement, looking up to heaven I said, "Huh? You took it! Oh, Jesus! You took my marriage! Oh, God, you took my marriage!" and now tears of pain turned into tears of unexplainable, uncontainable joy and relief! And… Oh yes, you guessed it right! I started dancing, rejoicing, and praising God! That is my friend the Holy Spirit! He is the most amazing teacher and friend. He doesn't like to see us suffer while we carry what belongs to God. He will reveal to you what you need to take care of, your part to play, and what God needs to take care of, God's part. When we try to play God, we will die prematurely because we were created to need God not to act God. We cannot be God and take His place, and neither will God take our place. We do our part, and He does His. We are children of God and God is our Father. We must realize this and stick to our roles. Stop carrying your marriage, it will destroy you! Let go and let God keep it safe for you.

My marriage door is now closed and securely locked, and the keys are with Christ. My marriage is hidden with Christ in God, where no weapon formed against it shall prosper, and every tongue that rises against my marriage is condemned in Jesus' name! You can have your marriage delivered from the enemy's manipulation. Release it to God, close all doors, and lock your marriage from all evil by living righteous and holy. Remember, we open doors to the enemy through sin. I love this God! I love my Helper! There is no losing when you have God the Holy Spirit as your Counselor.

- **My friend taught me that worrying is sin.**

When God says not to do something, and we do it, it is disobedience. Disobedience is sin. There is a reason why God told us not to worry. He knows that there are circumstances beyond our control that will come our way. God allows these things in our lives so that we can have a relationship with Him. We know Him intimately from these situations as He works them out for us. Only God could and did stop Abraham from sacrificing Isaac. Abraham never worried about it because he had come to know God's amazing ability and he trusted that if God gave him Isaac at such an old age by his wife Sarah, He could do it all over again by resurrecting Isaac from the dead. (Hebrews 11:19)

Had Abraham been worried, he would have brought some extra sheep or oxen to try to negotiate with God. He would have offered to sacrifice all his flock and his servants and their children so he could keep Isaac. Abraham never once negotiated, questioned, or tried to help God again. He had tried to help God before, and he learned his lesson the hard way with Ishmael who was born out of it. Abraham had to separate with him by sending him and his mother away which caused him great pain. Abraham had allowed worry to belittle God by insulting His ability to do what He said He would do, and Abraham was not about to repeat this sin again. He had come to know and trust in this powerful God. He now had unwavering faith in God.

Abraham's faith moved God so much that God not only provided the sheep for the sacrifice, but He also blessed Abraham more than He had blessed him before. God realized that the trust Abraham had in Him was very high. This trust moved God so much that God called it righteousness and credited this to Abraham. If childlike, complete faith in God is righteousness, then the opposite must be true. Lack of faith in God and in His ability to be God is unrighteousness. Abraham had no problem losing all he had but remain a friend of God. Is that so with us? Are we willing to lose everyone and everything to obey God? Is God that important to you, or is He only a means to your blessing?

My friend the Holy Spirit helps us to crucify this evil nature that wants to use God as the servant instead of reverencing Him as the Master. God is the one who instructs us, not us instructing Him. We report for duty, not Him reporting to us. We are the created; He is our creator. We, therefore, must submit and yield to His will. We must trust in His ability to be God in our lives and not worry.

- **My friend helps me to submit to God's will.**

The Holy Spirit helps us to submit to God's perfect will no matter how difficult or painful it may be. Jesus was full of the Holy Spirit when praying in the garden of Gethsemane. He asked His Father to take away the suffering He was about to experience. Christ knew what He was about to face because He understood how much hatred His Dad had for sin. He was about to take up all of humanity's sin and the punishment for it. He knew sin was going to separate Him and His Father for the first time ever in His life. He did signs and wonders before because, as He said, it was the Father doing it all through Him. He spoke His Father's words and did what He saw His Father do. He even said that His Father was teaching Him to do greater things. (John 5:19–21)

This relationship was about to be cut short, and the Father was going to leave His Son. The Father was going to turn against the Son in wrath and anger, and great punishment for the sin of the world was going to be laid upon Christ. The Father was not going to help like He had been since Jesus' birth. God is an all-consuming fire. His Word says that the soul that sins shall surely die (Ezekiel 18:20). Christ was going to face death alone! The giver of life was going to die, so He may give us life more abundantly—everlasting life. Christ laid down His life so we may live forever. He traded His perfect life for our filthy lives of sin so that if we believe and receive this sacrifice, we will have everlasting life and a great relationship with God the Father. The Holy Spirit helped Christ to pray in the right way. He taught Him to ask what He desired but also taught Him to align His desires with God's.

Jesus asked God to take away the cup of suffering from Him three times, and with each request, He submitted His will to God's will. "He went forward a little, fell on his face, and prayed, saying, "My Father, if it is possible, let this cup pass away from me; nevertheless, not what I desire, but what you desire." Again, a second time he went away, and prayed, saying, "My Father, if this cup can't pass away from me unless I drink it, your desire be done." He came again and found them sleeping, for their eyes were heavy. He left them again, went away, and prayed a third time, saying the same words." (Matthew

26:39, 42–44)

Christ wanted the will of His Father to be accomplished. He knew that there would be a great recovery of victory, dominion, and authority for God's children and Kingdom which had been stolen from Adam by the devil in the Garden of Eden. After this great accomplishment, He would be crowned King of kings and Lord of lords and given the name that is above every name! That is why it is written about Christ that for the joy that was set before Him, He endured the cross. (Hebrews 12:2) Christ would not have done this without the help of God the Holy Spirit. If Christ needed the Holy Spirit to submit to God's will, how much more do we need the Holy Spirit to guide and teach us how to die to self and yield entirely to God's will?

I once heard a story about dying to self, which helped me understand what dying to self really means. A man went to his pastor and asked what it meant to die to self. The pastor was busy doing something, so he told him that he would answer him, but first, he asked the man to do something for him. The man agreed. There was an Elder in the church who had died recently and was buried in a nearby cemetery. The pastor asked the man whom I will name Bob, to go to Elder John's (not the real name) grave and tell him all the good things he had done while alive and Bob agreed. He went and showered the late Elder John with praises of all the wonderful deeds he had done in his life. Bob reported back to the pastor, having fulfilled the pastor's request. The pastor asked him, "What did Elder John say to you?" Bob responded, "Nothing!" The pastor looked very shocked, and this time, he sent Bob to say even greater things about Elder John and asked Bob to really exaggerate, giving the Elder more praises than he deserved. Bob went back and did as asked and brought the report back. Seeing him, the pastor excitedly exclaimed, "Surely the late Elder must be very pleased now and he must have responded to you! What did Elder John say this time?" Bob responded in disappointment, "He said nothing!"

The pastor acted even more surprised. He then sent Bob again to the grave site, only this time, he asked him to remind Elder John of all the bad things he had done and not spare him anything. Bob did this and came back with his report. He reported that he reminded Elder John of his scandal and all the past mistakes he could remember hearing about him, but Elder John still said nothing. In dismay, the pastor sent him one more time to do the best job he could in insulting Elder John and lying about him. The pastor asked Bob to place on Elder John every evil thing he could ever imagine or think of. He asked the man to destroy the elder's reputation beyond repair completely.

The pastor said, "Surely, this time, the elder will say or do something about it." The obedient and spiritually hungry man who sought a simple answer went in obedience one last time and did significant damage to the elder's reputation, that there was no hope for a comeback after trashing him as much as he did. Bob felt so bad and ashamed when going back to report the outcome to his pastor.

The pastor asked enthusiastically and with extremely high expectation . . . "Yes? Yes? Can't wait to hear this . . . What did Elder John say to you?" He responded, "I have trashed him more than anyone has ever been trashed! I had nothing else left to say, and he still said NOTHING!!" The pastor sat down slowly in his chair, signaling Bob to sit next to him. The pastor looked at Bob and said to him, "The reason Elder John never responded to you when you praised him or when you slandered him, is because he is dead. Neither praise nor slander affects dead people. That is how a believer is when they die to self. Nothing said to them or about them moves or bothers them. They only live for God and to God. They do not receive glory. Instead, they give God the glory by the sacrificial life they live unto God. They do not retaliate with anger because they realize that their persecutors are persecuting Christ not them therefore, they pray for them to know and love Christ. These dead-to-self Christians cannot be moved!" What a lesson! Only the Holy Spirit can help us put to death the deeds of the flesh.

"For if you live after the flesh, you must die; but if by the Spirit you put to death the deeds of the body, you will live." (Romans 8:13)

One day, when I was completely done with my marriage, on my way to file for a divorce, God asked me a very simple question. He said, "How many times have you wronged me, and I forgave you? How many times have you committed the same sin against me, and I took you back?"

Right there and then, I felt broken, and as much as I was justified to leave my husband, I went into a library and meditated on God's Word. Then I went back to my broken home as much as I hated the situation. I had to die to self and allow God to heal me, heal my husband, and heal our marriage. Are you at a place where God's will doesn't feel good, but it is the right thing to do? Trust Him. I'm glad I did because my husband is my best friend today! God revealed to me that He was using my husband as a pressure washer to make me into what He wanted me to be. My marriage brought out of me more than I could imagine was ever in me. My husband and I would not want to go through it again, but we would not trade the lessons learned or the change we have experienced, including intimacy with God and knowing God in a deeper level, for anything!

- **My friend helps me with academics.**

When I took my Baccalaureate degree in nursing at Kennesaw State University, organic chemistry was a subject I learned to love because of my friend the Holy Spirit. Before I was accepted to the nursing school at Kennesaw State, I wanted to pursue an associate's degree in nursing at Georgia Perimeter College. I took the associates of nursing entrance examination and failed. Discouraged, my husband advised me to apply for the licensed vocational nurse (LVN) instead of the registered nurse. Before I began schooling, I told my husband that I would not do the LVN license because I did not like the limitations they had. I was going for the RN or none at all.

When I did all my required classes before the entrance exam, I had all 'A's and a couple of 'B's. I was not supposed to fail the test. I had no way of knowing how they determined the scores, but it was not fair that I worked so hard with two kids and high grades to be failed and demoted to a lower level of nursing. When my husband proposed the LVN, I started thinking that maybe he was right. But then something inside of me reminded me of the scripture that said, "Now the Lord is the Spirit, and where the Spirit of the Lord is, there is liberty. But we all, with unveiled face seeing the glory of the Lord as in a mirror, are transformed into the same image from glory to glory, even as from the Lord, the Spirit." (2 Corinthians 3:17–18)

I immediately realized what is true in the spirit is also true in the physical. I took the scripture and applied it to my situation, and by the Holy Spirit of God, I declared my academic situation is from glory to glory. I had asked God what He wanted me to do . . . music or nursing, and He said He wants to minister healing through me. Because I was in the will of God, I had Kingdom backing. I was a threat to the kingdom of darkness because of the healing God was going to do to multitudes through me. That is why there was a barrier. But when the enemy does something against the Kingdom of God, God turns it around for our good just like Joseph said in Genesis 50:20, "As for you, you meant evil against me, but God meant it for good, to bring to pass, as it is today, to save many people alive."

I reasoned that if God allowed this associate's degree door to close, it means that I was limiting Him, and I needed to go higher. It meant that He had opened the door to the Bachelor of Science in nursing degree, which was currently the highest level of RN entry. I told my husband I would apply for the BSN degree because God works with His children from glory to glory. It is like the checkers game when sometimes you will allow someone to take your chips because it creates a way for you to get to a higher ranking and higher authority than if you protected every chip. When the devil thinks he has pulled a genius move on God, God pulls an even more significant move with higher ranking and promotion on him.

Trust me; I know this because it has happened to me several times. That is how I came to really love my enemies and pray for those who persecute me. I love them because if they don't maliciously take a few of my chips, they cannot make way for my advancement, and thus, the Word of God that says He will prepare a table in the presence of your enemies. Enemies precede the promotion and glory. They must take your chips to open the way for you to be crowned king! They did it to Jesus and do it to all of God's children who are doing the Father's will.

Don't confuse this with the discipline you receive from disobedience. This is like when you make a wrong move on the checkers board and lose your chips with no gain. There is a difference. The glory to glory measure is for obedient children of God. Many times, I have been placed in positions that by human standards, one has to know someone in authority to get the position, and I have even been asked who I knew to get the position. I often answer, "I know Jesus!" Jesus created everyone and is in control of every man and their status on earth and heaven. That is why scripture is so clear when it says that promotion comes from the Lord, not from other sources.

Psalm 75:6–7 (KJV) says, "For promotion cometh neither from the east, nor from the west, nor from the south. But God is the judge: he putteth down one, and setteth up another."

I love this God! When you realize who the boss is, and who you need to know and trust and live for, you will enjoy the perks of having Jesus as your Lord because He will demote those not doing His will and promote His obedient bride. The resources on earth are for the sake of the Kingdom, not for our selfish use. The wealth on earth is for the purpose of God's Kingdom that many may know God through the love shown and His gifts to His church.

I was advised by many not to bother applying to the university because this university gave priority to those who had completed the pre-courses of the BSN program at their university. They also had an entrance interview and exam. *Oh, my goodness!* I thought to myself, according to the human point of view, *I am very disadvantaged because in pursuing a BSN degree,*

I needed to take more core classes per requirement, which disqualifies me. I had taken all my other classes at the community college where I was planning to do the associate's degree, which disqualifies me from the second requirement. I also had failed the entrance exam for the associate's program, and the BSN program required me to take another exam to be selected. I am already at a disadvantage here. After the test, those who pass must go through an interview panel to filter out applicants. What would you do if you were in my position?

If my trust were in man, I would have given up and followed my husband's advice. However, I declared to myself that I could do all things through Christ, who gives me strength. (Philippians 4:13) I applied to the BSN program by faith—and was accepted. I passed the exam and did great in the interview. I graduated with my BSN! What a mighty God we serve!

Chemistry was a subject I disliked because I had a very soft-spoken teacher in high school who never explained it to my understanding; therefore, I struggled with it. However, in the university, I had asked God the Holy Spirit to help me understand all I am taught and remind me in the test so that I may spend more time with Him than with my books. Because I asked according to His will, He did it.

Once, during a quiz, I came across a difficult problem, and as I thought on it, the Holy Spirit shouted the right answer. I heard it so loud that I looked up from my paper and looked around to see who spoke. Everyone was busy taking the test, and the professor was walking around the class. I then realized it was God who spoke. I wrote down the answer, and it was correct! On my way home from school, I began worshiping and praising God, and I cried as I felt and knew His love for me. I said to Him in the middle of my tears, "You love me so much that you even shout the answer at me?" and the Holy Spirit responded, "As long as you put me first in your life, I refuse to let you struggle."

I love this God! I ended the class with an A, and the professor tried to recruit me to change my major to chemistry instead of nursing because I was his best student.

Another time, in my nursing exam, I came across a question which we had not learned. The Holy Spirit led me to ask Him what the answer was and the rationale behind it. I said, "Holy Spirit, what is the answer? And why is it the answer?" He immediately responded to me by giving me the solution to the problem and the rationale behind it. I was so excited beyond explanation. During the test review, when the teacher got to that question, she asked what the answer was and why it was the answer. She knew that she had not taught us this concept, so everyone was silent. I had learned my answer from the Holy Spirit, so I raised my hand and repeated what He had taught me. She was so proud of me that she asked me to stand up and repeat the answer so everyone could hear. The Holy Spirit is full of wisdom and knowledge. He knows all things and teaches all things. With Him, I am unstoppable, unbeatable, and no one can outdo Him.

- **My friend teaches me to cook.**

There is a Kenyan bread we cook, the dish is borrowed from the Indians called chapati or in short chapo, that I could not cook well at all. I usually relied on other people to prepare it for me. It was my husband's favorite food, and one lady used to cook it for my family when she cooked it for hers. I got tired of relying on others, and as much as I tried their recipes, it never turned out right. I turned to my friend the Holy Spirit and asked Him to help me. The Holy Spirit taught me the ingredients, the mixing, and even how to be efficient in making them. My family enjoyed this and all who tried it loved it. With the efficiency taught by my friend, although preparing and cooking chapati is lots of work and time-consuming, my family can eat it fresh for breakfast, snacks, lunch, and dinner . . . All freshly made, not warmed up. He is an amazing God who gives great ideas, and there is nothing you can ever ask that He doesn't know. When I need to know anything, I ask Him.

- **My friend teaches me to do hair.**

One day, I had washed my hair and dried it. I usually wait for the Holy Spirit to tell me when to braid my hair. He either tells me in a dream, or He speaks to me and says it's time to do it. This time, He said to me, "We are going to do hair." I said, "OK! I will call the hairdresser and make an appointment." He said, "No, you will do your hair." I was shocked, but knowing Him, I said OK. I went into the beauty shop, bought what I needed, stood by my mirror, and began to follow His direction. I liked twists, but it was the hardest thing to do for most people, and it cost more. The Holy Spirit took my hands, and I saw my hands moving and twisting my hair! Oh, what an amazing God! I started crying in awe of what I saw. I did the small braids, enjoyed it, never felt tired at all, and never stopped to rest. I sat on the couch with my husband keeping me company as I did my hair and we watched TV. My husband was shocked because he knew I that disliked doing hair, and I did not know how to braid. I always had someone do my hair. He stayed with me till I was done, and he said, "I don't care about the hair mess. I will clean up the mess for you because this saves us a lot of money." I used to pay about $200 to get my hair done and be away from my family for hours. The Holy Spirit knows how to get back resources we lose to others because He knows how to do all things!

- **My friend gives me words of knowledge.**

He reveals a kidney problem in a former coworker.

One day, upon using the bathroom, my urine had a very strong smell. My husband is sensitive to smells, but he never commented on it. The smell each time I went into the bathroom was so overwhelming that I knew there was something wrong with my kidneys. I waited for my husband to comment on it, and he never did. I never told him my concern, but I was triggered to pray for my kidneys and for anyone else with the same issue, each time I used the bathroom. I hydrated well, but it never resolved the issue. I had never experienced this before.

After about a week or so, the smell went away and never returned. I thanked God for the healing. Almost immediately, I met with a lady I used to work with, and she was very excited to see me. She shared with me that she had been to the doctor and had been told that her kidneys were in the final stage of failing, and she would need dialysis. She was in her early forties. She was terrified! The doctor had performed one last test before starting her on dialysis, and she would get the results by the end of the week.

I asked her, "When did you receive the news that your kidneys had failed?" Her answer verified that the same time she had received the news of her kidney failure was the same time I started smelling my urine. The Holy Spirit quickened me that my urine smell experience was for her, and that He wanted me to pray. That was why the smell was hidden from my husband because the message was mine not my husband's. I shared this with her, and I told her not to worry because the smell was lifted, meaning her kidney failure was totally healed. She was excited, and when she got the results back, the doctor was amazed. He said that he could not explain the numbers and how or what corrected her kidney function. She told him it was Jesus! What a glorious God we serve! I thank God the Holy Spirit as He intercedes for us.

- **My friend helps me with fasting.**

When I began the journey of knowing Christ and intimacy with God the Holy Spirit, He told me that my life would be a life of prayer and fasting. He leads me in various fasts, just like He did Christ, without warning. I would wake up to get ready for work, and as I would be grooming, He'd tell me something like, "Today, we start a fast." I would ask Him how many days He wanted to go for, and He would mostly answer "forty days".

He led me into very many fasts like those, and He literally turned off my stomach so that I could cook and be around food, but I was not hungry at all. I never desired food either. He turned on my spiritual hunger, and this I love! My husband and children from when they were young knew when mom was not eating, Jesus was feeding her. They never could tell whether I was fasting or not as our schedules were hectic; we hardly ate meals together or at the same time.

Once I was on a forty-day fast and had one more week to go. My children were in Africa, visiting my parents, and my husband traveled a lot. As I came home from school and sat on the couch, my body felt so weak that I could hardly move. I was in so much agony that I spoke to Jesus and said, "Jesus, when you were in the wilderness on your forty-day fast, the angels came to minister to you. You had spiritual assistance for the weakness in your physical body. What about me? Where is *my* help?" I said that and gathered enough strength to go to bed. I did not cheat by eating any food. I knew that man shall not live by bread alone but by every word that comes from the mouth of God.

I fell asleep on my back. I dreamt that I was in a glass room where I could see outside, but I did not know if the people outside could see me. Some of the men looked rough, and I hoped they could not see me because I lay in bed too weak to get up and fight. I was still as weak as I had been going to bed. As I lay helplessly in bed, I thought to myself that if the rough-looking men decided to come for me, I would never be able to fight them off.

As I was anxiously thinking about my helpless situation, suddenly there was an earthquake and a very high rushing wind, and Jesus Christ, dressed in His full war armor, came into my room through the glass. As He stepped in, the ground shook heavily, and the wind about Him was so strong that inside my stomach felt like a big fan was in me blowing every part of my organs. I woke up at once and sat up in bed, holding my abdomen firmly to stop the feeling of flying organs. The feeling of the fan in my stomach lasted awhile, and I said out loud, "Jesus, please come back; let me go back to sleep, and I'll hold my stomach so that when you come, I can stand your presence."

I went to sleep and woke up stronger than I had ever been

when not fasting! I was skipping and jumping and very energetic. Jesus Himself had come to help me fight this war. We are in a spiritual battle, and Christ is our commander in chief of His army. He never sent His angel to assist me; instead, He came down from His dwelling place to help me. I am forever grateful and amazed at His love, humility, and kindness. Jesus will never leave you out in the cold. As long as you are in His army, He is the commander who takes care of His own. What a mighty God we serve!

- **My friend told me that I would get a new car.**

In my last year of nursing school, I was driving our Ford Expedition when the Spirit of God said that I would get a new car. I called my husband and told him what the Holy Spirit said, and he responded, "No! We just finished paying for that car. We will keep it. There is no point in getting a new car." I told him that I never said it. I'm just relaying information from God. My husband then was tired of my relationship with the Holy Spirit, and he had demanded that I choose between him and the Holy Spirit. There was no choice to make because, in the first place, he does not even compare to the Holy Spirit to stand on the same plane with Him for selection. The devil was the one fighting me, not my husband.

The Holy Spirit taught me this a long time ago. We must, like Jesus did, know who is speaking to us, and address the right person. Jesus knew when God spoke through Peter, and He never glorified Peter. Instead, He gave God the glory by saying that the Father revealed to Peter who Jesus was. Peter was not that smart to know this. Christ also knew when the devil spoke through Peter trying to divert Him from His assignment, and

He rebuked the devil, not Peter. We too must know when to give glory to God as He speaks to us through other people and to rebuke Satan when he speaks to us through people.

"Jesus answered him, "Blessed are you, Simon Bar-Jonah, for flesh and blood has not revealed this to you, but my Father who is in heaven."" (Matthew 16:17)

"But he turned, and said to Peter, "Get behind me, Satan! You are a stumbling block to me, for you are not setting your mind on the things of God, but on the things of men." (Matthew 16:23)

The next week, the car started turning itself off as I drove. It did that in the middle of the highway and on the side streets. No one could fix it. My husband started looking for a car, but none was a good deal. When he asked me to look for a vehicle I desired, the Holy Spirit led me to the dealership which had the perfect vehicle! My dream car. I had longed to own this particular make and model. About seven years before, my husband and I had visited the dealership and admired it, but all we could afford was to sit in it.

I loved the Lincoln Navigator SUV. It was fully loaded and had a DVD player, and my children were excited. The price was perfect! Oh, I loved the white color with tan interior and classy steering wheel with a full navigation system. This is the advantage of being a friend of God! He gives you your heart's desire when you least expect it. Just like I think of what I would do for my children as they obey and do all I ask them to do, God is the same way. He remembers our desires, and He makes it happen.

- **My friend revealed what God placed in me during creation.**

As I continued a close walk with my friend the Holy Spirit, he opened my eyes to see what God placed in me during creation. He revealed that I was an author of many books through a prophet who happened to be at the same birthday party I was invited to. I disliked writing then. Now, I cannot stop writing. It is my life! God had revealed that I was a worshiper, and I would receive from Him songs to sing and write and lead many into His presence. I have written songs beyond my comprehension in anointing, some in languages that I am not fluent in, but the song is fluent because the Holy Spirit composes these songs through me. He also revealed to me what my children would do for God, what my husband's gifts and calling were, that I loved horses, and I had what it took to ride and care for them even when I had never had an interest in horses. I loved horse movies and horses but had never been on one when He revealed this to me.

When I went to train, my instructor said I was a natural, and she had never seen or known someone who had never been on a horse, ride as well as I did. My friend the Holy Spirit revealed to me many intimate things which I can use and work toward for the sake of God's Kingdom. My passion is for the lost, children, orphans, or those without a loving home. I love children so much that it overwhelms me. He revealed to me about ministering to women, rescuing children, including the ones up for abortion. My heart is to take all these children and provide homes, bringing them up in the ways of Christ.

- **My friend shows me what the Father is doing.**

Healing ministry.

I once received a call to go in and work overtime at the hospital where I worked in the intensive care unit (ICU) because they were very short staffed. I went in to be their resource and meal break RN. As I was giving the telemetry monitor tech a break, the Holy Spirit said to me, "I want you to go and pray for that man." He pointed to a room right in front of me. I did not know whether the patient was a man or a woman until He told me. This is because the patient was not assigned to me, and I had never taken care of him before. I looked at his name, and sure enough, it was a man.

I then asked my friend the Holy Spirit, "How do I go into the room and pray for him legally? He is not my patient, and due to patient confidentiality, we are not allowed to access any patient information unless we were dealing with the patient as the nurse." Immediately, as I asked Him the question, the monitor tech came back from his break, and the intravenous (IV) pump in the patient's room started beeping. The Holy Spirit said, "There is your cue!" I immediately made my way toward the room.

For those not medically versed, when an IV beeps in any intensive care unit (ICU), it is everyone's responsibility to respond immediately because it could be a drip that is keeping the patient alive, and running out of it may be fatal. Many drips are very critical, and if it is occluded, meaning there is no proper flow, or if it is running empty, the patient might code and die, lose their blood pressure or wake up from sedation and pull out their tubes. Intubated patients can extubate themselves, which is very dangerous. I now had a valid reason for going into the patient's room as the Holy Spirit asked me to.

When God gives you an assignment, He makes provision for it. Never say no. Just like the women who went to put perfume on Jesus' body that early Sunday morning, they never stopped just because the stone at the tomb was too heavy to roll away. They still did their part. They woke up early, went to get their perfume, started walking toward the tomb, and asked the question, who will roll the stone away for us? Notice they asked the question as they were on their way to their assignment. Some of us would have been discouraged and asked the question while still in bed. We then would go back to sleep because there was no one to roll away the stone for us. We, therefore, would have disobeyed and missed out on God's supernatural provision. God never gives you an assignment which you can do all by yourself without needing His supernatural help. If your task doesn't require God's intervention, then it is not a God assignment; it is man's assignment, and there is no reward in it. God never gives us a Kingdom assignment without a Kingdom provision. This means He will never ask you to do anything that does not require you to have faith in His ability to perform it. Anything not of faith is not of God.

> When the Sabbath was past, Mary Magdalene, and Mary the mother of James, and Salome, bought spices, that they might come and anoint him. Very early on the first day of the week, they came to the tomb when the sun had risen. They were saying among themselves, "Who will roll away the stone from the door of the tomb for us?" for it was massive. Looking up,

they saw that the stone was rolled back. Entering into the tomb, they saw a young man sitting on the right side, dressed in a white robe, and they were amazed. He said to them, "Don't be amazed. You seek Jesus, the Nazarene, who has been crucified. He has risen. He is not here. Behold, the place where they laid him! But go, tell his disciples and Peter, 'He goes before you into Galilee. There you will see him, as he said to you.' (Mark 16:1–7)

Paul did not tell Timothy to just fight the good fight, but he included which good fight he was talking about. The good fight of faith. The one thing the enemy contends with us for is our faith. We must fight the good fight of faith. (1 Timothy 6:12a) Without faith, we cannot please God. Therefore, we cannot see Him working in and through our lives. God is longing for us to believe in Him and have faith in His ability and faithfulness to do exceedingly above our imagination. In other words, be still and relaxed and know that He is God! The problem with many today is that the name or title "God" has been diluted so much because of the many fake gods, so when you mention the title "God", people do not know the real meaning, strength and authority that the name carries. The devil does this to destroy people's faith.

That is why God the Father always mentioned His title to declare His power, might, and authority. God is all-powerful, all-knowing; there is no limit to His wisdom, knowledge, and might! He said to Moses in Exodus 3:14, when Moses asked Him who He was, that He was "I AM who I AM." You cannot describe Him or summarize Him with one name. He said in Psalm 46:10, to be still and know that He is God. We must come back to the full knowledge of God and complete trust in His name and title, in His ability and love, trusting that He will do any and all things for us according to His will and purpose if we believe.

Back to my story... The patient was in isolation as he had an infectious disease, and so, before going into the room, I had to gown up. Nurses dislike the isolation rooms because it delays their patient care. When the primary RN saw me gowning up to go into the patient's room, she was very grateful because she was very busy with another patient. I walked into the room and went to the pump. I fixed the beeping as I explained who I was and why I was there. I suctioned the patient and did some oral care as I spoke with the wife at the bedside. It was a young couple in their late thirties or early forties.

I asked the wife if she believed in prayer, and she responded, "Yes! Everyone is praying for us." I went on to tell her, "The Lord sent me here to pray for your husband. When God does this, it means He wants to heal your husband. I don't know what is wrong with him, or what the prognosis is, or what the physicians say about him, but I know what God says He will do. So believe and have faith. Do not believe any other report, but the report God is giving you today."

She agreed, and I said a simple prayer. I then walked out of the room. I asked his children not to worry, but to go to school and work hard because their dad would be all right. Needless to say, the man's prognosis, according to the medical wisdom, was very poor. He was basically waiting to die as he had suffered multiple strokes and had no chance of survival. His brain was declared damaged and he was not responding to stimulation. The physicians and nurses thought the wife was in denial and crazy. They spoke about it at the nurse's station; they all said he was dead and could not make a comeback. I would hear this and rebuke these words silently, claiming the healing power of God.

The patient was in the hospital for over a month, and because of his case, nurses wanted to alternate and have everyone take turns taking care of him. God made sure that I was never chosen to be his nurse because He was protecting the faith in me. Eventually, the man was discharged to a long-term care facility where all medical personnel knew he would die there. A few months later, he came back walking into the ICU with his wife to thank the staff for taking care of him! The physicians and nurses were all shocked. They said that his medical records did not match up with his current health and situation. He was not supposed to be alive or have any brain function from all the brain damage he had suffered from the strokes. He went back to performing normal activities like running and driving! He was a medical miracle, and God used him to glorify Himself. I then revealed to the staff that I had never been his RN. They were shocked and in disbelief! They said it was impossible because everybody had to take turns caring for him.

There was a nurse whom I used to tell about God's healing power, and he would say that there was nothing like healing in this day and age. One day after the fact, he was giving me a hand-off report on a patient as I was taking over the care, and this particular case was of anoxic brain injury. The patient had been found passed out on his bedroom floor with no oxygen supply to his brain, and his brain was severely damaged. He was unresponsive, intubated, and the RN said "He was down for over half an hour before the wife discovered him, so he was as good as dead." Then he corrected himself really fast and said, "Wait a minute! I will never call anyone dead that God hasn't called dead because the man we called dead came back walking to thank us!" I was so excited and amazed that God proved Himself to the RNs and MDs, and they now know that He has the final word!

- **My friend was my babysitter.**

When I was a stay-at-home mom, it was hard to do my hair all at once. That is, wash, dry, and style it without my baby's interruption. I decided one day to ask the Holy Spirit to babysit for me and give my child sweet sleep until I got done doing my hair. He did it perfectly! As He babysat, He kept me company, teaching me many biblical concepts as I did my hair. Even before I had read in scripture about Abraham's obedience to God and the sacrifice he almost made of his son Isaac before the Lord stopped him which was counted as fulfilled sacrifice (righteousness), the Holy Spirit had already taught it to me. I was amazed! God wants to know if our hearts love Him more than the gifts He gives us.

God did this for me when He wanted to see if my loyalty to Him was because of the gifts I had received from Him or because of my love for Him. After I had finished my first music audio CD production, and the producer was finishing up the mastering, God the Father told me to give it all away. He said that I should not sell my first music CD to anyone. I had worked so hard for this and paid so much for it. Many people tried to talk me out of it saying that God would want me to grow my ministry, and that I should sell so I could pay back my expenses. Some among them were pastors and prophets. But I knew what I had heard from God, and I was going to obey Him regardless. I was going to sacrifice my firstborn, my only child in ministry. I believed that if God truly changed His mind, He would tell it to me, just as He spoke to me initially.

Remember the story of the prophet whom God spoke to and gave instructions not to be entertained by anyone? Then a false prophet came and told him that God had changed His mind and said through an angel (I believe the angel was one of the fallen lying angels) to him that it was okay for him to go to the false prophet's house and eat? The true prophet believed the false prophet, and as soon as he ate, the false prophet was used by God to pronounce judgment upon the prophet who had initially heard from God; yet, he disobeyed by following the other false prophecy. That is why I believed that God was able to speak to me just as He had spoken to me in the first place when He gave me the initial instructions. See 1 Kings 13:14–24.

It is a terrible thing to be led into disobedience. However, it is easy even for a seasoned prophet to be led astray when we do not trust God enough to wait for Him to speak clearly to us. God wants us to ask Him if we are in doubt. He will gladly answer us. Be patient and wait. The Holy Spirit is our helper. Let us ask Him what the Father is saying. He will reveal it to us. His ultimate goal is that we constantly live in obedience to God.

God spoke to Abraham and told him to sacrifice his son, and then on the day of sacrifice, just before Abraham sacrificed his son Isaac, God spoke to him again and stopped him from making the sacrifice. God never sent a man or woman to give Abraham the second message. I wish we would trust God enough to test the spirits. When you are in an intimate relationship with God, He will tell you what He requires of you, and the prophets you encounter should only be confirming what God has already said to you.

In my situation, God never reversed His instructions to me. However, I reasoned that God is the gift giver, and I could not sing or compose songs without Him. Therefore, who am I to say no to His instructions? I am only a vessel, and I do not belong to myself. I belong to God. I yield in my Master's hand that He may use me. My husband was very much in agreement with God's instructions. I saw the disappointment but felt the support of my mother and brother, who had begun calculating the income which would come from the music because they were my babysitters and very supportive of me while I went to record the music, hours at a time.

From that sacrifice, I received numerous Spirit-filled songs that minister to me and to many people around the world. The music brings healings, deliverance, and glory to Almighty God! God was setting me up for a harvest when He asked me to plant the seed of music! What instructions have *you* received from God that the enemy knows if you follow, it will destroy his kingdom? Don't fall for his tricks! Stay in obedience to God, and when in doubt, consult my friend the Holy Spirit.

- **My friend tells parents what their children are doing.**

My mom and I are close friends. When I was in middle school, a certain boy with whom we attended family fellowships gave me a very precious necklace. It was made of gold and blue hearts. It was stunning! This boy had a brother who was competing with him to have me for his girlfriend. This necklace was a real treasure to me. It was pretty, looked real expensive, and I loved it. I wore it secretly because I did not want my mother to ask me about it. One morning, I secretly wore it under my clothes and sat in the living room when my mom said that she had a dream about me. She dreamt that someone had given me a very filthy rag, but I treasured it so much. I was very disappointed that what looked stunning, precious, and adorable in my eyes was filthy rags in God's eyes. I revealed the hidden necklace, took it off, and told my mom how I got it. I returned it to the boy and told him I couldn't accept it. I thank God for His protection from evil even when we do not see.

For me . . .

When my sons were younger, two in elementary school and another about a year old, they had their friends over for a sleepover. My house's backyard opened up to a lake, and we had a private beach. The boys asked me to take them to the lake for a swim, and I promised to take them once I was done with cleaning the yard and when the baby wakes up from his nap. As I was busy cleaning the backyard fellowshipping with my friend the Holy Spirit, He told me that the boys were waking the baby up. Sure enough, a few minutes later, the boys came running to me, shouting, "It's a miracle! It's a miracle! We held hands and prayed that the baby would wake up so we could go to the beach, and when we finished praying, Ken (not his real name) went to check on the baby and found him awake! It's a miracle!"

I smiled as I watched their excitement and said to Ken, "You woke the baby up, didn't you?"

He denied it at first, but when I told him that I knew the truth and lying would get him in trouble, he confessed to it revealing that after they had prayed, he told the other boys to wait for him as he went to the baby's room to see if their prayers had been answered. He found the baby still asleep, so he woke him up and ran to tell the others about the "miracle" which he had performed. The other boys felt cheated and were furious at him. From then on, we called him the "miracle worker." To this day, when I ask my sons if they remember the "miracle worker," they laugh and shake their heads.

Another time . . .

I had a dream of my second son, that there was a plan to kidnap him because I had just inherited a lot of wealth which was being hidden from me, but I discovered it, and there were people who were very unhappy that I inherited it, and they wanted to take it back. These people had burnt my birth certificate in hopes that I would never know that I legally qualified for the inheritance. They tried chasing me, but they could not catch me, so they figured out a plan. They said that if they kidnapped my son, they could ask for a ransom of all the wealth I had acquired. I woke up and prayed against their evil scheme. The next day, I dreamt with the same son that he was very sick and when we went to the physician, he had a terrible diagnosis. I woke up again, prayed against it, and told my son about it this time.

I was thinking of what the dream could mean on my way to work, and as I went down the stairs from my bedroom, my friend the Holy Spirit said to me, "He has opened doors." I went on to work, and that evening, sitting in the living room, I called out my son's name twice, but he never responded. He was sitting at the homework table, so his older brother went to get him. He walked toward me fast as he took out his earbuds. I asked him what he was listening to, and when he showed me, I was shocked! He had terrible secular music talking about clubbing. I asked him why he did that when he knew that he was opening doors for the demons to come into his life. He said he liked the beats. I told him whatever one loved, that belonged to the devil and opened doors of invitation into their lives. My son had opened an entryway for the enemy to come and attack him, and by attacking him, he wanted to stop my ministry as the first dream implied. We dealt with it in repentance and discipline.

- **My friend reveals the promotion Dad (God) had given me.**

Once, on a forty-day fast, I was meditating upon the greatness of God and His faithfulness . . . I was resting on my bed facing upward. I was even more amazed because we had just visited San Diego's Sea World Park and had seen animals I had never seen since birth. I was in awe and amazement of God's wonder. As I sat there, I received a song from the Holy Spirit in my mother tongue, which I am not fluent in, but the song was perfect. It speaks of God's greatness. When I sang it later to my husband, he was amazed at the fluency and accurate pronunciation of lyrics. The Holy Spirit can speak any language.

In the same episode, He said to me, "You are the house supervisor in the county hospital."

At the time, I worked in two hospitals, and both were looking for house supervisors. I had not thought of applying for the position. I worked as an ICU (Intensive Care Unit) RN (Registered Nurse) when I received this information from God. I then went downstairs to tell my husband of the great news, and we agreed with God. I then updated my résumé and took it to the county hospital. When I submitted it, I was informed that the position had been filled two weeks ago, and there was no other opening. I thought to myself, *God did not speak two weeks ago; therefore, He must know something I don't.*

I then told them to keep my résumé and call me if anything changes. I went home and announced to my children and husband that I was the house supervisor in the county hospital. I went ahead and ordered some white coats with embroidery on them of my name and title on them of the position God told me in the nursing administration. I occupied the position in the spiritual realm, and by faith, did all within my power in the physical realm to fill the position. That is what faith is. It consists of substance and evidence. The substance is made of the things you hope to get, and the evidence contains information on what you have not seen yet. This you must make evident. Evidence is what activates your faith.

Like a little child, I heard what my Daddy had said. I believed my Daddy's words and even with obstacles, I did not doubt His ability to dispossess whoever was occupying my position. I even met the lady who had been hired, and she was glorifying God for her job. She had come from a smaller hospital therefore, this was a great promotion for her. I was genuinely happy for her and celebrated with her. About three weeks later, I received a call from administration stating that the position was open again because it did not work out with the lady who had been hired. Apparently, the hospital was too big for her to handle. By that time, my jackets had arrived, and I was ready to work!

What a great and awesome God we serve! A week or two into my new position, I got a huge raise as negotiations were going on with the union behind the scenes which God knew about. It is amazing how God works. The day I got hired as a new grad, the pay rate that I had been quoted was increased due to the union negotiations; then as I changed into a Per Diem position as God instructed me to, I received another significant raise a week or so later. Now in this new position, God's faithfulness made them negotiate better pay for the supervisors. When you trust in God to let you know where to go and when to go, you will be in for a treat because He knows the end from the beginning. Remember, the steps of a righteous man are ordered by God. (Psalm 37:23)

Another time, I worked in a different place where the contract I had with them was ending. I had been informed that once the contract ends, I would not be needed since they had hired someone permanently for the job already. Immediately, my friend the Holy Spirit told me not to worry; there was a lot of work for me to do there. I laughed and again informed my husband of this. As always, we agreed with God and sealed it in the spiritual realm. Again, God said to me that I would not have to negotiate the pay because He had already settled it for me. Needless to say, I got the promotion, with the highest salary and excellent benefits. I marvel at this God who promotes His own.

At one point, they told me that the pay I was asking for was too high, that even one with a Ph.D. did not earn that much. I confessed to myself and to the spirit realm that I do not know what kingdom the person with the Ph.D. works for, but I work for the King of kings and the Lord of lords, and He is an extravagant paying employer. My Dad is great at compensating me.

Which kingdom has employed *you*? The kingdom of darkness where you work to promote the enemy, the kingdom of man where you work for man to please and promote their agenda, or the Kingdom of God where you work as unto the Lord, pleasing and advancing the Kingdom of God? You have a choice. Remember, God commands us to do whatever we do as unto Him. (Colossians 3:23)

Sometime back, I had an offer of a promotion, a higher position with higher pay and title. I told my boss that I would inquire of God, then get back to them. When I asked God, He said no and directed me to accept another position in a dream. There was a teaching position for the less fortunate students who had just completed high school. My friend the Holy Spirit instructed me to assist the school by accepting only half the pay they offered me. He said to me in a dream three times, "Seek first the kingdom of God! Seek first the kingdom of God! Seek first the kingdom of God!"

I rejected the promotion and accepted the teaching position. The school offered me very poor pay, and I accepted half of their offer. This takes being sold out to God, to trust and inquire of Him even when you think the deal is perfect. I worked wholeheartedly with the students, giving it all I had, and their lives were changed. All of them expressed their gratitude.

After the teaching job, another offer came, and again, I inquired of God, and He said no. He made a delay on the position posting that when the job was finally posted, my family life could not allow me to work those hours. After He closed that door, a great promotion followed it. I received an amazing position with a great team and a higher position than what I was being offered, twice before. Less stress, better pay, greater benefits, and amazing hours.

I would have missed my blessing twice if I took the bait of the counterfeit promotions that looked good. I have truly learned to trust in the Lord with all of my heart and not rely on my own understanding. The Holy Spirit knows the end from the beginning. He sees the greater picture! He is setting you up for success. Trust in His leadership and guidance.

- **My friend leads me to perform deliverance.**

One time after my devotions, I had been taught by my friend the Holy Spirit how to apply and sprinkle the blood of Jesus on myself and different areas of my life. I did this faithfully and had the blood of Jesus on my hands, and rubbed it on my palms as I applied it on me and sprinkled it over me to get the blood of Jesus speaking on my behalf as scripture states that the sprinkled blood of Jesus speaks better things than the blood of Abel. (Hebrews 12:4) I forgot about it and went from my prayer room and about my business. Earlier in the day, I had a conversation with someone who had a powerful urge to do something that was a bad compromise to get what they wanted as they had been waiting to get it for too long.

They tried to "help" God do His work. Forgetting that I had the blood of Jesus still on my hands when I touched the person, a very dark spirit with a profound deep and demonic voice spoke out as it left the person saying, "AG . . . RESS . . . IOO . . . N . . .!"

I looked at the person, and they did not even know what had happened. The person went about their business, and that was the last they ever spoke of the sin of compromise that they felt an urgency to commit. God opened my spiritual ears to hear the spirit speak and know what He had done for the person because of the blood of Jesus on my hands. Sometimes when one has a powerful urge to sin, and they are convinced that committing the sin is the only way out, there is a dark force working in them persuading them to sin against God. The blood of Jesus is sufficient for them. Jesus came to deliver our loved ones and us from these manipulating powers of darkness. When He said it is finished, it really was finished. We have the authority in Jesus' name by His Spirit.

- **My friend reveals to me a spiritual deliverance secret. Acting as my spiritual Lawyer, He advises me of my spiritual legal rights.**

"Women received their dead raised to life again: . . ." (Hebrews 11:35a, KJV; emphasis added)

Deliverance, as we saw, sets us free to live fully sold out to God. How many wives know that men have a certain pride in them, and if they are not careful, they can remain bound by the kingdom of darkness because they are the heads of the family? If they remain bound and evil dwells within them, this means war in your marriage and family as long as you remain married. As long as the devil has a foothold, he will take over your marriage. Remember, marriage, as God intended and still intends, is a union between a man and a woman. Marriage represents the kind of relationship the church of Christ should have with Him. When there are division and chaos in a marriage, people cannot understand the beauty of having a relationship with Christ. The enemy uses this discord to hinder us from desiring intimacy with Christ in fear of Him being like our husbands, or wife, for the men whose wives are too proud to receive deliverance.

When my husband said no to deliverance because my mother was the deliverance minister, I understood the dilemma and respected his decision but did not leave it at that. I was done fighting the same demons in my marriage for twenty years! There had to be a way out. I went through my deliverance and was excited. However, I still was not complete because my husband and I are one, and we will still struggle in marriage if he doesn't get delivered. I sought the Lord, and He graciously answered me. He opened my eyes to see my purpose in my marriage. I was my husband's helper. I was supposed to help him where he could not help himself. Another truth God revealed to me was that my husband and I are one in the physical and spiritual realm, so it was legal for me to take up his cross for him to set him free like Christ did for me.

"We know what real love is because Jesus gave up his life for us. So *we also ought to give up our lives for our brothers and sisters.*" (1 John 3:16, NLT; emphasis added)

With this scripture and Hebrews 11:35a, I had the legal right to take deliverance for my husband. I did this with so much power and great results that my husband says he doesn't know what happened, but he is not the man he used to be. I fought and went through a great battle with generational and ancestral bondages and ones we ourselves brought about by sins we had committed in our marriage. I was not ashamed to expose my wounds because God cannot deliver you from your friend. He is faithful to deliver you from your enemy.

I had an enemy in my marriage, and enough was enough for me! I was not going to continue living with the devil talking to me whenever he felt like it through my husband. I wanted the fullness of the love of Christ to flow through my husband, without any hindrance, to me. I was so thirsty and hungry for real love from my husband, the same extravagant love Christ has for me. It was a mystery for the deliverance minister because they had never experienced such a deliverance of someone through another.

I told them that it was not about what they were used to; it was about working with God and moving into a higher dimension of revelation and glory as He leads. I cannot begin to tell you how much love, joy, peace, and fulfillment this revelation and deliverance has brought into my marriage. I am in awe. Truly, people of God perish for lack of knowledge. Had I known this twenty years ago, I would have had a very happy marriage all this time. But this was God's timing for me to acquire this knowledge so that I can share it with you.

Marriages do not have to break or be unhappy; there is a way out. We are legally covered when we take the lead and cover each other. One of the spouses may be more mature than the other in Christ the Holy Spirit can help us act in wisdom. I did not ask for my husband's permission to fight the enemy for him and our marriage, because if both of us are under attack, it doesn't matter who does what, as long as we take out the enemy. One partner may be down, but if we do not step it up a notch, we will all be destroyed.

Scripture says that two are better than one. If you don't stand in the gap, what difference do you have with the person who is alone? Don't just stand and watch helplessly as the enemy destroys your communication, love, trust, unity, marriage, and family! Do something!! You and your spouse are victims of Satan. "Two people are better off than one, for they can help each other succeed . . . Likewise, two people lying close together can keep each other warm. But how can one be warm alone? A person standing alone can be attacked and defeated, but two can stand back-to-back and conquer. Three are even better, for a triple-braided cord is not easily broken." (Ecclesiastes 4:9, 11–12, NLT)

You cannot help your spouse if you need help yourself. So, get delivered first, then take deliverance for your spouse. Stand in the gap and rescue your marriage. Like Jesus said, first take the log out of your eye so you can see clearly to take the speck out of your spouse's eye. "And why worry about a speck in your friend's eye when you have a log in your own? How can you think of saying to your friend, 'Let me help you get rid of that speck in your eye,' when you can't see past the log in your own eye? Hypocrite! First get rid of the log in your own eye; then you will see well enough to deal with the speck in your friend's eye." (Matthew 7:3–5, NLT)

The day after deliverance, I was on my way to a studio recording and was praying in the Spirit when the heavens opened over me, and the Father smiled at me, looking very proud of me as He said, "Thank you for doing this for my son." (Son meaning my husband). This kept me smiling for a very long time while in His presence that my mouth felt exhausted when the experience was over. I remembered the Father doing this for Christ. He popped His head on earth every so often to appreciate Christ. This time, the Father peeked on to earth to appreciate me. Oh, what joy I felt! Now my husband and I teach couples how to live in the fear of the Lord and in love with Christ being led by God the Holy Spirit. When our relationship with Christ is perfected, it will pour out and overflow into the marriage. What a God! Full of revelation, power, and keys to the Kingdom for all spiritual access.

In this case, my friend the Holy Spirit acted as a lawyer would. He helped me to understand spiritual laws and what my legal rights were and how to go about it. That is why Ecclesiastes 4:12 (NLT) says that three are even better than two because a triple-braided cord is not easily broken. As long as you invite my friend the Holy Spirit into your marriage, your marriage will not be broken. He will be your anchor, personal advisor, lawyer, and spiritual intelligence so that you can destroy the enemy when they are planning an attack on your marriage before they even execute the attack. I love my friend so much! THANK YOU, Holy Spirit!!

- **My friend tells me of water issues in a church.**

The Holy Spirit will reveal things to us in dreams too. Once, I had a dream about some water problems in a church which was out of the country. I called the pastor and asked what problem they had with the water. They said there was a pipe burst at their house that day, and they were trying to fix it. I clarified that I was not speaking about water problems in their home but in the church. When they checked, they found out that the person who was supposed to pay for the Church water had forgotten about it, and the owner had not been paid for over a year.

When in prayer, the Lord said He wanted to bless them and did not want any hindrance to these blessings, so He revealed this to them through me. The pastor called the owner of the water supply, expressed her apologies, and the owner forgave them and did not charge them a dime for the past payment. They were given a new beginning. The pastor did not know this mistake was happening, but God knew it and, in His faithfulness, revealed it to them. What a mighty God we serve! The enemy saw that they were "stealing" water even if the pastor did not know about it. This was an open door for the enemy to attack the church and to stop blessings from flowing to them. Thanks be to God for He is a revealer of hidden things. Thank you, my friend, the Holy Spirit.

- **My friend is the revealer of secret things of God.**

He opens my eyes to see scripture in ways I have never seen or heard!

Which cross are you carrying?

One summer evening after work, I asked my sons to put something on TV so we could watch it together. They know that I only watch programs which grow my spirit, and I have no time to waste on secular programs. My baby asked if I wanted to watch Christian TV or the movie of Jesus on Netflix. I chose the movie of Christ. We had watched the Bible episodes, and now we were at the Last Supper, betrayal, persecution, and crucifixion episode. As I watched the movie, my friend the Holy Spirit opened my eyes to see Simon from Cyrene, who was forced to carry the cross for Jesus in a whole new light. "Along the way, they came across a man named Simon, who was from Cyrene, and the soldiers forced him to carry Jesus' cross." (Matthew 27:32, NLT)

My friend the Holy Spirit said, "I just didn't allow things to be written in God's Word for nothing. Everything has meaning. Simon helped Jesus carry His cross of suffering for the sake of God's Kingdom. As he helped Christ, he endured suffering and persecution for the sake of Christ. When men were spitting at Christ, the spit would also fall on Simon. As they hurled insults, he would get insulted too because of Christ. When they threw things at Christ, Simon would get hit too by those things.

Therefore, do not feel bad or take offense when you experience the same suffering when you help Christ carry the cross. As you do His will and draw many to the cross, you will be persecuted. But remember, you should not feel sorry for yourself but for Christ. This is because the persecution is not directed at you but at Him. Those not carrying the cross were not persecuted with Christ, only the one assisting Christ. Be glad that you are being persecuted because you are in Christ for great is your reward. That was why Christ said to Saul, who was persecuting Christians in Acts 9:4–5 (NLT), "He fell to the ground and heard a voice saying to him, "Saul! Saul! Why are you persecuting me?" "Who are you, Lord?" Saul asked. And the voice replied, "I am Jesus, the one you are persecuting!""

The Holy Spirit went on to teach me saying, "Christ never asked why Saul was persecuting His servants. Instead, He asked why Saul was persecuting Him. The persecutors should be the ones persecuted and carrying the cross, but because they are totally blind, Christ took it all for them. The righteous Christ served the death sentence for sinners. When these persecutors receive their eyesight, they will love Christ so much for what He has done for them just like you love Him. This was the same revelation I gave to Stephen, and that was why he willingly forgave his persecutors, then he courageously and boldly prayed out for their forgiveness."

WOW is right! That's what I said as I took it all in. My friend continued to say, "Do you know why I never allowed anyone to help the thieves carry their cross? Because the thieves were paying for their sin. No one should partake of a sinner's suffering. Sinners carry their own cross, but they can be forgiven just as the thief on the cross was forgiven when he saw his wrong and repented to Christ after acknowledging Him as his Savior, King, and Lord. He even confessed Jesus as Lord to his fellow sinner. The other sinner remained blind to his sin and the Lordship of Christ, and he was destroyed eternally. The forgiven thief was not excused from the consequences of his actions; rather, GRACE gave him eternal life, a second chance in eternity. Just because you forgive your children doesn't mean you do not discipline them. They must learn not to repeat their wrong."

The Holy Spirit gave the repentant thief on the cross heaven's intelligence that he may be the first to tap into the warm fountain of the blood of Jesus. This gave Christ more encouragement to endure the cross, as He saw His sacrifice already saving the sinner. Someone was already accepting His sacrifice even before He said it was finished. God the Father did this for His baby, Jesus Christ. The Holy Spirit softened the dying thief's heart and unveiled him that he was able to see things through God's eyes and he understood heaven's plan and the glory that awaited Christ. The conversation between the believing, repentant thief and Christ is what pushed Christ to the next level, where He was strengthened that He prayed for those who were persecuting Him. God the Father has a way of coming into the most painful times of our lives to provide endurance and encouragement just as He did for His Son. The Father allowed the Son to see the result of His sacrifice, heaven's joy and celebration for this one sinner who repented before Jesus died. Christ saw what joy and glory awaited Him, and He finished strong! We too will finish strong if we yield to my friend the Holy Spirit, following His guidance and leadership.

Whichever cross you are carrying, you know what to do now. Endure for the sake of Christ, forgive, and pray for your persecutors to be forgiven and for them to know the truth. There is a reward awaiting these lovers of Christ, those who help him carry the cross. If your cross is that of sin, acknowledge the wrong, be remorseful for your sin, confess, repent, and receive forgiveness and salvation from condemnation and eternal death. Those who help Christ carry the cross help sinners to see Him. He cannot do it alone. That is why He partnered with human beings to do this. He might not have made it to the place of the skull where He was crucified to save many if Simon had never helped Him.

Even now, He cannot save many without our help. He needs us to bring sinners to the cross, the place of the skull, the same place David killed Goliath and buried his head, where the spiritual Goliath—the devil—was defeated forever.

If Christ died before getting to the crucifixion site, the repentant thief would have been destroyed eternally. He had to make it to the cross! The scripture that says he took our curse away because cursed is the man who hung on the cross would have been a lie. Marriages would not have been healed and restored from the spear that pierced His side. That was why it was and still is essential for us to assist Christ with the cross. Remember, without Christ, we are nothing.

Without us telling others about Christ, He will not be made known on earth. Let us love Christ and God the Father back by diligently following the leadership of the Holy Spirit, and faithfully with joy, help Him carry His cross by carrying our cross for His namesake. We bring sinners to the cross, and He dies for them. Simon of Cyrene helped Christ to carry His cross, but he never died for anyone. Likewise, do not die for man. This was Christ's assignment, which he successfully completed. Instead, we are to love them enough to lead them to Christ for cleansing. Don't play savior, play your part by leading sinners to the Savior in word and deed, and leave salvation to the Savior.

- **My friend reveals to me trials coming, and the end result.**

"He will not die until he sees this!"

The end of the year 2010 and the beginning of the year 2011, I was in a Holy Spirit-led fast. During the fast, I turned off all volumes in my life, including my phone, and the only people who had access to me were my husband and children. At the end of my fast, the Holy Spirit revealed to me the impending future in a dream. I dreamt that I was in a huge bus full of children, and the rails on the bus were transparent with oil running in them. The oil looked like olive oil. I was standing in the bus speaking to the children while my dad was driving the bus. In the bus audio player, there was a song playing in the Kikuyu language that said, "*Ni Roho wa Ngai uria umatogoragia, no bata no mahoya na wetereri Ngai.*" In English, the song says, "It is the Holy Spirit of God who leads them; they only need to pray and wait upon the Lord." Then the Holy Spirit pointed right at my dad and spoke to me saying, "He will not die until He sees this!" pointing at all that was in the bus. The children ministry.

The Holy Spirit revealed to me that He was the oil on the bus and that He has anointed me for the children's ministry, and my father will assist me. I was amazed at the dream! I was excited that my friend revealed to me yet another assignment I was created for. I was also thrilled that my dad, who loves children extravagantly, is my designated assignment helper! My dad, at the time, was the best driver I ever knew. He was very safe and always alert while behind the wheel. To this day, my father stays awake as long as he is in the car, even as a codriver. The day after my fast, my cousin, who lived in Georgia, visited me. He said that he was concerned because he and my mother had tried to get a hold of me, but they could not. He went on to say that my father had collapsed and was now admitted into the hospital in a very critical condition.

I was very calm through it all because I remembered the dream. I knew that my father was not going to die until he saw the children's ministry come to pass. I thanked my cousin for the news and immediately called to speak with my mother. She was calm and did not seem to understand the severity of the situation.

My mother told me that she had been led to fast for three days by the Holy Spirit before the incident. I remembered that a few months before this, my father had visited my family during my graduation and had been very proud of me. Before his visit, a prophet had instructed me to take him for a physical checkup when he arrived, but I forgot all about it and remembered it only after he had traveled back to Africa.

I remembered it because dad had a transient ischemic attack (TIA) and was unable to move his extremities. After the TIA resolved, my mother and sisters called me to report the attack, not knowing what it was, but they were celebrating that the devil had been defeated, and dad was now back to normal. I explained to them that the symptoms were a warning sign for a stroke and asked them to take dad to the doctor immediately. The physician found that my dad had hypertension (HTN) (high blood pressure).

He then prescribed some blood pressure medication for my father for a few weeks, stating that the hypertension was triggered by traveling and that it should resolve once the medicine ran out. The doctor never gave my father any follow-up appointment to be sure that his prediction was accurate. I only learned of this after my father suffered a major hemorrhagic stroke and passed out after complaining of an excruciating headache at a funeral he had attended. He had run out of his blood pressure medication and did not have a refill for his prescription.

My father lay in the ICU (Intensive Care Unit) in a coma.

My friend the Holy Spirit had prepared me for this situation by telling me of the end. He revealed the victorious end from the tragic beginning. That my father would not die until he sees the children's ministry come to pass. This revelation of the end brings to mind the scripture where God answered the prophet Habakkuk. "Yahweh answered me, "Write the vision, and make it plain on tablets, that he who runs may read it. For the vision is yet for the appointed time, and it hurries toward the end, and won't prove false. Though it takes time, wait for it; because it will surely come. It won't delay. Behold, his soul is puffed up. It is not upright in him, but the righteous will live by his faith.""(Habakkuk 2:2–4)

God knows that the human soul faints and does not like to wait. Human pride causes many to be impatient and discouraged. But those who put their trust in God and wait patiently upon the Word of God to be accomplished in their lives, God will credit their faith in Him as righteousness, just like He did with Abraham. People who live by faith and not by sight will not be destroyed. They will live because of their faith in God. When hard times come upon these believers, they always seek God's wisdom. God reveals to them the end result. No matter how painful the process is, these believers put their faith and trust in God and in His Word, not in their situation's ability to destroy them.

During this season, I had another dream. I dreamt that my father was in a police car in the trunk, placed inside a black body bag. Alongside him was a lady who was also in a body bag. My mother and the family members of the lady were sitting in the back seat of the car mourning, ready to go to the mortuary from the hospital. The police officer stood outside the car having a conversation with someone. As he got ready to drive off with the bodies and their mourning families, I ran toward the car shouting and waving at him to wait and open the trunk.

When he opened the trunk, I saw two black body bags. When I opened the one on my left, I saw my father lying in it, and he was extremely weak. I told him to get out of the bag. He got out, and I helped him to a chair that was on the side of the road. I went back to the trunk to see who was in the other body bag. I saw a lady whom I did not know. I asked her to get out, but she said: "No, it's OK. I'm comfortable here, thank you." I left her to her wishes.

A few days later, a lady who was in the same hospital and unit as my dad, who had also suffered a hemorrhagic stroke, died. Her family and my family had met at the hospital because they were going through the same battle. My father survived the stroke, and a few weeks later, he was transferred to rehab. Thanks to my friend the Holy Spirit who directed me in prayer to fight this battle, my prayer took my dad out of the body bag and would have saved the other lady's life if she was willing.

- **My friend the Holy Spirit revealed that my school friend was physically legal but spiritually illegal.**

My "Jonah."

In nursing school, I met a Christian friend who lived on campus. We often studied together in her room. Because she was a Christian and a nursing student, she was physically legal to me. However, I made the mistake of not inquiring about her spiritual legality from God. On one occasion, we studied together and did the practical test as partners, but to my surprise, we both failed the first try. We had one more attempt left, but this time, we had to get 100 percent on the practical test, or we would be disqualified from moving on. Failing meant that we would have to repeat the class, be held back for a whole semester, and our graduation would be postponed.

As we went back to her room very disappointed, she confessed that she knew why she had failed the test. She said it was because she had been told to do something by God, but she was walking in disobedience. On the other hand, I had no reason why I failed the test. I was living in obedience to God, I loved Him, and had a very intimate relationship with Him. I also took my studies very seriously. When she confessed this, my spiritual antennas rose, and immediately, the Holy Spirit told me to separate from her and not study with her anymore. That was a warning I heeded like nothing before. I did not want to know what she did to disobey or why; all I knew was that she knew better, and I had to get away from her company just like Psalm 1 exhorts us.

The following weekend, my husband and I were invited to a pastor's meeting where I was asked to minister in a song from my first CD "Ushindi." Usually, before I minister anywhere, I inquire of the Lord, and the Holy Spirit always confirms where He wants to go and minister through me. He does this in different ways. This time, He showed me the meeting in a dream. In the dream, I saw the pastors who would be in attendance and their exact sitting places at the meeting. I also saw myself leading praise from one of my recorded songs, "Ushindi," meaning "Victory." That was my confirmation.

As we sat in the room waiting for the meeting to start, the Holy Spirit walked me through the book of Jonah in just a few minutes, with great revelations like I had never experienced before. He told me to tell all the pastors that they MUST always inquire of the LORD before appointing anyone to any position in their ministry. This was because the person might be physically legal but spiritually illegal like Jonah was; otherwise, it would cause their ministry to sink and suffer a significant loss. If someone can sing or play instruments perfectly well, that does not mean they qualify in God's eyes. To people who only see the outside and not the inside, they may be eligible, but not to God, because God looks on the inside—the *real* you.

See examples in the Old Testament battles—when leaders inquired of the LORD, they won the battle long before they began because victory begins in the spirit and then manifests in the physical. When King Jehoshaphat inquired of God before the battle, God told him to praise. As he praised, God sent confusion into the enemy's camp, and their enemies destroyed each other. However, there was a time when King Jehoshaphat did not inquire of the Lord, and his works were later destroyed because he allowed a "Jonah" on his ship.

"After this, Jehoshaphat king of Judah joined himself with Ahaziah king of Israel. The same did very wickedly: and he joined himself with him to make ships to go to Tarshish; and they made the ships in Ezion Geber. Then Eliezer the son of Dodavahu of Mareshah prophesied against Jehoshaphat, saying, "Because you have joined yourself with Ahaziah, Yahweh has destroyed your works." The ships were broken, so that they were not able to go to Tarshish." (2 Chron. 20:35-37)

Another example was when Joshua and the Israelites did not inquire of the LORD. They were deceived by the travelers who said they were from a far land because the travelers were afraid of being destroyed, but in reality, they were their next-door neighbors. (Josh. 9)

From the look of things, these people seemed physically legal. The travelers knew that people relied on physical evidence, instead of spiritual evidence. The mistake Joshua and his troops made was that they did not consult God, who looks more in-depth than the physical evidence of legality. We must be wise enough to ask God to reveal what is in the hearts of those around us and among us.

Just because a car has a body frame of a luxury car like a Lamborghini, it doesn't mean that the engine is a legitimate Lamborghini's engine. It could be Ford's engine. The evidence is only seen when we open the hood and expose the engine. Have you taken people at their face value, their body frame, and not their spirit? Have you been deceived into entertaining demons instead of relying on the Holy Spirit to guide you like He did Christ so that Christ knew His betrayer, the one who would deny Him, and the thoughts and hearts of men around Him during ministry? I like to have this intelligence that I may live wisely around people. I had rather have a Lamborghini's engine in a Ford's body than having Ford's engine in a Lamborghini's frame.

My friend the Holy Spirit reveals people's real identity in the spirit realm as we all are spirits living in a human body. One time my friend allowed me to hear a lady's thoughts of me that when I told her what I heard her think, she was shocked and embarrassed. Another time, He revealed to me that a lady who was visiting me had been sent by demons to find out my plans on a specific issue so that they could plan their evil mission to stop me, and He warned me not to speak anything of it in her presence. She did not know she was being used, but I knew it from my friend the Holy Spirit.

My nursing-school friend was physically legal to me because she was in the same nursing program, and she was a Christian and was kind enough to babysit for me on several occasions, but she was spiritually illegal due to her disobedience to God. Having her in my company would cause me great loss or even sink my ship. There is no other remedy for any Jonah in our lives but what is written in the Bible. Throw them into the storm they caused, and let them deal with their storm. In this way, they learn from the consequences of their disobedience, and maybe they will turn back to God and be saved, both in the spirit and in the physical. (Jonah. 1:10–16)

God will not calm the sea for you unless you throw Jonah into the sea. If you try to take Jonah back safely to shore, you will be destroyed. The reason being, Jonah is not a regular person who doesn't know God; he or she is a person who knows better but is intentionally walking in disobedience. Jonahs should be thrown into the stormy sea so they can get right with God. To avoid all this drama, don't board any Jonahs in your ship. Ask my friend to reveal to you the Jonahs in your life and repent for not consulting with Him before allowing these people into your life. God knew how to get Jonah's attention. Trust God. He loves those Jonahs and cares for them more than you will ever know. He creates a storm that only Jonah can handle, not you. Let the Jonahs in your life deal with their storm.

In my case, I obeyed God and separated myself from my nursing-school friend and never studied with her again. I passed my practical exam the second time, and she failed. She was held back a semester, and I graduated as scheduled. All glory to God in the highest! During this time, I had a dream. In the dream, some people had come to my house to steal from me. I looked around to see what they had taken and found that they had stolen some of my nursing books.

Shortly after, there was a knock on my door, and when I opened, I saw a small boy standing there with all the books they had stolen from me, and he said, "Take these books. Those men . . ." (he pointed to where they stood about a mile away), ". . . told me to bring them back to you. They said that they could not steal from you because you are a very prayerful woman." Hallelujah! My education could not be taken away from me because when we pray and live in obedience to God, we allow God to fight on our behalf. "Oh that my people would listen to me, that Israel would walk in my ways! I would soon subdue their enemies, and turn my hand against their adversaries." (Psalm 81:13–14)

- **My friend reveals to me the importance of names.**

Names: The power of names, and how my name and my children's names put us in bondage.

Naming started with God. God names people according to their assignment. He lets them know their origin, so they do not forget who they are but makes sure they understand their purpose and their assignment description.

Before one works for a company, the company posts a job opening to solve a problem or need they have. Once the person is hired, they receive a name badge with their title. They also sign paperwork of their job description, which is their assignment, stating that they fully understand the company's expectations of them. In this case, the title would be considered a name which identifies your assignment in the company, and your personal name tells of your origin. The hired person still keeps their own name, but their name is irrelevant when it is unattached to their company's given title. However, when their personal name is attached to their title, their name gains value and commands respect. How many times have you heard of someone's name but because you do not know what title they hold in the company, you treat them as ordinary people?

As a hospital administrative supervisor, I was doing my rounds in the hospital one day, but somehow my badge was turned the other way. As I made my rounds, I greeted people with a smile. One lady, a certified nursing assistant (CNA), started a conversation with me, and she went on jokingly. I listened to her and engaged her. She acted casual and playful. Just before I left, she asked what my title in the hospital was. By this time, she felt comfortable enough to turn my badge the right way to see my title even before I could answer her. That was how I knew that my badge had turned the wrong way. When she read my title, she immediately let go of my hand and went down almost on her knees, begging for forgiveness.

I reached out to her and told her it was okay, but she was so shaken. When she finally composed herself, she said, "Why are you so kind, humble, and nice? You are not supposed to be that good with such a title. I have never met anyone so kind who carries a big title like you. You should not be that nice." She kept repeating the same thing as if to accuse me of making her feel very comfortable with me. I told her that my title means nothing to me if I do not represent Christ well. I believe that people should be themselves and at ease as they work. People give just what they are required to and do not go beyond their call of duty if they are working in a hostile and punitive culture or environment. My name had no meaning to the CNA without my title, but after she knew my title, when my name is mentioned, it has a lot of meaning to it.

Once, I was administering a vaccination, and the person I was giving it to wrote on the consent form that they worked in administration. I asked her where in administration she worked, as I prepared the vaccination just to make conversation because the administration department has many titles from office assistant to all the big administrative titles. She said lightly, shrugging her shoulders, "Just administration." I had a great conversation with her as I gave her the immunization.

After she left, I looked at her name and asked my secretary who she was. He said that she was the chief executive officer of the hospital. I was shocked! Really? Wow! I gave her a shot but treated her like an ordinary person, but with respect. Thankfully, I treat all my patients as VIPs (very important person) no matter who they are, so I had nothing to worry about. Once I learned of her title, her name gained meaning. By itself, her name meant nothing to me. It just told me of her origin or race, which doesn't make any difference to me since I love all races and all people equally, no matter who they are.

Human beings name objects according to the object's task. A spoon to eat with, and a knife to cut with. If we are so smart to name our creations according to their assignment, why is it that we name each other or our children according to everything out there *but* their created assignment?

We do not qualify to name any human being because we never created them. Only God is qualified. Adam never saw how God created humans because he was asleep when Eve was being created. Adam never saw what God put in Eve when He created her.

However, Adam watched God create the animals, and God allowed him to name them because Adam saw what God put in each animal as He created them.

Beloved, we are not human beings first. We are spirits first (male or female spirit); then a human body was created to house our spirits. A spirit cannot legally operate on earth unless it has a body.

Before God created anything, He saw the problem which He wanted to solve. He then called out the solution's name. In human terms, God posted a job opening; then He created the person and equipped them to solve the problem. That is, God hired the person. This proves that the assignment came before the person was created. God never created man and then had him jobless, trying to look for something for Him to do. God is purposeful. He does not promote idleness. Just like someone once said, an idle mind is the devil's workshop. That is why high crime rates are found where there is joblessness. A job position is always created first, then the person is hired. It is never the other way.

If you have nothing to do, the devil will give you something to do. Remember, he is a spirit and also needs a body to operate effectively on earth. Satan likes idle humans because he can go to work through them. That is why there is so much evil on earth. God is not responsible for it. We are. We are the ones with the body, and we host in us the Spirit of God or evil spirits. God cannot legally operate on earth out of a body. That is why He used prophets of old, made a body for Christ, and still uses those who yield to Him as I have. He is writing this book through me. The more people remain oblivious to their God-given task, the more evil prevails because the devil has more than enough people to hire for his evil works on earth.

Adam was created to solve a problem which God had. There was no one to till the ground, no one to manage God's estate, which was the earth He created. That was why a male body was formed first to do the work with both male and female spirits in it. He created them both with the same ranking and title. Both were called managers. After Adam (male and female), which is the origin name of man which means, "made from earth," was created, God was ready to cause plants to grow because the managerial position for His estate had been filled.

> No plant of the field was yet in the earth, and no herb of the field had yet sprung up; for <u>Yahweh God had not caused it to rain on the earth</u>. *There was not a man to till the ground,* but a mist went up from the earth, and watered the whole surface of the ground. Yahweh God formed man from the dust of the ground, and breathed into his nostrils the breath of life; and man became a living soul. Yahweh God planted a garden eastward, in Eden, and there he put the man whom he had formed. Out of the ground Yahweh God made every tree to grow that is pleasant to the sight, and good for food, including the tree of life in the middle of the garden and the tree of the knowledge of good and evil. A river went out of Eden to water the garden; and from there it was parted, and became the source of four rivers. (Genesis 2:5–10; emphasis added)

A porter thinks of what object he needs before it exists. Then he or she creates the item to serve the purpose he intended it to. If he needs to drink, he will make a cup so he can solve the problem and drink from the cup. When people wanted to travel faster, they manufactured cars. The problem, which was the need to travel faster, came before the solution, which is, manufacturing cars. A solution never comes before a problem. Before man was created, there was no one to have dominion over earth. That was a problem God needed to solve so He came up with the idea of creating someone like Him. Man.

> God said, "Let us make man in our image, after our likeness: and let them have dominion over the fish of the sea, and over the birds of the sky, and over the livestock, and over all the earth, and over every creeping thing that creeps on the earth." God created man in his own image. In God's image he created him; male and female he created them. God blessed them. God said to them, "Be fruitful, multiply, fill the earth, and subdue it. Have dominion over the fish of the sea, over the birds of the sky, and over every living thing that moves on the earth." God said, "Behold, I have given you every herb yielding seed, which is on the surface of all the earth, and every tree, which bears fruit yielding seed. It will be your food. (Genesis 1:26–29)

"He created them male and female, and blessed them. On the day they were created, he named them "Adam."" (Genesis 5:2)

At creation, both male and female were called Adam. Then when God realized there was another problem with Adam being alone, and not being able to fellowship with animals, He took the female spirit out of the body of Adam. He then created a body for her and gave her the name after her assignment, "Helper." The name God had called the female before he got her out of male to solve the problem on earth, that is, for her assignment, was "Helper." This is the same name as God the

Holy Spirit.

"Yahweh God said, "It is not good for the man to be alone. I will make him a helper comparable to him."" (Genesis 2:18)

"Yahweh God made a woman from the rib which had taken from the man and brought her to the man. The man said, "This is now bone of my bones, and flesh of my flesh. She will be called '**woman**,' because she was taken out of Man."" (Gen. 2:22–23; emphasis added)

Adam named her "**woman**," according to her origin, where she came from, and not according to her assignment, which was "Helper." Adam never explained to the woman why she was created. He never attached a title to her name. Remember my story? Authority comes from the title, not the name of origin. Because of this origin name, "woman," and not taking time to explain Eve's assignment to her, Adam introduced the first identity crisis ever on earth, and the devil took it and ran with it. The devil knew that Eve did not know who she was, or that she originally came from God and was also a god just as Adam was. That is why the devil told her that if she ate the forbidden fruit, she would be like God.

"for God knows that in the day you eat it, your eyes will be opened, and you will be like God, knowing good and evil." (Gen 3:5)

If she knew who she was, her title, and ranking, she would have said, "I am already a god. I was created in God's image and likeness; therefore, I don't need to be what I already am." The devil would not have had an open door to walk through. Adam opened this door for the enemy through the wrong name. Adam was both male and female. Eve was supposed to be called Adam as well. When Adam renamed her, he diluted her origin and made her inferior. He never gave her a title and her assignment description. The devil can access anyone who has a name of origin but does not know their Kingdom title.

When a person leaves their place of work, they cannot exercise their authority outside the company because their jurisdiction is limited only to the company's business transactions. To the rest of the world, they are just ordinary people when they are not conducting company business. Once their badge is gone, their authority goes with it. That is why the first thing that is required before getting the final check when a person resigns, retires, or gets fired, is to submit their title badge. Individuals hired in any company do not own their title. The company does. The title and badge belongs to the employer.

The badge carries authority and access to all company business. That is why God told Elijah to go and anoint Elisha when Elijah was hiding because he was afraid of Jezebel, and he wanted to die. Meaning, he was to orient and be a preceptor to Elisha and prepare to hand off his badge. Elisha was smart enough to catch on and ask for the badge when Elijah retired but with a double promotion, a double ranking title which was higher than what his preceptor had. (1 Kings 19 and 2 Kings 2)

Eve never wore a title or badge, so she was just an ordinary person to the devil. Without your God-given task, you are too regular and accessible to Satan because he does not respect your origin. Your origin means nothing to him. The only time you have authority and demons tremble is when you know why you were created, and you are living according to your God-given task. Your Kingdom title. The demons shook when Christ appeared where they were. They even confessed to knowing Paul and Jesus in Acts 19:11–17.

Paul was given a name change from Saul, and with it came a Kingdom title and new assignment which he lived up to.

Jesus was given a name and Kingdom title before birth, with a job description which He lived up to. What about *you*? Are you easily accessible to Satan because you have no title attached to your name? Having no title means you are nobody in the spiritual world. Jacob, whose name meant trickster, was easily accessible to the demon of trickery because he had no Kingdom title. He tricked his brother into selling him his birthright.

Later in life, Jacob had an encounter with God. During this encounter, Jacob asked God to bless him. The Man whom Jacob wrestled asked what Jacob's name was, and then he changed Jacob's name to Israel because the name Jacob was not found in heaven's titles—assignments—. The name Jacob was found in the assignment in the kingdom of darkness. Whose payroll are *you* on? You may, like Jacob, be working for the wrong kingdom without knowing it. Nabal's name meant "fool," and he lived up to his name and died a fool. (1 Samuel 25:25)

The man said, "Let me go, for the day breaks." Jacob said, "I won't let you go, unless you bless me." He said to him, "What is your name?" He said, "Jacob." He said, "Your name will no longer be called Jacob, but Israel; for you have fought with God and with men, and have prevailed." (Genesis 32:26–28)

Beloved, knowing your God-given Kingdom title is your blessing! Your blessings are connected to your title just as paycheck is connected to your job title.

The name Israel is what saved Jacob from Esau's wrath. Israel's title gave Jacob authority over Esau because Esau was just an ordinary person, with no title. Esau was looking for Jacob for revenge, but he saw Israel instead. He saw a man with power and authority from God, a co-ruler with God. Esau saw a king and priest, a broken, limping, and chosen man who belonged to God. Heaven troops backed up Israel and the devil had no chance or courage to confront Israel. Authority had been bestowed upon Israel, just like one would receive a promotion with a new title and higher authority.

Gideon was another man who did not know his title and authority. When he realized this, even the devil warned the enemies about him. His enemies had nightmares of being destroyed by Gideon. The devil knew that heaven had gained a mighty man of war, and they were in trouble. The kingdom of darkness trembles when a believer knows that they are a god, and when they discover their title and job description. Satan cannot contend with God's authority because he has power but no authority. Christ stripped his authority and gave it to God's children.

Authority is bestowed upon someone or taken away, but power is a gift, and it cannot be taken away. However, power without authority is useless because power submits to authority, but authority never submits to power. God is more powerful than the devil. Therefore, since we have the authority to use the name of Jesus, we can call upon a greater power to destroy Satan's power, and Satan must submit. Insubordination is nonexistent in the spirit realm. Satan learned this the hard way when he was in heaven and was cast down, dismissed from duty and his badge recalled so he would not repeat the same mistake he made before. He was fired! Just as on earth insubordination is grounds for dismissal, Satan knows better than to operate in rebellion again.

Instead of calling Eve woman, which was obvious, Adam should have looked at the woman in excitement and exclaimed, "Hello, god my helper! It is so nice to put a face to the name finally! We lived in one body together until God the Holy Trinity saw that it was not good for me to be alone. God, therefore, took you out of our male body and created a female body for you to wear so we can have fellowship, and most importantly, you can be my helper! Your body is new, but your existence is not. We both were created at the same time. We rank the same, and we had one body, but now we have two and still are one flesh."

"Therefore a man will leave his father and his mother, and will join with his wife, and they will be one flesh. The man and his wife were both naked, and they were not ashamed." (Genesis 2:24–25)

That is why when man and woman join together, they form one flesh. This oneness is the original creation which produces fruitfulness and multiplication. That is what the enemy fights so much. As long as Adam was both male and female, the devil never showed up as he could not even approach this union! He had no chance! Satan was no match for the unity in male and female. After the separation, the enemy knew that the strong bond had been weakened, and a door opened by Adam of the identity crisis in Eve; therefore, he had the courage and upper hand over the first family.

As long as a husband and wife are one, and they both know each other's identity in Christ, when they pray for and with each other, support, encourage, strengthen, help, complement, and challenge each other to fulfill their God-given task, the enemy has no opportunity or chance of defeating them. But when they are separated and do not know each other's created assignment, the enemy has the upper hand on them. Satan will use them to destroy each other, and they will suffer pain and loss just as we see happening with the first couple in Genesis.

It was Adam's responsibility to speak what God spoke over Eve. How many times do couples speak what God speaks over their spouses? If Adam spoke what God spoke about Eve, it would have kept Eve up to date on her identity and assignment. Most men speak few words to women instead of taking time to explain and be clear on what they need their wives to do to help them. These men are only harming themselves. They do not take time to lift up their helpers, and/or equip them to be the helpers they need. Instead, they work for the devil by following his advice and looking down on their helper. In doing so, they foolishly disable themselves and end up not reaching their full, created potential.

Now that we have this information, in this knowledge, can you tell who caused the fall? Adam caused the fall, not Eve. Adam did not think it was necessary to explain to Eve why she was created, or let her know that she was, and still is, equal to him in ranking but different in assignments. Adam was created to till the ground, and she was created to be Adam's helper. They ranked the same. They only operated differently for harmony. Just like God the Father, Son, and the Holy Spirit. They all rank the same but have different operations and assignments for harmony. If they ranked differently, they would not be three in one. They would be three in three.

Eve knew God's command about the tree, but even with the word of God, she was still susceptible to fail without knowing her title and assignment. If I study a company's policy and know all about it but have no title or authority to enforce it, how effective would I be? Would anyone listen to me if I were to enforce the policy? I would have to go through someone with a title to try to enforce it. But if I had the title, I would immediately enforce it without pushback. That is why the sons of Sceva in Acts 19:11–20 tried to cast out demons in the name of the Jesus who Paul preached, and the demons refused to comply.

Instead, the demons asked them their title saying, "Jesus we know, and Paul we know, but who are you?" Then the demons turned around and beat them up, stripping them naked, causing them to bleed, and the seven sons of Sceva ran away because they had no title of their own. They had no Kingdom authority or backing. Your title, which is your God-given task, gives you the authority to operate under Kingdom power and influence. God and His angels only offer backup to those with Kingdom authority.

Beloved, names are significant because they reveal the authority and jurisdiction a person has in the spirit realm, which manifests in the physical realm. Names are meant to reveal your God-given task. Names are very spiritual. If the enemy can distort your identity, he will defeat you because you will never show up for your assignment. With an identity crisis, you will never be a threat to the devil, nor will you please God. That means that you will not get rewarded because you never worked your assignment.

Some people follow other people and get the wrong titles and assignments. This is worse than not doing anything because you will still not get rewarded. Why? Because you worked in the wrong department. If a company hires you to be a manager, but you show up in housekeeping and work there without any breaks, including putting in some overtime, when it comes time to pay you, you will not get paid. This is because the housekeeping department does not have you on their payroll, so they cannot pay you. However, the administration has you on their payroll but with no hours worked because you never showed up for duty as a manager. You will not get paid. How sad for these people at the end of time, when they stand before God, having done so much work that counts for nothing because they worked out of their assignment. Will you be one of these people?

If a car is manufactured, and it does not get used, it will be useless and eventually not work anymore. What if it is built but given the wrong title and assignment? If someone named it a plane, the vehicle would waste all its time on the runway trying to fly, but it will never be able to. But if the car would have known that its name was "car" and not "plane," the car would have been more useful to the owner and others by changing its location from the runway to the street and the freeway. Are you a car on the runway? Or are you a plane on the streets? Do you know who you are? Have you asked your creator? What does your badge say your title is? Who gave it to you? That determines which kingdom you are working for. What is your role in God's Kingdom? Do you have a title other than your name of origin?

Any name or title which God has not given you, comes from the enemy. One can only work for one of the two kingdoms. God will not allow you to work part-time in His Kingdom (being a lukewarm Christian) and the rest of your time in the kingdom of darkness. Knowing that God only hires and pays (rewards) full-time employees who work solely for Him due to conflict of interest, the devil doesn't mind if you are part-time in his kingdom or on an as-needed basis, as long as you work some hours for him. Why? Because he knows that if you give him any kind of service, you belong to him. Satan knows that God will never accept you in His Kingdom as long as you still work for the enemy. If our earthly organizations will not allow you to work any job that poses any conflict of interest to the hiring company, why do we think that God will?

The title or name that has people working for the kingdom

of darkness may have been obtained through your parents naming you, like mine was, knowingly or unknowingly through traditions, baby name websites, or thoughts of "cute" names. Some were initiated into Satanism, and the devil changed their names like one who was delivered from the powers of darkness gave a testimony that Satan could not use his given name "Moses" because it belonged to God's Kingdom, so he called him "Moroni." In scripture, this is made clear when the children of Israel sinned and were taken into captivity in Babylon. The king changed the names of the three Hebrew boys and that of Daniel. Names belong to kingdoms, not the person. Because they were now in a different kingdom, they had to receive a different name that worked for and not against the kingdom which had hired them.

"Daniel, Hananiah, Mishael, and Azariah were four of the young men chosen, all from the tribe of Judah. The chief of staff renamed them with these Babylonian names: Daniel was called Belteshazzar. Hananiah was called Shadrach. Mishael was called Meshach. Azariah was called Abednego." (Daniel 1:6–7, NLT)

Have you reported to duty on your God-given assignment? Are you working on the wrong assignment because you don't know your title or your name was changed to work for the enemy? Everyone is working, either for God or Satan. Satan will never let you stay idle. Are you assisting the devil in introducing identity crisis to your children and grandchildren? May the Holy Spirit illuminate this to all people in Jesus' name!

My story:

I am originally from Kenya, East Africa, a town called Kinoo. For those who know this town, it is always made fun of in Kenyan comedy. Someone would be justified to say, "Can anything good come from Kinoo?" just like Nathaniel said about Jesus, "Can anything good come from Nazareth?" According to the Kikuyu tribe and custom which I was born in, people are named after their family members. This naming system ensures that the family member's name lives throughout many generations. To this day, this naming continues even among Christians. This is a demonic naming system. It is a sin of ancestral worship, hidden in innocent traditions. Africans used to be idol worshippers, and when they embraced Christianity, they incorporated it into their traditions and, unaware, kept some of the idol worship traditions. In this culture, the first child is named after the husband's parent.

If the child is a boy, he would be named after his dad or if a girl, after his mum. Then, if the second child is a boy, he would be named after the wife's father, and if a girl, the husband's side of the family is named first, so it would be his mother, and so on, including naming them after brothers and sisters. This tradition tells you that when a child is born in my culture, people do not have to ask for the name of the child. All they did was ask for the gender of the child, and they automatically knew the name of the child. This tradition introduced favoritism, partiality, and rejection, depending on who one was named after.

My older son was named after my father-in-law, "Kiriga," which meant "difficult to comprehend." He struggled in school and could not comprehend even the simplest concepts. My husband and I were very frustrated at his lack of simple comprehension. Our son was always frustrated when it came to doing his homework. One day, I followed him to the bathroom after he had excused himself from the homework table as we, my husband and I, were frustrated at him, thinking that he just did not want to think because his younger brother would effortlessly figure out his assignment. As I stood outside the bathroom door, I heard my baby crying deeply and in prayer, pleading with God to help him comprehend what he was being taught. He was only seven years old at the time.

I was deeply moved, heartbroken, and I knew that there was a force greater than stupidity working against my son. I spoke to my husband about this. We prayed, repented, and changed our son's name to only using his first name, Trevor, which meant "wisdom." We did this without worry about any consequences of breaking the Kikuyu tradition. We had to set our children free! We repented, denounced their ancestral names, and called them what God calls them. Beloved, the change was instant! They broke out into a rush, both the first and second son. The baby had not been named after anyone. However, our cute name for him "Trestyne" meant "horns of a deer."

We repented of this too because he had started being defiant, which triggered me to find out the meaning of his name, and I called him what God called him when he almost died in my womb. During prayer, after receiving the bad news from the doctor and I called my mother to inform her to pray, God said to her, "Peace is all well." My husband wanted to name the baby after himself, but I refused and told him to go and inquire of God and come back with a name from Him. He came back, not knowing the conversation I had with my mom months before, and said that he found a name which was "Amani." Amani is a Swahili name for "Peace." This confirmed what God had spoken earlier in my pregnancy through my mother while she was in prayer. To this day, our third child goes by the name Amani. He is the most peace-loving and peaceful child I know.

From that day on till now, our first son Trevor is the head only and never the tail, above only and not beneath. He used to be in special education until I disenrolled him after a big fight with his school counselor who said once children are on special education, they never get out as they will do poorly and fall back. She explained that this was so because they do not get the individualized help they need. She was wrong! Trevor thrived and became an "A" student with no one's help but Jesus'! He became the most popular kid in school for great achievements behaviorally, academically, and in sportsmanship. He made us famous in his school. All we had to say was we were his parents, and then everyone wanted to meet us and congratulate us on raising such a great son. This went on all through middle school and in high school. He is a great student and is always on the honor roll. He graduated high school with great honors and as a student athlete.

My middle son's name was "Kibuiya," which means "a Kikuyu traditional dance." Yes, you guessed it right! My son was a dancer like no one else! He would come up with amazing moves as any song played. In preschool, all the students and teachers would come to his class to watch him dance. The problem was that he danced to all music, even secular music which was not pleasing to God. When music played, he would start dancing until it was turned off. At times, he could not stop himself from dancing, and he would cry, asking us to turn off the music so he could rest. After prayer and name change, the bondage was broken. Now, he is not the addicted dancer he used to be. In fact, he can hardly dance. I came to realize that it was the "kibuiya" demon which was dancing through him.

As for me, I had been named after my father's mother because I was the first girl. Esther Warigia. "Warigia" means the "last one." I struggled in school, trying not to be the last one in my early years. I remember being celebrated when I got a C+ in my senior year in high school, and my brother got in trouble when he got anything less than an "A" because he was brilliant. My grandpa used to jokingly call me his wife because I was named after his wife, and he would favor me. My mother could not discipline me in my grandmother's presence because if she did, my grandma would tell her to place the punishment on her instead. My grandmother took it personally. She thought my mother wanted to get back at her through me. It was very personal that my mother would be scolded in public by my grandma.

I grew up very proud, and like my grandma, I had anger issues. I held on to grudges from when I was a little child just like she did. In most of my childhood pictures, I was angry. This was a great bondage for me. My grandmother later had multiple strokes due to uncontrolled high blood pressure. She was nonverbal when she died. I would refuse to talk to teachers all day in kindergarten because my mother had annoyed me that morning, or I would refuse to speak to or respond when my mother talked to me late in the evening because she had spanked me earlier in the day. I held on to grudges a lot even as a grown-up.

One day, as I walked to my car from class in Georgia, I had a terrible headache on the left side of my brain. It was a stroke like headache. I happened to look at my watch. It was 3:30

p.m. I went home praying that the headache would leave, but it remained until later that evening. The following day after class, the excruciating headache returned. When I looked at the time, I didn't know why I looked at the time then, but I later knew that my friend the Holy Spirit was telling me something. It was 3:30 p.m. again.

I remembered that the devil could program bad things to happen to someone at certain times because he cannot be in all places at the same time. More like a timer. I immediately called my parents and told them what was going on, and they both said, "Change your name!" They knew this was spiritual because they had just learned about names and the importance of them. I prayed and disowned my name. I prayed against all curses and demonic activities programmed through that name on me to be destroyed in Jesus' name.

Demons gain a portal of entry through a name. They can continue the destruction of one person to the other with this connecting bridge. Remember in Mark 5:12–13 when Jesus went to the other side of the lake and met a demon-possessed man, and the demons begged Jesus not to get them out of a body, but to send them into the pigs, who have a body, so they could still operate legally on earth? The enemy cannot do anything to you if he is out of a body. That is why Satan caused man to sin.

Sin and ignorance open the door for him to come into us and do evil on earth. He can use humans or animals. The devil uses animals because they have no willpower. Satan is a bully and a thief, but God gives us the free will to love and serve him. Just like God needs a body to minister healing and deliverance and to perform Kingdom business because He is a Spirit, the same is true with the evil spirits. Understand that spirits outside a body cannot operate on earth. That is why when people die, they cannot be effective or legal anymore on earth unless they leave behind teachings which others can carry on.

God cannot do things for us. We must allow Him in us and obey Him as He leads us into bringing His Kingdom and His will on earth. Evil spirits perform their wicked acts through people. A lying spirit must use a person's mouth to tell a lie. A suicide spirit or murder spirit must use the human body to perform these evil acts. Remember when Jesus healed a demon-possessed man and the demons were sent to the pigs? The pigs were minding their own business, having a great time, feeding and playing in the dirt, enjoying their day. They did not want to drown themselves, but when the evil spirits got into them, they forced the pigs into the lake and killed them.

Evil spirits like to remain legal on earth and in the territory they have mastered. That was why they did not want to leave the area and begged Jesus to let them stay. When we evict them from us and allow the Holy Spirit to lead us, we will bring more good on earth as Jesus did. The man was uncontrollable when the demons lived in him, but after the demons left him, he was very calm and collected. His sanity and dignity were restored. He must have had a lot of open doors and all 6,000 demons—a legion—took advantage of this and drowned all 2,000 pigs! What a relief this man must have felt. No wonder Jesus was led to this town to set him free. Then He asked him to tell others what God had done for him. Spread the gospel!

"Send us into those pigs," the spirits begged. "Let us enter them." So Jesus gave them permission. The evil spirits came out of the man and entered the pigs, and the entire herd of about 2,000 pigs plunged down the steep hillside into the lake and drowned in the water. The herdsmen fled to the nearby town and the surrounding countryside, spreading the news as they ran. People rushed out to see what had happened. A crowd soon gathered around Jesus, and they saw the man who had been possessed by the legion of demons. He was sitting there fully clothed and perfectly sane, and they were all afraid. Then those who had seen what happened told the others about the demon-possessed man and the pigs. (Mark 5:12–16, NLT)

The following day, my mother and I decided to attack this evil headache spirit before it struck again. The next morning, I had a home health practical lesson and was out in the field with my preceptor. I grabbed a book which I had been given awhile back by a pastor and his wife, who were teaching on deliverance. I had not read it before, but for some reason, the Holy Spirit led me to read it. The topic of deliverance was not very well accepted in the church then. Christians were ignorant of the fact that they can be born again but not delivered. In the *Deliverance for the Delivered* book by Stephen Mwanaliti, the Holy Spirit led me to a place where he discussed ancestral worship. The author explained that naming people after others is ancestral worship. God revealed to me this hidden sin, which I did not know of. As David prayed, I prayed . . .

"Who can understand his errors or omissions? Acquit me of hidden (unconscious, unintended) faults." (Psalm 19:12, AMP)

I repented as I rode in the car with my preceptor on our way to the patient's house. At 3:20 p.m., as my preceptor was speaking with the patient, I laid my hand on my head and began praying against that ancestral spirit curse and evicting the demons that had access to me because of this sin. At 3:30 p.m., the headache had not returned. The curse was broken! I was healed and free! Glory to Jesus and the power of His blood. My mother told me that as she was praying, she experienced a terrible headache. She could hardly believe the pain I had experienced. She prayed through the headache, and when the curse was broken, she knew it because the pain she experienced was gone. Sometimes, God will allow you to experience someone else's pain as you pray for them so you can pray with deep intensity since you are in the same shoes. Christ became a curse so that we could be blessed. Don't live in the curse anymore. Receive deliverance in Jesus' name!

My grandma's name had been shared among my cousins too. Through this name, my cousin and I suffered HELLP syndrome, which caused me to have a premature baby at six months, while my cousin could not make it to the hospital in time. She died with the child in her stomach. Years later, my mother learned how to do deliverance ministry, and as she was ministering deliverance to someone, demons spoke through the person saying that they wanted to kill me, but they failed, so they killed my cousin. They said they failed because my mother was very prayerful.

After this victory, I was nameless waiting for God to name me, and He did! My mother had a prophet visiting her church who did not know her. He was a guest speaker in her church through someone she knew. He prophesied to her, saying, "You have a daughter in the United States, and she is in the medical field. God says she is a gift. He calls her Gift. is her name Gift?" I was nameless then, which he had no idea of. When I called my parents, my mum answered the phone and said, "Hi,

Zawadi." (Zawadi means "Gift" in Swahili.) I was amazed at her greeting, and she went on to tell me all that God had said through His prophet.

I asked God to confirm to me this new name. One night, in my sleep, I saw my old name written in full and then crossed out with a big "X," and the name "GIFT" was written above it. When I woke up, I was excited! I woke my sons up to go to school, excitedly saying, "Good morning, boys. It's time to wake up!" On the way to school, my older son said, "Mum, when you woke us up, did you say 'Good morning, boys, I have a new name!'?" His brother laughed and said, "No! She said, 'Good morning, boys. It's time to wake up!'" His brother was right. I then revealed to them the dream I had, and how God had given me a new name, and how my older son was used to confirm that it was real. I had received a new name given by God the Father. I love God because He confirms His Word if you trust Him. I did not go looking for a name. I allowed God to name me. I now go by my new name, Gift, or Zawadi.

How about you? Who named you? Remember, even nicknames are names. Do not let anyone, circumstances, or trials in life name you. Let God tell you what He calls you so you may live in His glory, authority, and power in Jesus' name!

The fall of man in the Garden of Eden was because Adam and Eve got diverted from their God-given task and began to operate in their own wisdom. They turned to the tree of human wisdom instead of being satisfied with God's wisdom. God kicked them out of His divine and supernatural provision because they started doing what they were not created to do. Because of this sin, they had to be fired, kicked out of Kingdom property, and an angel placed there with a sword as a security guard. They had Kingdom authority with earthly wisdom which is very dangerous. Just like operating against your employer under their title and authority access. You become an enemy and a threat to the company. These people are usually walked out of the company by security and warned never to return or they will be trespassing and the police will get involved.

The police of heaven, (an angel), was placed on guard when God walked Adam and Eve out of the Garden. The angel was there to guard a specific tree. The tree of life. God in Genesis 3:22–24 shows how man was foolish not to eat from the tree of life but instead, chose the tree of human wisdom. Their humanity is what made them realize that they were naked. They were now more sensitive to the flesh, its nature and looks than to the spirit, who they really were. It was therefore very dangerous for them to eat from the tree of life and forever live in this shallow mentality of valuing their outward appearance more than the spirit which lives forever. That is why we all must die, and this body must return to dirt. Then we will receive the immortal body and eat from the tree of life, and we will live forever just like Christ. His body now is a forever body. This tree of life is only reserved for those who receive Christ and are led by the Holy Spirit. This is the wisdom of God which when we eat from the tree of life we will live forever in His Kingdom.

"Anyone with ears to hear must listen to the Spirit and understand what he is saying to the churches. To everyone who is victorious I will give fruit from the tree of life in the paradise of God." (Revelation 2:7, NLT)

God will not allow us to run His Kingdom's business in human wisdom as it is too shallow for the Kingdom. It will cause a significant loss. Adam and Eve's vision was limited, and their wisdom was foolishness to God. They thought they were just human. They did not see themselves as gods anymore. They had a distorted vision and mind-set which the enemy could easily manipulate. Their eyes were open to the wisdom of man and blinded to the wisdom of God.

They began lying to God and hiding from Him even when they knew clearly that no one could lie to God. Human wisdom makes people shortsighted and foolish. It stripped them of God's glory. God could not partner with such foolishness, nor could He fellowship with fools. Before human wisdom, humans had God's wisdom alone. They knew that they were spirits wearing a body, and they were gods. That was why God and man walked and talked together in fellowship.

How successful a fellowship would you have with a drunkard? It would be impossible to do so because their realty is not your reality. This is the case with those who do not have the mind of Christ. It is impossible to have fellowship with a spirit when you are in the flesh. The flesh and the spirit desire opposite things and therefore they are always in conflict. Paul made this clear in Gal. 5:17 NLT "The sinful nature wants to do evil, which is just the opposite of what the Spirit wants. And the Spirit gives us desires that are the opposite of what the sinful nature desires. These two forces are constantly fighting each other, so you are not free to carry out your good intentions."

Even now, the only way we can fellowship with God and be at the same wisdom level with Him is only through my friend the Holy Spirit. He must live in us to give us the right words to say, as well as reveal to us what God the Father is saying for effective fellowship with Him. Without the Holy Spirit, man and God cannot relate. Man will never achieve the wisdom of God without God in him. Christ had to explain everything to His disciples because they did not understand His wisdom.

Christ had the Holy Spirit, who is the Spirit of God's wisdom in Him.

The initial plan, as my friend the Holy Spirit explained to me, was to have man live holy just like God, with no sin. When Satan introduced evil, by sinning against God, the tree of knowledge of good and evil came to existence because God had to separate good and evil. The tree in the Garden is symbolic of God's book, which had a list of all evil and good, and a way to differentiate it. Without this knowledge, we would have been holy, because we would not know that any evil existed. If all you read is the Word of God and all you see is heaven and all you fellowship with and hang out with is God, how can you do any evil?

Just as we teach our children good things, but when they see evil on social media and in school they encounter bad behaving children, they become polluted with the evil they are exposed to. Before this exposure, all they knew to do was the good we taught them. Likewise, God was protecting man from this pollution by keeping them from the existing evil. Satan, however, knew God's plan, and he went behind Him to convince men to do evil, disobey God, which polluted them, and this sin drove them out of God's presence and divine protection, provision, and grace. God is the only one who can see and know evil and not get polluted by it. Imagine all He has seen and still sees; yet, He never gave up on humanity. Instead, He came to die for us. What kind of love is this!

Isaiah 55:8–9 confirms this truth . . . "For my thoughts are not your thoughts, and your ways are not my ways," says Yahweh. "For as the heavens are higher than the earth, so are my ways higher than your ways, and my thoughts than your thoughts."

1 Corinthians 1:18–31 also says that the foolishness of God is wiser than the wisdom of man. Christ is God's wisdom, but the human mind and wisdom cannot receive Christ. That is why only by the Holy Spirit can one confess Jesus Christ as their Lord and Savior. The Holy Spirit is the only one who can convict us of sin, that we may receive Christ, the wisdom of God. Once the Holy Spirit puts this wisdom in us, He teaches us how to think, speak, and live like God. He transforms and renews our minds and mentors us to think like God because we are to be married to Christ, and the marriage cannot work if we do not have the mind of Christ. The Holy Spirit has the assignment of getting us back to being gods. He is preparing us to be like Christ. Human beings only marry human beings, not animals.

Likewise, God marries god, not a human being. We must be at the same level with Christ. Kings rule together and sit together on the throne. We are being trained by the Holy Spirit to rule and reign with Christ. Disobedience gives people a slave mentality, and they cannot rule with Christ in the heavenly places. The reason for the financial struggle among Christians is because God will not fund our agendas. He only supports Kingdom business according to His timing, plan, and will. Are you living in your own wisdom instead of the wisdom of God? Remember, if the Holy Spirit leads you, you are a son (mature child) of God.

A lady from the Philippines once told me that in their culture, if a child often got ill, they would change the child's name, and the child would experience better health. Don't give the enemy legal right to your life through a name. Don't perish for lack of knowledge. You have no excuse now because you know.

Another wonderful change happened in my marriage. I

used to delete my husband's name and phone number from my phone when we were not on good terms, until one day, the Holy Spirit gave me God's wisdom that replaced my foolishness. I still knew my husband's name and phone number off the top of my head no matter how many times I deleted it. The devil is a liar! The devil was my enemy, not my husband. My friend the Holy Spirit asked me what I wanted from my husband. I told Him that I needed my husband to love me like Christ loves His church. Then He said to me, "Then call it! Give your husband the name Love, and every time he calls you, especially in trying times, know and confess that you are in the marriage because of God's perfect love for each other, and declare the love of Christ in him until it manifests."

When I did this, I never deleted him again. Every time he called me, I would remember what love is, and up to this day, his name is Love. I now experience the selfless and extravagant love that Christ has for His church through my husband's love for me. I asked my friend the Holy Spirit to teach my husband how to love me as Christ loves me, and to have my husband make Christ his best friend and hang out with Him until he becomes like Him. I also asked my friend the Holy Spirit to make me the bride of Christ and the bride to my husband like God needs me to be. I must admit that it is easy to submit to a man who is like Christ. It gives me great pleasure to do so.

See more details on names in my book, *Your God-Given Task*.

- **My friend taught me how to forgive.**

In the first incident, a junior (first year) doctor came into my patient's room, and in the presence of the patient, she started quarreling me and asking questions about a leaking ileostomy into a wound next to it which everyone, including the wound-care specialist, had tried to deal with but was unsuccessful. The wound was so close to his ileostomy, and he had terrible diarrhea. No matter how many times we dressed the wound and changed the ileostomy bag, it leaked beyond control. I tried to explain this to the doctor but was unsuccessful because before I could even answer her, she would rudely interrupt me with another question, and another, with scolding, and it was nonstop! I gave up trying to reason with her; therefore, I kept quiet and let her talk. I then kindly asked her what her name was, because I had had enough of her unprofessionalism, and I was going to write her up. I politely asked, "Doctor, what's your name?" She rudely responded, "Go find it in the chart where I have written some orders!"

By this time, my patient, whom I had led to Christ during my shift and who had seen how hard I worked all night to care for him, looked at the doctor and sternly said to her, "STOP IT! She is a great nurse!"

The doctor was shocked at his response to her behavior. She had been very kind to him, but extremely mean to me. I was shocked too, but very glad he spoke. At least someone, the one I was serving, and who mattered most to the organization and me, saw and appreciated my care for him. I knew that the devil was angry because the patient had received Christ as his Lord and Savior. I went home that morning and prayed, but before I did, I quoted scripture back to God and said to Him, "You said to love my enemies and pray for those who persecute me. Well, this had better work for me now . . ."

You have heard the law that says, 'Love your neighbor' and hate your enemy. But I say, love your enemies! Pray for those who persecute you! In that way, you will be acting as true children of your Father in heaven. For he gives his sunlight to both the evil and the good, and he sends rain on the just and the unjust alike. If you love only those who love you, what reward is there for that? Even corrupt tax collectors do that much. If you are kind only to your friends, how are you different from anyone else? Even pagans do that. But you are to be perfect, even as your Father in heaven is perfect. (Matt. 5:43-48, NLT)

I prayed for God to forgive me for taking offense and to give me His forgiveness and love to forgive and love this doctor with. I felt His love and forgiveness all over me as I prayed . . . "In Jesus' name, I forgive the doctor with God's forgiveness, and love her with God's love."

Immediately, I had a great release in my spirit. I began praying for her, her family, her school, and her prosperity, that she would know God and be all she was created to be. I prayed as if I were praying for myself or a friend. I had a sense of great peace in me and was FREE! My relationship with God always means more to me than anything or anyone. I did not want to allow unforgiveness and offense to come between God and me.

The following day at work, my assignment changed. I always asked God to make my assignment, and I believed He did. I never argued at all with the charge nurse about my assignment. I accepted it gladly because I worked for God and not man. I believed that where I was assigned was where God wanted to work through me. I accepted my assignment and worked it. I did not have the same patient from the day before. Only he had been taken out of the assignment while all the other patients were left on for no reason at all. In the morning, the same unprofessional doctor, in the presence and hearing of everyone at the workstation where other doctors and nurses were working on their computers, saw me passing by and she said to me sternly and with such authority, "Hi! Did you know that it is leaking again?"

I looked at her and said very gently with a smile, "Hi. No, I didn't know this because I am not his nurse today."

She was shocked and felt so embarrassed, and she looked down. I went on and said to her, "See, it was not my nursing skills that had a problem. I tried to explain this to you yesterday, but you were so rude to me that my patient had to stand up for me." She said politely, "I am so sorry. I did not mean that your nursing skills were a problem. I was just angry because it had happened over and over, even before you were his nurse, and I was tired of it because I have great compassion for my patients."

By this time, everyone was listening in on our conversation. I was hoping they would so that her fellow doctors would never treat nurses with such dishonor. I replied, "You and I both. I am here because I have great compassion for what I do and for my patients, but that does not make me disrespect others. You have a license, and I have a license. You are a professional just as I am. You need to respect me, and I respect you as we work together to better our patients' outcomes. If you had listened to me, maybe you would have known where the problem was and fixed it instead of blaming nurses who have nothing to do with the surgery."

She apologized, and I forgave her. From that day on, she

knew my name, addressed me respectfully by name, using the words "please" and "thank you." We worked together very well after that. I am almost sure no other nurse will have to suffer humiliation from her again, or from other doctors who listened to the conversation. God provided a great opportunity for reconciliation. I took Him at His Word, and it worked!

In the second incident, the doctor was a neurosurgeon senior. He was very rude to me on the phone, because I informed him that his patient was in pain and needed pain medication. He wanted me to place the pain medication order for him in the chart, but rules had changed, and the doctor had to put in his order. He was asleep and did not want to wake up to put it in. He was so upset that he hung up on me. He called back after a few minutes, but I refused to answer. I gave the charge nurse my phone to answer him. The charge RN gave the doctor the same answer I had given him, so he was not happy. He asked the charge RN for my name so he could write me up. I wrote up the incident and took it to the assistant manager. Apparently, he had been written up before for the same behavior of insulting and being rude to nurses. The assistant manager that night said she was going to report it to his attending. I went home and did the same thing. I prayed in the same way I had prayed in my first incident.

One day, about two weeks after the incident, I had a patient where he was the doctor. He needed to have a conference with some family members, and he wanted the patient's nurse to witness the meeting. In the meeting, he was so kind to the family members. It was like day and night compared to his previous behavior on the phone. He did not know me, but I knew him. After the meeting, I felt the Holy Spirit say that this was my opportunity for reconciliation. I asked the doctor to remain behind, which he gladly did. I started the conversation by telling him how much I appreciated his work, and how he handled the meeting very well.

I reminded him of our incident over the phone, and I told him that I had forgiven him, and had prayed for him, his family, his school, and all that concerns him. He said he remembered that day and admitted that he was rude and apologized for his behavior. He said that he was also a Christian, but had failed and wished he was half the Christian that I was. I knew that I was not good, but Christ was good in me. I told him I didn't get there easily. I had to ask God for His grace to be a doer of the Word, not just a hearer because God's Word works! We shared God's Word and spoke about our families, and from that day on, I have not heard of any more incidents reported on him.

Beloved, it is not foolish to make the first step toward reconciliation. God says that as long as it depends on you, live at peace with all people (see Rom 12:18–21) and that if you go to pray and remember that someone has something against you, stop praying, go and reconcile, and then come back to pray so that God may answer you (see Matt. 5:23–24). You see, God is not asking about your offender. He is concerned about *your* spiritual and physical health.

Forgiveness and reconciliation set you free and gives you great health both spiritually and physically. You cannot be used by God and fulfill your God-given task successfully with unforgiveness. Brethren, God's Word is proven to be true! You don't have to try it. Just do it because it has already been tried and proven, and God has guaranteed it and honored it over His name. It is forever settled in heaven.

"Every word of God proves true. He is a shield to all who come to him for protection." (Prov. 30:5, NLT)

"Your eternal word, O Lord, stands firm in heaven." (Ps. 119:89)

"The grass withers and the flowers fade, but the word of our God stands forever." (Isa. 40:8)

It works! I do this with all who offend me, and God opens up a door for reconciliation. Sometimes I used to get tired of being the first one to make peace, but God says in Matthew 5:9, "Blessed are the peacemakers, for they shall be called children of God."

Love and forgiveness are divine. By our strength, we can't love or forgive as God commands. Ask for God's love to love others with and His forgiveness to forgive others with. He will gladly give it to you.

(More on forgiveness can be found in my book, *Your God-Given Task*, by Gift Zawadi.)

A prayer to forgive like Christ:

"Father, in Jesus' name, you command me to forgive from my heart, to love my enemies, and pray for those who persecute me. I can't do this with my strength, but with your strength, I can. Please put your love for all humanity in me that I may love them the way you love them. Put your perfect forgiveness in me that I may forgive them with it. I confess and repent of every sin of unforgiveness and offense in my life. Please cleanse me from all unrighteousness, create in me your heart, and renew your Spirit within me. With the authority I have in Christ, I rebuke the spirit of offense and any other spirits that came in from this sin of offense in Jesus' name! I receive the spirit of love, the peace of God, and the grace of God in Jesus' name. I forgive all my enemies with your forgiveness and love them all with your perfect love. In Jesus' name, I pray, believe, and receive with thanksgiving. Amen!"

Now, pray for your enemies with believing that God has put His love and forgiveness in you. Pray for them as if they were your friends. Pray in the same way you would pray for yourself. In this way, the devil loses, and the Kingdom of God wins! Our real enemy is in the spirit. We fight against principalities and powers of darkness, not fellow humans.

- **My friend ministers healing through me.**

A patient healed instantly of a bleeding disorder.

Once again, in ICU, we received a patient from the telemetry floor who was bleeding profusely from his lower gastrointestinal tract. He was not my patient, but it was an emergency, so I went in to help the nurse. The doctor had ordered a rapid blood transfusion, and I was hanging the blood and IV fluids as ordered when I heard the patient's wife say to him, "We are back to square one."

That statement led me to ask what she meant. They went on to explain that this same thing had happened to him a few months ago, and he was hospitalized in ICU where he almost died. I asked them if they believed in Jesus Christ and His healing power. They said they did.

I asked the man, "Do you want this to stop and never come back again?"

He responded, "Yes!"

I began to pray and commanded all bleeding to stop and

never return in Jesus' name. It was a simple but on target prayer as I continued to hang the blood. At the end of the shift, the man asked his nurse to call me.

He said, "Thank you so much for praying for me. The bleeding stopped after you prayed."

I glorified God with him for Jesus! Then, the following night when I went back to work, he was no longer in ICU. The doctor who had treated him the night he was bleeding walked to me and said, "Remember the man who was bleeding profusely yesterday? They scoped him from the top and bottom, and they could not find any trace of blood or opening that caused the bleeding! Strange!"

I said to him, "It's Jesus! We prayed, and Doctor Jesus healed him!"

The man had been transferred to the medical-surgical unit, the lowest level of care in the hospital and was going to be discharged home the following morning. When I went to see him, he and his wife were very grateful for my obedience and courage to pray, and for Jesus' healing power!

Another healing:

Formally declared brain-dead patient alive and well.

I was in ICU again taking care of my patient, who looked very familiar, but I could not remember where I saw her. As I was taking care of her, her husband walked in and was so grateful that I was her nurse. He said, "I remember you! You are the same nurse who took care of our nephew who had been declared brain dead by the doctors, but you prayed for him and told us not to lose hope but to have faith and keep praying. We did that, and now our nephew is at home and well. Thank you so much!" I then remembered where I had seen my patient. She had come to visit her nephew. Beloved, God is still in the healing business!

- **My friend the Holy Spirit reveals my patient's stronghold.**

Once during my senior practicums in nursing school, I had a patient who was a believer, living with her pastor because she was homeless. She was trying to get her life together, but every time she did, there was a setback, and she could not get ahead. We spoke and prayed. As I was going about my shift, the Holy Spirit told me, "Look at the back of her neck." She had hair that fell down her shoulders, and I could not see as she lay in bed. I put it off for later on when I assessed her, but I forgot to follow up. I remembered that I failed to check when I was in the elevator going home. The patient was going to be transferred to another facility that night, meaning that I would not have the chance to see what the Holy Spirit wanted to reveal to me. I prayed and repented of this sin and asked God to keep the patient in the hospital for one more night, and I promised to check the back of her neck first thing in the morning.

God answered my prayer! I found the patient still there with her transfer postponed till noon. I asked her to rollover to her side so I could listen to her lungs. At this point, I pulled her hair to the side exposing the back of her neck . . . and there it was! A tattoo of a horoscope! I was shocked but grateful to God. The Holy Spirit told me that she had given her life to be controlled by the horoscope and not Jesus, and that is why she always has setbacks. I gave her this revelation, and she agreed to pray and break this stronghold. We did so, and by the grace of God, she was delivered from the power of darkness. Glory to Jesus!! Horoscopes and tattoos are not of God. These are an abomination to God. Fortune tellers, star gazers, palm readers, and magicians are all demonic powers. God forbids against these practices and warns us of destruction. Many have opened demonic doors in their lives from these practices. (Lev. 19:28 & 31, Lev. 20:6 & 27, Rev. 21:8)

Once, in the same hospital as a nursing student, there was a blind patient who would not allow anyone to come near her. She would curse and kick whoever went near. She was elderly and did not allow the nurses to take her blood pressure in order to administer her blood pressure medication. I asked the nurses to allow me to go to her. They warned me to be careful. As I entered her room quietly, she immediately submitted, greeted me with a wave before I even said a word to her as if she could me. Everyone was shocked! She did not curse at me. She responded to me as if she could see me. She gave me her arm before I asked her for it so I could take her blood pressure. It was a shock to me and everyone who stood outside her door witnessing this interaction. She opened her mouth and took her medication and responded "yes ma'am" when I spoke to her. The Holy Spirit quickened to me that she submitted because the evil spirits in her saw me and submitted to God in me. The spirits in her were afraid and did not want to be cast out. I did not know deliverance then, because if I did I would have cast them out of her in Jesus' name to set her free. Beloved, God in us makes the devil tremble.

- **My friend guided me to rebuke the spirit of fever**

I began my nursing acute care career on a step-down unit where I worked this particular day, and my patient reported to me that every night he experienced high fevers that went away during the day but returned at night. He said the doctors could not find the cause. This confirmed the report I had received from the outgoing RN. I told him, "I believe in Jesus Christ, and His healing power. Do you believe in Christ?"

He said he did. I told him that fever was a spirit, and that it was no longer welcome in his room. I spoke out loud and said, "Spirit of fever, I command you to leave and never come back. You are not allowed in this room in Jesus' name." I put a blood line at the door, and said, "You cannot cross over in Jesus' name! Amen."

That night, the patient slept so soundly that I had to wake him up to check his blood pressure and temperature. He had not slept for many nights due to the high fevers and discomfort, so it was hard to get him to wake up now. After that night, he told everyone who visited him or took care of him what had happened that night. I was very excited to know how much power we have over the kingdom of darkness in Jesus' name! Glory to Jesus for He came to set the captives free!

- **My friend leads me to minister to my patient and prepare her for eternity.**

My patient had dementia and respiratory failure. She was on comfort care, as she was in her late 80s with a poor prognosis. I spoke to her about Jesus, and she said that she loved Jesus. I asked her if it was okay to pray with her, and she was excited. We prayed, repented of all our sins, and forgave all who have sinned against us. After the prayer, she kept saying, "Thank you, Jesus! Thank you, Jesus! Hallelujah! Hallelujah!" Fifteen minutes later, her breathing slowed down, and she died peacefully. Her family was called, and I let them know how she spent her last hour on earth. They were very grateful knowing that their mother had gone to be with Jesus! They reported that she used to suffer unforgiveness but they were glad we dealt with that before she transitioned to heaven. What a blessing and privilege to be used by my friend the Holy Spirit to usher a child of God into glory. I was so blessed to be used in that capacity. Glory to Jesus!

- **My friend is the Spirit of worship. He writes and sings songs through me.**

I usually get songs supernaturally from the Holy Spirit . . . in my sleep, in worship, or as I am going about my day I hear the Holy Spirit singing in me like a radio, and then I record it. The Holy Spirit is the greatest songwriter I know. He gives me all the songs I sing as I do not know how to write songs from my understanding. I ask Him to reveal God the Father to me through music and give me my heavenly Bridegroom's and Dad's favorite songs so that I may worship them with and teach others to do the same.

One morning at three a.m. as I was breastfeeding my baby, I asked my friend to reveal to me what the Father wants to hear. He immediately gave me a very anointed song. The song is made in the throne room, Revelations 4. It is in Swahili language. It says, "As you are enthroned on high, you receive continuous worship from the angels, four creatures, twenty-four elders, day and night. No other king on earth is worshipped like you are. You alone are everlasting! All praise and honor belong to you. You do not share your glory with any man. Receive all the glory and honor, Jesus."

My friend often takes me to a place where I tap into the throne room of God, and I worship Him there in tongues; then He translates the song into an earthly language. This is my favorite, most complete moment, and I long for it daily. I worship and praise God with these amazing songs until my spirit masters them. Then I share them with the world after I draw from them myself. Glory to the name of Jesus!

- **My friend delivers me from the spirit of suicide.**

I was at the edge of a cliff ready to commit suicide when God...

The spirit of suicide was introduced to me when I was about thirteen years of age when one middle school teacher demanded that Jane (not her real name) and I, along with one other homeless kid, go to the school office. We were trying to go through the school fence into the slums. Jane and I had been busy having fun at the swings as we waited for our parents to pick us up, but the teacher said we were also trying to go through the fence, which was untrue. She made us all kneel with our hands lifted up, and then she put ropes around our necks, making a knot as if she was going to strangle us. She then said, "Be prepared to die today. I will kill you because you wanted to die anyway, going into the slums!"

We all cried so hard trying to explain that we were not going through the fence, and the homeless kid said she was sorry for trying to go through the fence. The teacher laughed at us and kept repeating those words: "Today, you will all die." I was rescued when a family friend came to get me because her mother had come to pick us up. I went home crying and shaken with the fear of death. I believe this was the beginning of the spirit of suicide in my life.

In high school, I was in a boarding school where bullying was allowed. They called it "monolization" I was bullied a lot in the first year. I had a very rough and tough high school life, and when I tried to report this, my parents only thought that I did not want to go to school. I learned to stay alone and was confident of who I was in Christ because I would turn to God, and He would fight my battles, putting my enemies to shame ALL THE TIME! One day, a girl in my class who was the class leader was jealous of me because teachers favored me, so she lied about me, saying that I had spread malicious slander about her. I had no idea what she was talking about. She said I spoke many curse words which were untrue because I did not curse then, and I still will not use profanity or even watch or listen to movies or music which contain profanity or swearing. My mouth will not utter such words.

One Saturday, as I sat in class doing my daily devotion, the bully walked in the class crying and commanded me to stand up. When I did, she gave me a double slap on both cheeks in the presence of the whole class as she called me all sorts of names. After she was finished with the drama, I gently asked her, "Are you done?" Then I sat down and continued with my Bible study as if nothing happened. She went out crying and acting out.

In school, students used to cut grass and mow the lawn using machetes because there were no hired workers to do it. The school was a boarding school, and the first two weeks of school were dedicated to cleaning the school and cutting grass that grew the month we were on vacation. When the bully divided portions of grass to mow, she would give me three times more than everyone else and warned the others not to help me, or she would punish them.

The following weekend when I went home because my joints hurt due to the cold weather, as well as to get away from the bullying, my parents said that I was lying about my pain because I did not want to go to school, so I got in trouble at home. My parents never listened to my side of the story. My dad threatened me, saying that if I did not return to school immediately, I should never call him my father. The school was far, and I was not allowed to go back at night or during the weekend. So I was miserable all weekend at home with my parents angry with me. I had no hope, and no one to love me, so suicide was my only option at fifteen years old. The suicide attempt failed as the acid I drank only made me throw up. No one ever knew about this. I went on in life and graduated high school. My bully never graduated, and she got demoted from a leadership position and was expelled from school in her senior year. However, I was promoted to a captain's position with two assistants under me from my second year in high school till I graduated.

When I got married at nineteen years old, my marriage was challenging and full of abuse. I went through so much that I wanted my husband to leave and never come back. He was a truck driver then. When that did not happen, I decided to go and never come back. I wanted to end my life. I told my brother of my intent to commit suicide one night. I said that I was going to go to work, and on my way, I would speed up my car and hit the dividing wall on the freeway head-on so I would die. We lived in Georgia U.S.A then. My brother, in his calm, laid-back, and very caring tone, opened my eyes to see how much I meant to so many people, even though I meant nothing to my husband. He hugged me and held me close to him as he spoke to me saying. . . "Why kill yourself for someone who can always be replaced? If you kill yourself, your children will lose their mother, I will lose a sister, our parents will lose their daughter, our cousins will lose their cousin, our uncles and aunts will lose their niece, and our friends will lose a friend . . ."

All of a sudden, I realized that I *was* valuable to many more people, and my husband didn't matter anymore. I had been deceived like Eve was in the Garden of Eden, when the devil magnified the one tree she should not eat fruit from so that she lost vision of all the fruit trees she had at her disposal for food. Only one tree did not matter if she could not eat it, because she had thousands more to eat from! I am forever grateful to God for my brother, who was used to rescue me from this spirit of suicide this second time.

The third suicide attempt was after I had all my three children and still had a terrible marriage! My brother was not around, and I was at a place of deep depression. I hit rock bottom over my marriage betrayal, and betrayal from all my close "friends." I wanted to hide under the earth. I felt tiny and worthless. I was at the lowest place I had ever experienced in my life. I had hit rock bottom, and I had to die this time, I thought. I would squeeze myself to fit under the bed because that was where I felt was the lowest point I could go. One day, I had contemplated suicide by a butcher knife, but I chickened out thinking it would be too painful and bloody, and if I survived, I would be taken to a mental hospital and given psychotic medications. This, to me, was worse than death.

I then remembered the cliff by the lake where I lived. It was very quiet and isolated. I told my husband to take the children because I needed to take a drive to clear my mind. I drove to the cliff, and I sat on a bench that had been dedicated to someone who was dead. I felt great courage and a voice urging me strongly to throw myself down the cliff, and then all my misery would be over. I would never have to deal with my husband ever again or betrayal from friends! That sounded like a dream come true! They might put up a proper tombstone for me, and the pain and suffering I felt would be gone. I stood and walked to the edge of the cliff and, looking down, I thought, *Great! This is perfect! I will jump and fall headfirst on the rocks, then bounce off to the lake. I will not be found until tomorrow, so that guarantees my death! Mission accomplished! No one is here to stop me.*

But . . .Just before I jumped, a voice and light flashed on my right side from the sky and got my immediate attention. I looked to my right. The voice asked me, "WHAT IS THIS IN YOU THAT THE DEVIL IS SO AFRAID OF THAT HE WANTS YOU DEAD SO BAD?!"

Immediately, it was like someone woke me up from a deep sleep! What? Is the devil the one behind all this? Not my husband? I grasped the revelation from God in my spirit, and angry at the devil, I spoke out loud, repeating what God had said, but this time, addressing the devil. I asked him, "Yes, devil, what is this in me that you are so afraid of that you want me dead so bad?! I will not die, but I will live to see what you are afraid of in me. I will live to see and declare the goodness of the Lord in the land of the living!"

All of a sudden, I was energized, courageous, and felt very lightweight, like I could fly. The spirit of heaviness, depression, suicide, and death was broken and defeated forever in me! I went back home now with a different perspective, knowing who my real enemy was, and what he was after! I was going to kick him out of my marriage, out of my husband, and out of myself. I was very curious and ready to live to see what he was so afraid of in me.

Since that day, I've been on a mission to destroy this spirit in many others as I have victory over it in Christ Jesus. No one around me who reveals this spirit will remain bound in Jesus' name! If this spirit has tormented you, today is your day of deliverance! Today is your day of salvation! Realize that God had put greatness in you, and that you are a significant threat to the enemy. Do not let him win! The devil wants to take you out before you take him out! He wants to destroy you and have it easy. Don't lose focus of who your *real* enemy is. We are here to destroy his kingdom of darkness forever!

My children would have never understood why I killed myself. The devil would have convinced them that I committed suicide because I hated them, and the rest of my generation would have been lost. Glory to God in the highest for His deliverance power! I thank God daily for this great rescue! God stepped in when man could not. He stepped in just for me. His love is unimaginable! He loves you with the same great passion! This spirit of suicide took its time and lingered in me since middle school, and it showed up in high school, then in my early twenties, and early thirties. It had no problem waiting, as long as it accomplishes its mission, which is to kill you. Don't allow it. Receive the same word I received from God, and ask the devil the same question I did. Destroy him with the same authority Christ our Lord gave me. Remember the spirit of anger in Moses lingered in him from Egypt, to the wilderness, and eventually made him not enjoy the Promised Land. The devil has no problem waiting for an opportune time to destroy you and your destiny. Stay alert and be led by my friend the Holy Spirit.

Now, declare God's Word in Psalm 118:11–17 (NLT), "Yes, they surrounded and attacked me, but I destroyed them all with the authority of the Lord. They swarmed around me like bees; they blazed against me like a crackling fire. But I destroyed them all with the authority of the Lord. My enemies did their best to kill me, but the Lord rescued me. The Lord is my strength and my song; he has given me victory. Songs of joy and victory are sung in the camp of the godly. The strong right arm of the Lord has done glorious things! The strong right arm of the Lord is raised in triumph. The strong right arm of the Lord has done glorious things! I will not die; instead, I will live to tell what the Lord has done."

You may ask why God never rebuked the devil for my sake or told him to stop. Instead, He spoke to me. It is because God has given us authority on earth, and He cannot take authority for me. I now rule the earth, and that was why the devil lost, because I knew who I was that instant. The devil has power but doesn't have authority. Jesus took this from him and gave it to us. When my identity was restored, I took authority. The devil had lied to me that my identity was good for nothing; that I was unloved, useless, and hopeless; that I meant nothing to anyone; and he went on and on with his lies. I believed his lies until God stepped in and woke me up from my identity crisis coma. Beloved, wake up! Know who you are in Christ! Nothing can or ever will separate us from the love of God that is in Christ Jesus our Lord! (See Romans 8:31–39.)

- **My Jesus asked to use my past experiences to draw many to His Kingdom.**

One night, Christ Jesus appeared to me in a dream. He walked toward me and came to where I sat on a rock. With both hands, He bent down and held my face by my cheeks. He moved closer and kissed me on my lips and said,
"*I am so sorry for all you have gone through.*"

I was so overwhelmed with His love, and as He stood in front of me, I reached out and attempted to express my extravagant love for Him, but the love was too much to form into words. I was so overwhelmed by my love for Him, and He understood it. Without my words, He responded with the most amazing smile as He reached out to touch my outstretched arms and said . . .

"*I know . . . Me too!*"

Then He turned gracefully and walked away. As He walked away, He stopped, turned around, and faced me. Then He called out to me asking,

"*But can I use these to draw many into the Kingdom of God?*"

Overjoyed and in awe, I replied,

"*Yes! Yes! Anything for the Kingdom of God! Anything!!*"

He smiled, turned, and walked away.

Christ feels our pain. He, in turn, takes it and uses it as a blow against the enemy's kingdom. He prays for our faith not to fail us, and when we are restored, we are to strengthen others. As in my book *Your God-Given Task*, the Holy Spirit revealed to me the meaning of the word MESSAGE. MESSAGE = MESS + AGE.

If we don't go through trials in life (MESS) and overcome them by the power of Christ (Maturity = AGE), we cannot strengthen others with our MESSAGE. Christ uses real people with real struggles to draw many to His Kingdom.

I, therefore, like Christ, will show my scars where He has healed me so that others may be strengthened and receive their healing as well. Some scars are not easily visible. Christ had to show the doubting Thomas His scars, including the ribs where the spear pierced Him. This means that Christ undressed for Thomas to see and believe. We too should not be ashamed to undress that others may see and believe and share in eternity. I will do anything for God's Kingdom. That is why I share my stories, my failures, as well as victories in Christ Jesus so that those who are now healing will have hope; those who have just been wounded will endure the pain in hope that they will be healed, and those not yet there will be strengthened when trials come. It is not about saving face; it's about saving the human race from the powers of darkness.

I have a promise to keep to Jesus. I have no reservations for the Kingdom of God. I am hidden in Christ in God where no weapon formed against me shall prosper, and every tongue that rises against me is condemned in Jesus' name. May God trust us to uphold the Kingdom and not live in fear. Instead, we must live in the confidence of His love and in the fear of the Lord.

"This High Priest of ours understands our weaknesses, for he faced all of the same testings we do, yet he did not sin." (Hebrews 4:15, NLT)

- **My friend directs my preaching.**

My friend the Holy Spirit tells me what He wants to speak about in the service. He gives me words and visions of what He wants to do or what He will do. Once when in worship before preaching, He showed me a vision of heaven and a very huge table full of food. The food was so much that the table had no space. All I could see was food, fruits, and more food. Then God the Father said that His table was ready and full, but it is only for the hungry. God will just feed the hungry, not those who will waste the food. The congregation had to hunger and thirst after His righteousness, and they would be filled. How amazing!

Another day I was getting ready to minister when God told me to wear my white robe because He wants to minister healing to His people. That day was the most amazing day and service. A drug addict who was looking for a quick job so he could get some money for drugs stumbled into the church where I ministered that day and had an encounter with Doctor Jesus. The man came back to church a few days later to testify that he had been delivered from drug addiction since that day. Glory to Jesus! Our God is just as powerful as He was in the beginning of creation. His blood is just as effective as it was on the cross when He was dying. It is the same blood which the repentant thief got cleansed with and was the first to be saved and enter into glory through the blood of the new covenant, glory to Jesus!

- **My friend writes books through me.**

My mother was an English teacher, and daily, after school, we had tutoring in our home. I disliked writing and was never a fan of essays or compositions as we called them in Africa, but my mother made us write one daily, and she then would grade it. This continued even during school break because my mother loved to teach. My cousins would visit, and we would have tutoring sessions daily. When in my late twenties when I asked the Holy Spirit to reveal what was put in me during creation, He said I was an author of many books through a prophet I never knew.

When I write, I never go to my laptop because I have an organized rough draft or set outline on what I am to write. Instead my friend gives me the content. He tells me the book title, the chapter titles, and the content as I am typing. Many revelations in my books are received at the same time I'm typing. He downloads information, and I write what I hear Him say. I am totally reliant on His authorship and cannot write any book in my own understanding. I actually get so excited that I do not get tired and can write all day and all night because my mind is yielded to Him for His use, and all I have to do is write what He says.

I must remain in constant fellowship with Him to hear Him clearly and accurately. My friend wrote the Bible through many writers in ancient times, and I am a witness of His continual authorship. He is still inspiring and writing God's Word to this day. God's Word is not limited to the words in the Bible, but it does not contradict His Word either, because God is not an author of confusion. My friend the Holy Spirit is awesome!!

CHAPTER 10

BAPTISM OF MY FRIEND THE HOLY SPIRIT AND FIRE

WHO CAN RECEIVE the Holy Spirit?

Anyone who comes to drink from the well of Jesus Christ that never runs dry. Whoever believes in Christ as the Son of God, and accepts His sacrifice, repents, and receives salvation, then asks for the Holy Spirit from the Father through Jesus Christ. This person must not only come to drink from the well of salvation to quench their thirst but must also be willing to go further and quench the thirst of God in worship and service to the Kingdom by fulfilling their God-given task.

God has a desire to be worshipped and adored. Rebecca not only gave the servant a drink of water, but she also served him by feeding his animals. Are *you* willing to serve God? The Holy Spirit is given to those in Christ Jesus who are eager to serve God, not those who want to quench His fire instead of allowing His fire to ignite their passion, making them hot for Christ. The Holy Spirit has gifts and fruit, which are for the benefit of the church of Jesus Christ.

The Holy Spirit is the personal trainer of Kingdom living. I remember the day when I asked God the Father through God the Son to give me the Helper, God the Holy Spirit whom He had promised me according to Luke 11:10–13 (NKJV): "For everyone who asks receives, and he who seeks finds, and to him who knocks it will be opened. If a son asks for bread from any father among you, will he give him a stone? Or if he asks for a fish, will he give him a serpent instead of a fish? Or if he asks for an egg, will he offer him a scorpion? If you then, being evil, know how to give good gifts to your children, how much more will your heavenly Father give the Holy Spirit to those who ask Him!"

To Receive the Holy Spirit, you MUST be Born Again.

God the Father sends God the Holy Spirit to us in the name of Jesus Christ His Son. If you do not have the power to use the name of Jesus Christ, you cannot ask for or receive the Holy Spirit. Only those who have made Jesus Christ their LORD and Savior have the right to be called by His name. They can ask for and receive God's gift, my friend the Holy Spirit. God could have stopped the work of salvation at the resurrection, and our sin would have been paid for by the blood of Jesus, but He did not. He added Pentecost. This means that there is no heaven without these three: Death, Resurrection, and Pentecost (baptism of the Holy Spirit). We must die to sin and resurrect unto righteousness, and be baptized with the Holy Spirit and fire to live like Kingdom citizens. Without Pentecost we cannot know God, be holy, or enjoy Kingdom privileges because we would not have the power of God through the Holy Spirit.

We die to sin by confessing we are sinners in need of a Savior, and we resurrect by accepting Christ into our hearts. This is symbolized by water baptism. When one is immersed in the water, it means that they are dying to their old sinful nature, and when they come up out of the water, it means that they are now resurrected in Christ. They are born again. After this comes the Pentecost experience, like Christ had after water baptism, when we ask for the baptism of the Holy Spirit. God gave us a Helper to help us use this newly found power in the blood of Jesus effectively for our salvation to destroy sin. Sin has a twin that must be destroyed along with it, and that is death. Death was never seen until sin came into play.

God killed an animal to sacrifice for man's sin and cover Adam and Eve's nakedness. This was followed by Cain killing Abel, and the killing and death went on and still goes on, but those who are in Christ have been delivered from sin and death. (Romans 6:23) "For the wages of sin is death, but the free gift of God is eternal life in Christ Jesus our Lord."

The reason Jesus never went to heaven straight from the dead but He had to resurrect, come back on earth and stay for another forty days to confirm and seal His resurrection before ascending to heaven, was because He had to destroy sin's twin, death. That is why He died and rose again on the third day to give us victory over both sin and death. These are the devil's greatest weapons against nonbelievers. They are the foundation upon which his kingdom is built. When you receive the sacrifice heaven made for you and accept Jesus Christ as your Lord and Savior, then you destroy the enemy's foundation from your life, and he has no more root or hold on you. He becomes homeless. Therefore, beloved, if you are born again, we have authority and power over the kingdom of darkness in the name of Jesus Christ by His blood because He shed all His blood for my sin, and He rose again for my freedom and victory over death that I may live forever as God initially intended.

Asking for God the Holy Spirit without having Christ as your Lord and Savior is asking for the right to receive access to all secret intelligence information from the Kingdom of God while you still belong to the kingdom of darkness. This information is usually kept confidential for the protection and benefit of the Kingdom. It is only accessible only to Kingdom citizens. Because the Holy Spirit of God knows the secret things of God, He is only given to citizens in the Kingdom of God for the benefit of the Kingdom. He is the KIA (Kingdom Intelligence Agent) revealing secret things of the Kingdom to aid in destroying the devil's kingdom.

If you are born again, you have the right to ask God to fill you with His Holy Spirit without measure and to ask the Holy Spirit to come in and cleanse you and rid you of all that is not of God in you. You can ask the Holy Spirit to fill you with His fruits and gifts. Ask Him to give you the gift of speaking in tongues. Believe you receive, open your mouth, and start speaking in the language He provides. The devil and your mind will try to work against your spirit, saying that the language is fake or made up. But keep speaking; don't give up, because you are allowing God to use your tongue to express mysteries that your mind can't comprehend, and neither can the devil. You are talking directly to God; it is the perfect prayer by the Holy Spirit through you to the Father. You must open your mouth and make a sound! Just like talking, you can't learn to speak with your mouth closed. When you open your mouth to speak, you allow the Holy Spirit to fill your mouth with heavenly tongues. Like a hungry child who opens their mouth in anticipation of food from their parent, your expectations will not be cut off. (Prov. 23:18)

How do you know you received the Holy Spirit when you ask? Luke 11:11–13 says, "Which of you fathers, if your son asks for bread, will give him a stone? Or if he asks for a fish, he won't give him a snake instead of a fish, will he? Or if he asks for an egg, he won't give him a scorpion, will he? If you then, being evil, know how to give good gifts to your children, how much more will your heavenly Father give the Holy Spirit to those who ask him?"

God gives the Holy Spirit because He wants you to prosper just like Christ prospered in His assignment on earth, and His disciples waited to receive the baptism of the Holy Spirit and fire to be witnesses of Christ and to fulfill their God-given assignments. We too must receive this baptism to please God in fulfilling our duties on earth.

Ephesians 1:17–20 says, "That the God of our Lord Jesus Christ, the Father of glory, may give to you a spirit of wisdom and revelation in the knowledge of him; having the eyes of your hearts enlightened, that you may know what is the hope of his calling, and what are the riches of the glory of his inheritance in the saints, and what is the exceeding greatness of his power toward us who believe, according to that working of the strength of his might which he worked in Christ, when he raised him from the dead, and made him to sit at his right hand in the heavenly places."

Romans 8:11 says, "But if the Spirit of him who raised up Jesus from the dead dwells in you, he who raised up Christ

Jesus from the dead will also give life to your mortal bodies through his Spirit who dwells in you."

For you to receive the Holy Spirit, you must do your part, and God the Holy Spirit will give you the language. Don't think about how much sense the language is making because the things of God are spiritually discerned, not carnally. 1 Corinthians 2:14 says, "Now the natural man doesn't receive the things of God's Spirit, for they are foolishness to him, and he can't know them, because they are spiritually discerned."

Your mind is too shallow for God, and that is why the language of God bypasses the mind, rendering it inactive. Your mind will never interpret God because it can't. The devil will lie to you and make you feel like you must understand God because he wants you to sin by lacking faith in God and in His Word or promises. Do not fall for this. Believe that when God says He will give you His Spirit if you ask, it is precisely what you will get. God never lies. All promises we receive from God are by faith only. It is not dependent on God. It is dependent on our faith in Him. His integrity and faithfulness are everlasting.

How I received my friend the Holy Spirit.

It all began with a word from God through a lady who was scared to tell me that God told her to tell me to pray. I told her never to be afraid to give God's message because if I didn't know what is required of me, I would not do it, and my downfall would be charged against her. That is what God says in Ezekiel 33.

I had received the gift of tongues as a teenager but never the intimate relationship like I have now when I asked for the Holy Spirit myself.

The Prayer

I obeyed God's Word, and I started setting aside time to pray daily even when I did not know how to pray long prayers. I thought the longer your prayer, the closer one is to God. I came to realize it was not true. The more you get to know God, you actually speak with Him continuously through the day, and your relationship with Him is so close that you can stay for a long time in His presence or a short while, and still accomplish the same thing. Just like with a spouse. When you speak throughout the day, you do not need hours set aside at a specific time to talk. You will have fulfilled each other's request better by staying in communication throughout the day.

One day as I was praying in the middle of my living room in the state of Georgia, I found myself very frustrated with the church in general, and their leaders who, although from different churches, took advantage of me. I had gone from church to church, looking for a good leader. I had been molested by two preachers, once as a teenager, and then in my early twenties. The problem was not the preachers, nor the churches. The problem was me! I was looking for a good leader in man instead of looking for a great leader in God! Cursed is the man who trusts in man. (Jeremiah 17:5)

I knew about God from church and my parents when I was growing up, but I had never known God for myself. The great leader is only found in my friend the Holy Spirit. At that point in my life, I was finally done! I was done with church! Done with their programs and their fleshiness.

There must be more to God than this . . . I thought to myself. With a lot of desperation and hunger to know God and angry about how His church was run, I heard myself pray this prayer out loud, which changed my life forever!

> *Father, in Jesus' name, I am tired of church as usual and of being used and abused by those You have entrusted to teach me Your Word. I want You to come and teach me Your Word and reveal Yourself to me, just as You say in Isaiah 54:1, that 'All your children shall be taught by the Lord, And great shall be the peace of your children.'*
>
> *"You also promised to send me a Helper, the Holy Spirit, who would teach me all things. Where is He? I need Him now, in Jesus' name." Then I said to my Helper, because I believed that I had already received Him when I asked, "Holy Spirit, You were there during creation, when God the Father said, 'Let US make humans in our own image.' You know what was put in me during creation. Reveal that to me and help me accomplish my assignment in Jesus' name! Teach me ALL things just as Jesus said You would."*
>
> *I then prayed to the Father and concluded, "And, Father, I want to see Jesus! I want to see my Savior! And don't send me any angels, in Jesus' name, amen!"*

I had not planned to pray this prayer at all, but this is what came from my Spirit when I knelt to pray. This was a bold, no-nonsense prayer! It was a Holy Spirit-inspired prayer. I had a deep desire to know and see my Savior! More so than a baby longing for its mother. The church had abused me, and now I wanted the owner of the church to teach me Himself that I may know firsthand how I was supposed to live as His church because His representatives did not represent Him well at all. When I got up from my knees, I never thought of that prayer again. To me, it was as good as answered. I believed that I had received what I asked the Father for and went about my business like a little child would.

Prophecy of Confirmation

A few days later, my music producer and his wife invited my family to their house for dinner, as it was one of their birthdays. That night, it rained so heavily, and I had four children to take with me to the party. My husband was out of town, and I thought maybe we should not go, but something powerful in me said to go. The roads were terrible with almost zero visibility. We finally got there and had a lovely time. In the home, there was a prophet who started prophesying as the anointing of God led him. He prophesied many things, confirming what God had said over my life, including being an author of many books. He also said, "You have asked God to reveal Himself to you intimately, and He says that He will do it."

The Prayer Answered
The Vision

About a week after the confirmation prophecy, I was directed by the Holy Spirit to go down to the basement of my house to pray. I knelt, prayed, and when I was done, and I got up to leave, the Holy Spirit stopped me, saying, "*Wait! Prayer is not a monologue. It is a dialogue. You spoke to God, and He listened. Now, allow Him to speak, and you listen.*" I was amazed at this as no one had taught me to give God a chance to speak to me or to answer my prayer by waiting upon Him. I remained on my knees and was still before God. The Holy Spirit was teaching me that prayer is a shared conversation, not a monopolized one.

As I waited on my knees with my eyes closed, my answer came! God answered me! We often forfeit our answers when we are not willing to be still before God and allow Him to speak to us. There in my Georgia basement, I saw Jesus coming down from heaven, walking graciously toward me. He had the most beautiful hair and robe. Half of His face on the left side from the nose down was shaded. The right side of His face was visible to me. He walked down and came to me. My eyes were still shut, but I could see Him very clearly. I believe these were the eyes of the spirit that had been opened.

His eye, Oh! wow! His right eye that was visible to me was more than *breathtaking*. I saw the most beautiful blue-colored eye I have ever seen. But something beyond my comprehension or imagination was happening in that eye. I saw the whole world in His eye! I saw people in different parts of the world performing various tasks, busy with whatever they did. Jesus was there, seeing all things and hearing all. He was in the whole world, everywhere, at the same time. Yet, He took time to come to me in my little basement. This was a revelation of His omnipresence. Amazing! Then as graciously as He had come down, He turned around and went back up to heaven.

I had to tell someone about it! I wanted to scream it from the rooftop! However, I knew if I told my husband, he would think I was now going overboard. I, therefore, tried as much as I could to hold my peace. Now I understand how the people who were healed by Jesus and told not to tell anyone felt. How can you hold your peace when you have had an encounter with

Jesus Christ and beheld His majesty and glory? The God of the universe who humbled Himself and made Himself lower than His creation to save us? Only a strong person can humble himself even unto death—the worst death of all times. Knowing that Christ had the power not to die; yet, He still chose to put Himself under the mercy of His own creation is mind-blowing! His creation had no mercy for themselves or their Creator. What kind of love is this!

After encountering Jesus Christ, my Savior, it was impossible to hold my peace. I had three sons at that time, and the oldest of them was about seven years old. I told him all about the vision, and he also was excited! I told him to keep it to himself. (Laugh out loud! Yes, I know. I couldn't keep it to myself; yet, I expected a seven-year-old to keep it to himself.) After I told him, I felt better for a moment.

The following morning as we were getting ready for church, I felt the urge in me to tell my husband—a grown-up—of my encounter with my God. I excitedly told him how I asked God to show me Jesus, and how God answered my prayer. My husband calmly replied, "Why are you so surprised that God answered your prayer? Did you not have faith that He would?"

If you knew my husband then, you would know that these were not his words. God the Holy Spirit was speaking to me through him. I was so excited about his response. I LOVE this GOD!

When I asked the Father in Jesus' name to give me the Holy Spirit, I believed that I had received the Holy Spirit without a doubt because of what we read earlier in Luke 11:11–13. Because of this scripture, I was assured that if I asked for the Holy Spirit, God would not give me anything less than what I asked for, just like a good father would give good gifts to his children. Why did Jesus use food that nourishes the body to talk about a father-and-son relationship and provision? Because food is a necessity of life. It is needed for us to live and grow. If we do not have food for the rest of our lives, we would die of hunger and starvation and have stunted growth. Jesus never used examples just for the sake of it. He had a meaning for every word He spoke. A good father provides food for his family. Without shelter, many people survive (homeless); without clothing, people can still live; but without food, people will die.

Likewise, as a good father, our Spiritual Father, God, cannot leave us starving in the Spirit. Just like we who are earthly know how to feed our children good food for their nourishment and livelihood, God our Spiritual Father, knows how to feed us spiritually. We must desire and ask for the Holy Spirit, who takes what God has prepared for us from God's kitchen and serves us on God's dining table, feeding us spiritually. God desires for all of us to be fed spiritually and grow big and strong in the spirit just like He is.

When Jesus taught His disciples how to pray, He included this significant request . . . to be fed by our Father God.

> Pray like this: "Our Father in heaven, may your name be kept holy. Let your Kingdom come. Let your will be done, as in heaven, so on earth. Give us today our daily bread. Forgive us our debts, as we also forgive our debtors. Bring us not into temptation, but deliver us from the evil one. For yours is the Kingdom, the power, and the glory forever. Amen." "For if you forgive men their trespasses, your heavenly Father will also forgive you. But if you don't forgive men their trespasses, neither will your Father forgive your trespasses." (Matthew 6:9–15)

However, God will not impose Himself on us. He has already made provision for our salvation, deliverance, healing, blessings, and eternal life through Jesus Christ His Son. However, it is up to us to receive the sacrifice. It is not automatic. For anyone to receive the baptism of the Holy Spirit, they must be born again. Meaning, they must accept the sacrifice that God and His Son Jesus Christ made for them. They must give their lives to Jesus and live for Him now, by letting Him be their LORD and SAVIOR, MASTER and RULER of their lives . . . born again from the kingdom of darkness into the Kingdom of light. Dying to sin and resurrecting unto righteousness.

Just like the Israelites on the Passover night when the spirit of death was coming to destroy the firstborn sons of the Egyptians, the Passover lamb had to be killed, and its blood APPLIED on their doorposts for their salvation from death. The lamb made the sacrifice, but the people had to take the initiative of taking the blood of the lamb and applying it on their doorposts for the angel of death to see the blood and not enter their houses to destroy. The blood in the bucket was useless, but it gained the meaning of life when it was applied onto the doorposts.

> They shall *take some of the blood, and put it on the two doorposts* and on the lintel, on the houses in which they shall eat it . . . "For I will go through the land of Egypt in that night, and will strike all the firstborn in the land of Egypt, both man and animal. Against all the gods of Egypt I will execute judgments: I am Yahweh. The blood shall be to you for a token on the houses where you are: and when I see the blood, I will pass over you, and there shall no plague be on you to destroy you,

when I strike the land of Egypt." (Exodus 12:7, 12–13; italics added)

The lamb's assignment was done when the lamb sacrificed its life for their salvation. The lamb never applied its own blood on their doorposts. In the same way, it is not enough for Jesus to die on the cross and pay for all our sins and shame, redeeming us from the kingdom of darkness into the Kingdom of His marvelous light. We MUST CONFESS our sin, take the blood of Jesus who was our sacrifice and apply it in our hearts, spirits, souls, and bodies. We must give our lives totally to Christ and live for His glory alone. We MUST DIE TO SELF and live in Christ.

Jesus Christ made the sacrifice, He died for us, but He will not apply His blood on us to save us. It is up to us to believe that He took away our sins and take action by applying His blood by faith in our hearts by confession, and we shall be saved. Just like having soap and water in your house doesn't guarantee your cleanliness, you must take the soap and use the water on your body to be clean. You must make a CONSCIOUS DECISION and take PURPOSEFUL ACTION to be clean in the spirit by cleansing yourself with the blood of Jesus.

> But what does it say? "The word is near you, in your mouth, and in your heart"; that is, the word of faith, which we preach: that if you will confess with your mouth that Jesus is Lord, and believe in your heart that God raised him from the dead, you will be saved. For with the heart, one believes unto righteousness; and with the mouth, confession is made unto salvation. For the Scripture says, "Whoever believes in him will not be disappointed."(Romans 10:8–11)

Jesus said that out of the abundance of the heart, the mouth speaks (Matthew 12:34). Therefore, after accepting Him in our hearts, we must confess with our mouths that Jesus is our Lord, and our salvation is assured. We must continually live our lives in obedience to Him because He is our Lord, Master, and Savior. We submit to Him.

"For He has rescued us and has drawn us to Himself from the dominion of darkness, and has transferred us to the kingdom of His beloved Son, in whom we have redemption [because of His sacrifice, resulting in] the forgiveness of our sins [and the cancellation of sins' penalty]." (Colossians 1:13–14, AMP)

If I pay off all you owe, that is, give you a check for a payoff of all your debt and give you more than enough to spend and give away to others, and you accept my gift, and cash the check, you will live a free and prosperous life. You will be more prosperous and wealthier, happy and without the stress of being a slave to your creditors. You will have the courage to be a blessing to many. You will never have to sweat again for the rest of your life. Never work for anyone; instead, you can now be a lender and not a borrower.

However, if you refuse the gift, or if you take the check but not cash it, you will live a miserable life as a slave to your creditors. You will be a borrower, work hard, and have more stress in your life trying to make ends meet. You will not be able to enjoy life and be a blessing to many. Instead, you will see others as a burden and may even become a burden to others. This is because I cannot force you to accept my gift. No one can force you to accept a gift from them. It is always dependent on you. It is your choice. In the same way, the sacrifice of Jesus Christ is a gift from God for ANYONE. If you believe in Him and in

His sacrifice, the gift is yours! If you believe that by His wounds you are healed, the healing is yours. If you believe the following scripture, the promise is yours!

"For God so [greatly] loved and dearly prized the world, that He [even] gave His [One and] only begotten Son, so that whoever believes and trusts in Him [as Savior] shall not perish, but have eternal life." (John 3:16, AMP)

"But [in fact] He has borne our griefs, And He has carried our sorrows and pains; Yet we [ignorantly] assumed that He was stricken, Struck down by God and degraded and humiliated [by Him]. But He was wounded for our transgressions, He was crushed for our wickedness [our sin, our injustice, our wrongdoing]; the punishment [required] for our well-being fell on Him, and by His stripes (wounds) we are healed." (Isaiah 53:4–5, AMP)

You must receive Christ in your heart, be filled with the Holy Spirit, and receive the baptism of the Holy Spirit to be a witness of Christ because the Holy Spirit is the Spirit of God, who is the witness of Christ on earth. When you say the prayer of salvation, believing in Christ's sacrifice, He will plant His seed in you and conceive you into the new spiritual birth (i.e., born again). This gives you the spirit of Christ, and the Holy Spirit marks you as belonging to God, and the spirit of eternal death has no more hold on you. The Holy Spirit becomes a seal, a deposit confirming that your owner is now Christ.

> Whatever you will ask in my name, that will I do, that the Father may be glorified in the Son. If you will ask anything in my name, I will do it. "If you love me, keep my commandments. I will pray to the Father, and he will give you another Counselor, that he may be with

you forever,—the Spirit of truth, whom the world can't receive; for it doesn't see him, neither knows him. You know him, for he lives with you, and will be in you." (John 14:13–17)

The Holy Spirit will not come to anyone who does not have the Son. This means that the Father will not accept anyone as His child who does not come to Him in Jesus' name. The only reason we have the right to be God's children is that we believe and receive Christ as our Lord and Savior. "But as many as received him, to them he gave the right to become God's children, to those who believe in his name." (John 1:12)

Before you become dead to sin and alive in Christ (being born again in Christ), the Holy Spirit works on you from the outside to convict you of sin, righteousness, and judgment. (John 16:18) He makes you realize that you are a sinner and a slave to sin, and makes you aware of your need for a savior to rescue you from this bondage of sin and death. Then, when you accept that you are a sinner and ask for forgiveness and cleansing by the blood of Jesus, and ask Jesus to come into your heart to be your Lord and Savior, the Spirit of Christ comes into you, and you receive the Holy Spirit as a seal that you belong to God. Jesus breathed on His disciples to receive the Holy Spirit in them as a seal for salvation in John 20:21–23 "So Jesus said to them again, "Peace to you! As the Father has sent Me, I also send you." And when He had said this, He breathed on them, and said to them, "Receive the Holy Spirit. If you forgive the sins of any, they are forgiven them; if you retain the sins of any, they are retained."

"in whom you also, having heard the word of the truth, the Good News of your salvation—in whom, having also believed, you were sealed with the promised Holy Spirit, who is a pledge of our inheritance, to the redemption of God's own possession, to the praise of his glory." (Ephesians 1:13–14)

"Those who are in the flesh can't please God. But you are not in the flesh but in the Spirit, if it is so that the Spirit of God dwells in you. But if any man doesn't have the Spirit of Christ, he is not his. If Christ is in you, the body is dead because of sin, but the spirit is alive because of righteousness." (Romans 8:8–10)

There is an exchange, a trade that happens when we accept Christ into our hearts. We give Him our sins and wickedness which He nailed to the cross, and, in turn, He gives us His righteousness. That is why we have the righteousness of Christ by faith. Salvation is by faith. Don't let the enemy talk you out of it by reminding you of your failures. Because our righteousness is as filthy rags before God (Isaiah 64:6), our righteousness can never save us. We must believe and rely on Christ's righteousness alone to save us. Don't wait to stop smoking or being a drunkard or to stop immorality before you accept Christ because this is false information from the pit of hell. Christ wants you *just as you are*, in all the filth, so He can take it and nail it to the cross and clothe you with His righteousness.

When you invite Christ into your life, He will cleanse you. He knows how to clean house; trust Him. You don't know how to do it and what He likes. For example, if you call someone to do a makeover on your house, and they arrive, knock on the door, but you refuse to let them in because you want to make it over *before* letting them in, what sense was there in calling them? If you knew how to do it, you would not be living in the unmade house, i.e., the filth of sin. So the best thing is to open the door and allow the experts to come in and do what they do best . . . a professional makeover. After all, God is the one making the house suitable for Himself, not for you. He knows what He likes. He just needs your permission to occupy and possess and make Himself at home. Are you ready to house the King of kings and the Lord of lords?

Once you accept Jesus Christ into your heart, then you can ask the Father through Jesus Christ to baptize you with His Holy Spirit. We need the Holy Spirit to come into us, so He may introduce Christ and witness Him to us and cleanse us by God's Word, making us ready for our bridegroom, Jesus Christ, who is the Word. Then the Son, Jesus Christ, introduces us to the Father because as we obey the Holy Spirit and the Son, the Father is pleased, and He then comes into us. The Holy Spirit prepares us to receive the Father through obedience, and then the Father, Son, and the Holy Spirit make their home in us and manifest miracles, signs, and wonders, wisdom, counsel, might, power, knowledge, and understanding, as well as the fear of God. They make themselves known to the world through us. Our lives become their glory.

God, therefore, uses your body, which you have yielded willingly as a living sacrifice, holy and pleasing to Him as worship to do the will of the Father on earth just as Jesus Christ did. Worship is, therefore, the complete yielding of our lives (spirit, soul, and body) to God for His use and pleasure on earth. "If we confess our sins, he is faithful and righteous to forgive us the sins, and to cleanse us from all unrighteousness." (1 John 1:9)

"Come now, and let us reason together," says Yahweh: "Though your sins be as scarlet, they shall be as white as snow. Though they be red like crimson, they shall be as wool." (Isaiah 1:18)

For, "Whoever will call on the name of the Lord will be saved." (Romans 10:13)

"All those whom the Father gives me will come to me. He who comes to me I will in no way throw out." (John 6:37)

Therefore, come to Christ with this confidence that He loves you so much that He died for you and He longs to be your Lord and Savior.

"in whom we have boldness and access in confidence through our faith in him." (Ephesians 3:12)

"Let us therefore draw near with boldness to the throne of grace, that we may receive mercy, and may find grace for help in time of need." (Hebrews 4:16)

Prayer to Accept Christ into Your life (to Be Born Again)

Father, in Jesus's name, I thank You for Your extravagant Agape love. Thank You for Your Son, Jesus Christ. Thank You Jesus for the greatest sacrifice and price You paid for me at Calvary. Thank you Holy Spirit for convicting me of sin. I realize and now acknowledge that I am a sinner. I confess and repent all my sin including the sin of offense and unforgiveness. Please forgive me. Cleanse me by the Blood of Jesus from all unrighteousness. Create in me Your heart and renew a right spirit within me. Please give me Your forgiveness and love that I may forgive and love those who have sinned against me with it. I believe that I have receive it in Jesus's name. I now forgive all my offenders with Your forgiveness and love them with Your perfect and unconditional love.

Jesus, I believe that You are LORD and You rose from the dead. Write my name in the Lamb's book of life, and make me Your child now. I now receive Your forgiveness and salvation with thanksgiving. Father, now as Your child, please fill me with Your Holy Spirit. Baptize me with Your Holy Spirit, teach me all Your ways and show me Your truths. I evict every evil spirit in me in Jesus's name. Empty me of anything in me that is not of You in Jesus's name. May Your Holy Spirit take full control over my life and take full occupancy of my spirit, soul, and body. Thank You, Lord Jesus, for saving me. Thank you, Father, for making me Your child. Thank You for the gift of Your Holy Spirit. Thank you Holy Spirit for being my personal Kingdom trainer. Grant me the spirit of wisdom and understanding, the spirit of counsel, power, and might, the spirit of knowledge, and the fear of the LORD. May I, like Christ, delight in the spirit of the fear of the LORD in Jesus's name, that I may live in total obedience to the Father's will and in humility walk with You. In Jesus's name, I pray, believe, and receive with thanksgiving, AMEN!

Now praise God for the greatest miracle of Salvation and infilling of the Holy Spirit! Buy a New King James Version of the Bible as it is easier to understand and it does not omit some words, and fill your spirit and mind with the Word of God. Ask God to teach you His ways and give you the understanding of His Word in Jesus's name. Pray for a sound bible teaching church, ask God to lead you to the church of His choice because not all churches preach the uncompromised gospel of Jesus Christ.

If you are born again but you have gone astray and do not live you life wholly submitted to God, here is a prayer for you to rededicate your life to Jesus Christ. He is waiting for you with open arms just like the prodigal son's story in Luke 15:11-32. The Father is longing for your return so He may restore you back to Himself as His child.

Prayer to Rededicate Your Life to Christ

Father, in Jesus's name, I exalt and lift You on High, for there is none other God but You. No one compares to You, LORD. Your love and power no one can fathom. I thank You so much for Jesus and for the finished work of the cross. I thank You for Your Holy Spirit who has convicted me of sin, righteousness and judgement. I confess all my sins, LORD. I acknowledge that I have turned away from You and have leaned on my own wisdom and understanding. Please forgive me. Cleanse me from all unrighteousness. Create in me Your heart, oh LORD, and renew a right spirit within me. Cast me not away from Your presence; take not Your Holy Spirit from me. Restore unto me the joy of Your salvation. I now by the power of the blood of Jesus evict every evil spirit that came in me while I strayed from You in Jesus's name! I rebuke the spirit of rebellion from my life in Jesus name! Fill me with Your Holy Spirit; teach me all Your ways and paths. Grant me the spirit of wisdom and understanding, the spirit of counsel, power, and might, the spirit of knowledge, and the fear of the LORD. May I, like Christ, delight in the spirit of the fear of the LORD in Jesus's name. May I live in total obedience to Your will and in humility walk with You. May I be a great representative of Your Kingdom. I thank you, Father, for receiving me back into Your Kingdom and restoring my position as Your child. In Jesus's name, I pray, believe, and receive with thanksgiving. Amen!

Prayer to Receive the Baptism of the Holy Spirit and Fire

Father, in Jesus's name, You said that every perfect gift comes from You. You also said that if I ask for the Holy Spirit,

You will not withhold Him from me. Father, I ask that You forgive me, cleanse me and purify me for Your name sake. Baptize me and fill me with Your Holy Spirit without measure, grant me the gift of speaking in Heavenly tongues now in Jesus's mane. Teach me all Your ways and truths. I receive the Baptism of the Holy Spirit and of Fire which is the fullness of who you are now in me in Jesus's name. I ask that You overflow me with the fullness of Your Spirit, the seven Spirits of God and your fire, in Jesus's name. I pray this, trusting, believing, and receiving Your precious gift with thanksgiving in Jesus's name, amen!

Now speak to the Holy Spirit and say…

Holy Spirit, you were there when I was being created, you saw all that was placed in me during creation. Please reveal it to me, and give me the grace, power, obedience, and all I need to fulfill my God-given task successfully just like you helped Christ. Please be my personal trainer in Jesus name I pray, believe, and receive with thanksgiving, Amen.

Now release yourself to God, open your mouth and allow the Holy Spirit to speak through you in other tongues in Jesus's name!

Prayer for Blessings

Father in Jesus name, thank You for making me Your child. I now repent all the sins of my ancestors, and I reverse every generational curse that has come to my family and I because of their sin. I denounce their bloodline, and cross over to the bloodline of Jesus Christ because I believe that Christ became a curse for me that I may be blessed. I receive all the promises, gifts, and blessings that my ancestors were meant to have that lay wasted in their graves due to disobedience in Jesus's name! I take it all back for my children and I, and for generations to come in Jesus's name. Just like you gave the promise to the Israelites, that they would go into the Promised Land, but because of sin, the promise was given to their children, I receive all the blessings my ancestors forfeited due to sin in Jesus's name. I receive the blessings of being in Christ in Jesus's name. I embrace perfect health in spirit, soul, and body. I uproot, tear down, destroy, and overthrow every curse and satanic programs against my family and I in Jesus's name. I receive every blessing, and promise that You have spoken of in Your Word for Your children now in Jesus's name. Thank You, Father, for Your blessing, thank you for the promise of salvation. I receive all these blessings with thanksgiving in Jesus's name, Amen!

Now that we have given and rededicated our lives to Jesus, and received the fullness of God in us through His Holy Spirit, we can now access heaven and claim our promises in Jesus's name!

Beloved...

I hope you now have a **BURNING, UNCONTAINABLE** desire to make God the Holy Spirit your **best** friend like I did. He is the witness of Christ, and the power of God within us. He is a **must** have for all who have made Christ their Lord and savior. For those who desire to see God's Kingdom come on earth and His will be fulfilled. He is here for those who want to get back to the original intent of God's purpose for man which is to live in His holiness and intimate fellowship.

My friend, the Holy Spirit is training those who long to be the brides of Christ, those who want to receive heaven's standing ovation as Christ introduces them to His Father and all His angels as His precious, and most beloved bride. He is here for those who want to hear the Father say to them at the end of this life on earth; "Welcome Home! Good and faithful servant." My friend is available to those who are tired of the ordinary life and realize that they were never created to be just ordinary, but extraordinary. Those who understand that their lives was never meant to be natural but supernatural. My friend, the Holy Spirit is ready for those who have been believers for many years and all they have to show for is years of church membership and service with no power, or signs and wonders following them.

Remember that those who are continually yielded to and are led by the Holy Spirit of God, they are the **MATURE** sons of God.

May God's Love, Christ's Grace, and the beautiful, refreshing, fellowship of the Holy Spirit always be with you now and forever in Jesus's name, Amen!

Agape...

www.ingramcontent.com/pod-product-compliance
Lightning Source LLC
Chambersburg PA
CBHW051535230426
43669CB00015B/2599